KB132656

내 교과서, All that 에서 찾아보기 '의사소통 기능'

단원	비상교육 (김진완)	올댓	동아출판 (윤정미)	올댓	동아출판 (이병민)	올댓	천재교육 (이재영)	올댓	미래엔 (최연희)
Lesson 01	• 관심 있는 것 말하기 • 문제 해결 방법 알려 주기	20 40	• 여가 활동 묻기 • 정보 묻기	20 20	• 조언 구하기 • 제안하기	40 80	• 의도나 계획 묻기 • 충고하기	20 40	• 능력 표현하기 • 확신 표현하기
Lesson 02	• 바라거나 기대하는 일 표현하기 • 어떤 일을 해야 한다고 알려 주기	80 60	• 길 묻고 답하기 1 • 길 묻고 답하기 2	40 40	• 확신 말하기 • 성격 묘사하기	100	• 음식 권하기 • 의미 확인하기	60	• 의향 묻고 답하기 • 위치 묻고 답하기
Lesson 03	• 들어 본 적이 있는지 묻기 • 설명 요청하기	60 60	• 물건 사기 1 • 물건 사기 2		• 선호 말하기 • 이유 말하기	100	• 증상 묻고 답하기 • 약속 정하기	100 80	• 경험 묻고 답하기 • 날씨 묻고 답하기
Lesson 04	• 격려하기 • 상대방에게 도움 제안하기	100 80	• 외모 묘사하기 • 정보 묻기	100 60	• 여가 활동 말하기 • 경험 말하기	20 20	• 허락 구하기 • 금지하기	100 40	• 도움 요청하기 • 감사하기
Lesson 05	• 좋지 않은 감정의 원인 묻기 • 고민을 해결할 방법 제안하기	100 40	• 문제점이나 증상을 묻고 답하기 • 당부하기	100 40	• 길 묻고 답하기 • 소요 시간 말하기	40 40	• 희망이나 바람 표현하기 • 외모 묘사하기	80 100	• 제안하기 • 약속 정하기
Lesson 06	• 궁금한 일 표현하기 • 비교해 표현하기	60 80	• 계획 말하기 • 약속 정하기	20 80	• 알고 있는지 묻기 • 용도 말하기	60	• 불만 표현하기 • 상기시키기	60	• 선호하는 것 묻고 답하기 • 추천 부탁하기
Lesson 07	• 구체적인 종류나 장르 묻기 • 둘 중에 더 좋아하는 것 말하기	20 100	• 알고 있는지 묻기 • 궁금증 표현하기	60 60	• 추천 요청하기 • 만족 여부 묻고 답하기	80	• 경험 묻고 답하기 • 절차 묻고 답하기	20 60	• 알고 있음 표현하기 • 상기시켜 주기
Lesson 08	• 상대방의 의견 묻기 • 상대방 의견에 동의 여부 말하기	100 40	• 허가 여부 묻기 • 금지하기	100 40	• 도움 요청하기 • 추측하기	80	• 사실 묻고 답하기 • 놀람 표현하기	60	• 관심 있는 것 말하기 • 빈도 묻고 답하기
Lesson 09									

※ 각 의사소통 기능의 **올댓 중학 영어** 수록 페이지 표시 중, 청록색은 1학기, 주황색은 2학기 교재의 페이지입니다.

올댓	능률교육 (김성곤)	올댓	천재교육 (정사열)	올댓	YBM (박준언)	올댓	YBM (송미정)	올댓	지학사 (민찬규)	올댓
40	• 관심사 묻고 답하기 • 허락 요청하고 답하기	20 100	• 의견 묻기 • 희망, 기대 표현하기	100 80	• 슬픔, 불만족, 실망의 원인 묻기 • 제안, 권유하기	100 80	• 바람, 소망 말하기 • 계획 묻고 답하기	80 20	• 주의 끌기 • 의도 표현하기	20
20 40	• 충고하기 • 추천 요청하고 답하기	40 80	• 계획 말하기 • 약속 정하기	20 80	• 상기시켜 주기 • 금지하기	60 40	• 충고하기 • 당부하기	40 40	• 걱정 표현하기 • 충고하기	100 40
20	• 경험 묻고 답하기 • 의미 묻고 답하기	20 60	• 알고 있는지 묻기 • 금지하기	60 40	• 능력 여부 묻기 • 좋아하는 것 표현하기	40 100	• 능력 여부 묻기 • 좋아하는 것 표현하기	40 100	• 도움 제안하기 • 칭찬에 답하기	80
80	• 걱정 표현하기 • 방법 묻기	100 40	• 기억 여부 묻기 • 생각할 시간 요청하기		• 의도 묻기 • 기원하기	20	• 걱정 표현하기와 안심시키기 • 의견 묻기	100 100	• 유감, 동정 표현하기 • 당부하기	40
40 80	• 도움 요청하고 답하기 • 제안하기	80 80	• 능력 여부 묻기 • 열거하기	40 60	• 길 알려 주기 • 선호에 대해 묻기	40 100	• 선호하는 것 묻고 답하기 • 희망, 기대 표현하기	100 80	• 설명 요청하기 • 열거하기	60 60
100 80	• 계획 묻고 답하기 • 소요 시간 묻고 답하기	20 40	• 설명 요청하기 • 놀람 표현하기	60	• 알고 있음 표현하기 • 궁금증 표현하기	60 60	• 경험 묻기 • 만족이나 불만족에 대해 묻기	20	• 의견 표현하기 • 확실성 정도 표현하기	100
60 60	• 능력 표현하기 • 조언 구하고 답하기	40 40	• 관심에 대해 묻기 • 칭찬하기	20	• 강조하기 • 설명 요청하기	60	• 의견 표현하기 • 가능 여부 표현하기	100	• 질문하기 • 희망, 기대 표현하기	20 80
20			• 불평하기 • 의도 표현하기	20	• 놀람 표현하기 • 요청하기	80	• 알고 있는지 묻기 • 설명 요청하기	60 60	• 알고 있는지 묻기 • 격려하기	60 100
							• 약속 정하기 • 상기시키기	80 60		

VISANG

중학 영어의 모든 것

All that

중학영어 2-1

구성과 특징

PART I 실력 다지기

All that Grammar

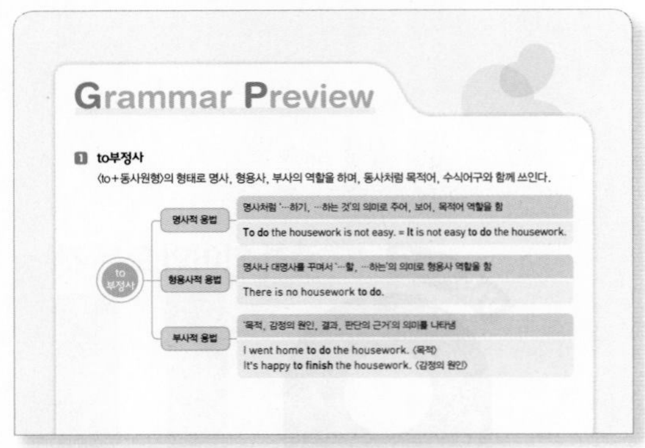
Grammar Preview

1 to부정사

(to+동사원형)의 형태로 명사, 형용사, 부사의 역할을 하며, 동사처럼 목적어, 수식어구와 함께 쓰인다.

명사적 용법: To do the housework is not easy. = It is not easy to do the housework.

형용사적 용법: There is no housework to do.

부사적 용법: I went home to do the housework. It's happy to finish the housework.

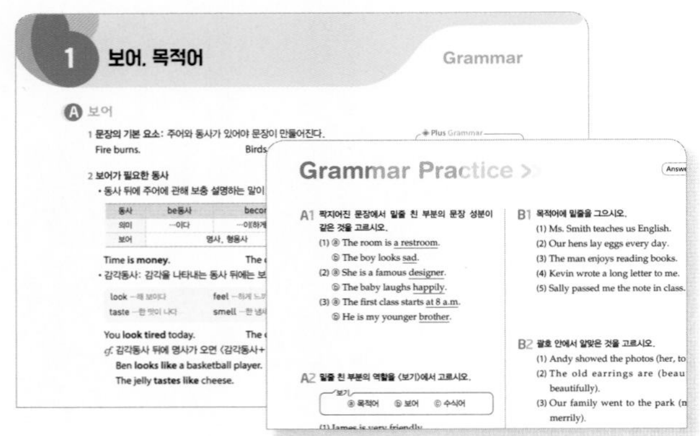
1 보어, 목적어 Grammar

Grammar Practice

- 단원을 학습하기 전에 꼭 알아야 할 핵심 문법 개념을 소개하는 자기주도적 학습 장치

- 주요 교과서를 철저히 분석하여 구성한 체계적인 문법 목차
- [개념 소개] → [Grammar Practice] → [Grammar Test] 3단계로 구성된 체계적인 문법 학습 시스템
- 출제 빈도가 높은 기출 문항들을 엄선하여 수록한 연습 문제

All that Reading

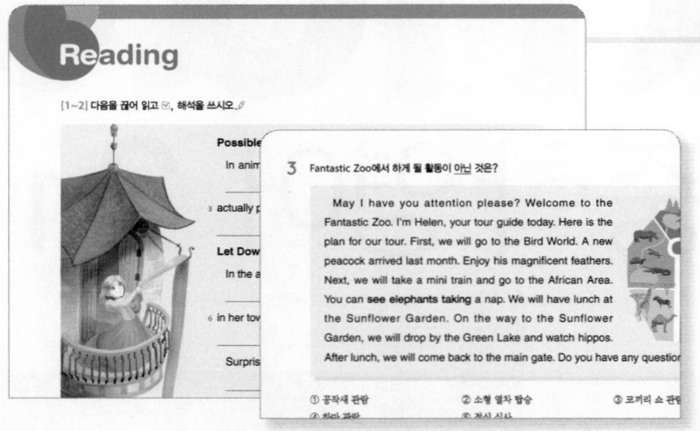
Reading

3 Fantastic Zoo에서 하게 될 활동이 아닌 것은?

May I have you attention please? Welcome to the Fantastic Zoo. I'm Helen, your tour guide today. Here is the plan for our tour. First, we will go to the Bird World. A new peacock arrived last month. Enjoy his magnificent feathers. Next, we will take a mini train and go to the African Area. You can see elephants taking a nap. We will have lunch at the Sunflower Garden. On the way to the Sunflower Garden, we will drop by the Green Lake and watch hippos. After lunch, we will come back to the main gate.

- 재미있고 다양한 소재의 지문 수록
- 교과서 지문을 이용한 끊어 읽기, 해석 연습
- 실제 시험과 유사한 독해 문항 유형을 다양하게 수록

All that Expression

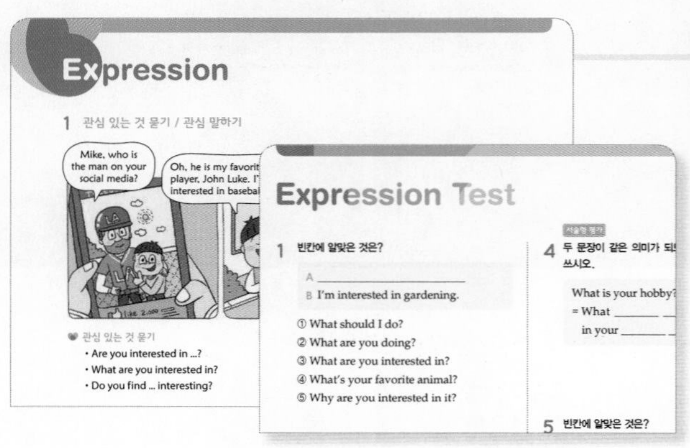
Expression

1 관심 있는 것 묻기 / 관심 말하기

관심 있는 것 묻기
- Are you interested in ...?
- What are you interested in?
- Do you find ... interesting?

Expression Test

1 빈칸에 알맞은 것은?

B I'm interested in gardening.

① What should I do?
② What are you doing?
③ What are you interested in?
④ What's your favorite animal?
⑤ Why are you interested in it?

- 주요 교과서에 소개된 의사소통 기능을 엄선하여 소개
- 대화 상황을 재미있는 만화로 생생하게 제시
- 다양한 유형의 기출 문항들을 엄선하여 수록

Test & Review

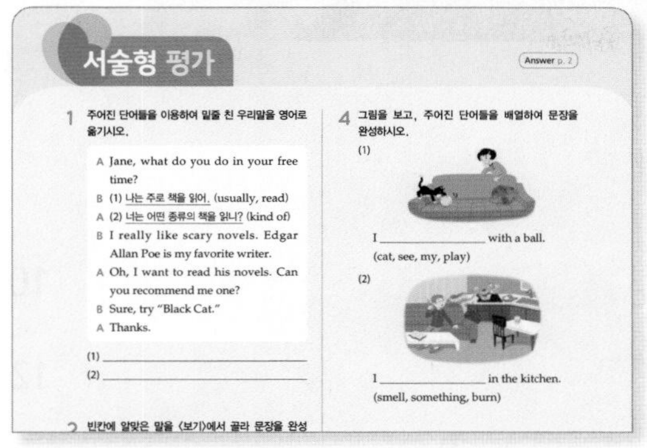

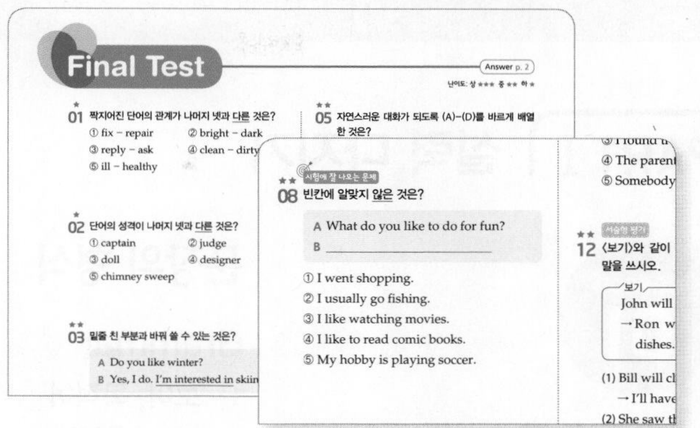

- 문법과 표현을 적용한 서술형 평가 제공
- 학교 서술형 평가 완벽 대비를 위한 다양한 문제 수록

- 실제 시험과 동일한 유형으로 구성된 종합 평가
- 여러 난이도의 문제를 빈출 유형 위주로 수록

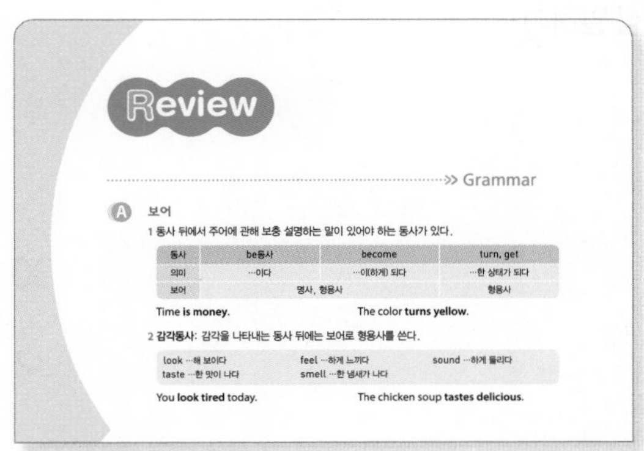

- 단원에서 학습한 문법과 의사소통 기능 복습
- 학습 내용을 도식화하여 신속한 이해 점검 가능

PART II 듣기 실전 모의고사

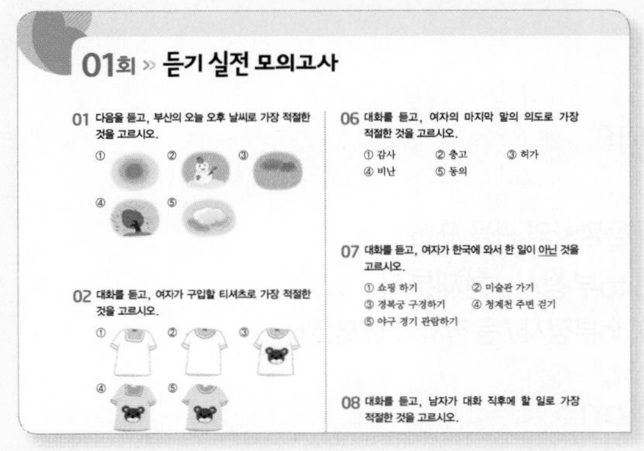

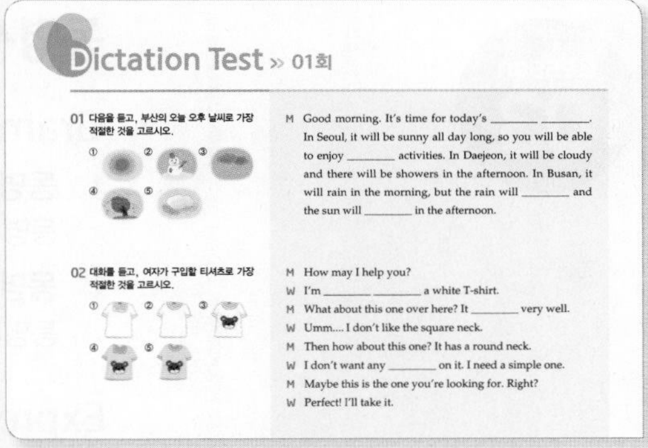

- 시 · 도 교육청 영어 듣기능력평가를 분석하여 반영한 듣기 실전 모의고사 5회 수록
- 실제 시험과 유사한 분량 및 녹음속도의 듣기 자료를 통해 실전 적응력 향상
- 듣기 능력을 향상시켜줄 Dictation Test 제공

차례

PART I 실력 다지기

PART II 듣기 실전 모의고사

How To Study

* 월간, 주간, 일간 학습 계획을 세운 후 공부하는 습관을 가져 보세요. 무턱대고 공부하는 것보다 훨씬 체계적이고 계획적으로 공부할 수 있어요.
* 먼저, 구체적으로 공부할 분량을 파악한 후에 학습 목표를 세워 보세요. 목표를 세울 때는 막연하거나 장황하지 않게 구체적으로 세우는 것이 중요해요. 그렇게 해야 계획대로 공부할 수 있고 목표한 만큼은 반드시 끝낸다는 마음으로 공부할 수 있어서 효율적이에요.

60일 완성 학습 계획표

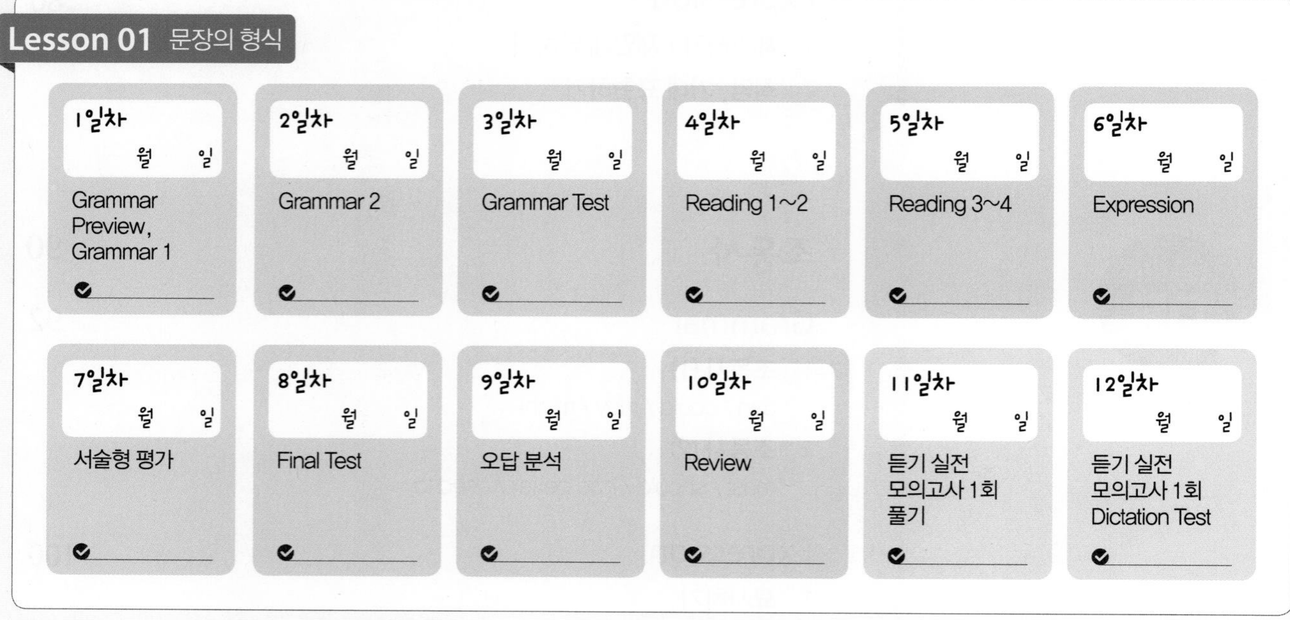

Lesson 01 문장의 형식

1일차 월 일	2일차 월 일	3일차 월 일	4일차 월 일	5일차 월 일	6일차 월 일
Grammar Preview, Grammar 1	Grammar 2	Grammar Test	Reading 1~2	Reading 3~4	Expression
7일차 월 일	**8일차** 월 일	**9일차** 월 일	**10일차** 월 일	**11일차** 월 일	**12일차** 월 일
서술형 평가	Final Test	오답 분석	Review	듣기 실전 모의고사 1회 풀기	듣기 실전 모의고사 1회 Dictation Test

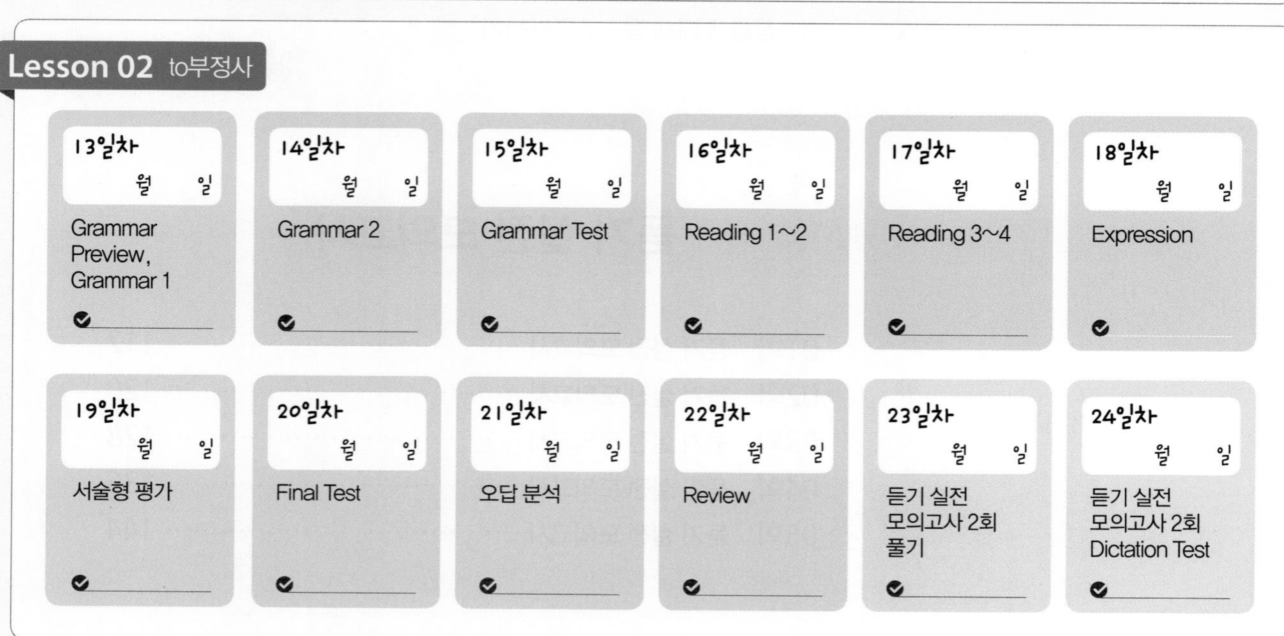

Lesson 02 to부정사

13일차 월 일	14일차 월 일	15일차 월 일	16일차 월 일	17일차 월 일	18일차 월 일
Grammar Preview, Grammar 1	Grammar 2	Grammar Test	Reading 1~2	Reading 3~4	Expression
19일차 월 일	**20일차** 월 일	**21일차** 월 일	**22일차** 월 일	**23일차** 월 일	**24일차** 월 일
서술형 평가	Final Test	오답 분석	Review	듣기 실전 모의고사 2회 풀기	듣기 실전 모의고사 2회 Dictation Test

Lesson 03 동명사

25일차 월 일	26일차 월 일	27일차 월 일	28일차 월 일	29일차 월 일	30일차 월 일
Grammar Preview, Grammar 1	Grammar 2	Grammar Test	Reading 1~2	Reading 3~4	Expression
31일차 월 일	32일차 월 일	33일차 월 일	34일차 월 일	35일차 월 일	36일차 월 일
서술형 평가	Final Test	오답 분석	Review	듣기 실전 모의고사 3회 풀기	듣기 실전 모의고사 3회 Dictation Test

Lesson 04 분사, 수동태

37일차 월 일	38일차 월 일	39일차 월 일	40일차 월 일	41일차 월 일	42일차 월 일
Grammar Preview, Grammar 1	Grammar 2	Grammar Test	Reading 1~2	Reading 3~4	Expression
43일차 월 일	44일차 월 일	45일차 월 일	46일차 월 일	47일차 월 일	48일차 월 일
서술형 평가	Final Test	오답 분석	Review	듣기 실전 모의고사 4회 풀기	듣기 실전 모의고사 4회 Dictation Test

Lesson 05 조동사

49일차 월 일	50일차 월 일	51일차 월 일	52일차 월 일	53일차 월 일	54일차 월 일
Grammar Preview, Grammar 1	Grammar 2	Grammar Test	Reading 1~2	Reading 3~4	Expression
55일차 월 일	56일차 월 일	57일차 월 일	58일차 월 일	59일차 월 일	60일차 월 일
서술형 평가	Final Test	오답 분석	Review	듣기 실전 모의고사 5회 풀기	듣기 실전 모의고사 5회 Dictation Test

미리보는 2학기 차례

Lesson	Grammar	Expression
Lesson 01	**현재완료시제** 1 현재완료시제 2 현재완료시제의 용법	1 경험 묻기 / 경험 말하기 2 계획 묻기 / 계획 말하기
Lesson 02	**관계대명사** 1 관계대명사 who, which 2 관계대명사 that, what	1 금지하기 / 충고하기 2 동의하기 / 반대하기
Lesson 03	**명사, 대명사** 1 명사, 관사 2 대명사	1 약속 정하기 2 아는지 묻기 / 궁금증 표현하기
Lesson 04	**형용사, 부사, 비교** 1 형용사, 부사 2 비교	1 비교하기 2 요청하기 / 요청에 답하기
Lesson 05	**접속사** 1 접속사 2 간접의문문	1 의견 묻기 / 의견 표현하기 2 허가 여부 묻기 / 허가 여부 말하기

PART

I

실력 다지기

Lesson 01

문장의 형식

Grammar Preview

1 보어, 목적어

• 보어: 주어에 관해 보충 설명하는 말

동사	be동사	become	turn, get	감각동사
의미	…이다	…이(하게) 되다	…한 상태가 되다	…한 느낌을 주다(가지다)
보어	명사, 형용사		형용사	
예문	Time **is money**. Luke **becomes a movie director**.		The color **turns yellow**. The chicken soup **tastes delicious**.	

• 목적어: 동사가 나타내는 동작의 대상이 되는 말

We must protect **nature**.

Tom wants to buy **a new computer**.

• 수여동사는 〈수여동사+간접목적어+직접목적어〉의 어순으로 쓰며 〈수여동사+직접목적어+전치사(to, for, of)+간접목적어〉로도 쓸 수 있다.

전치사	to	for	of
동사	bring, give, lend, send, show, teach, tell 등	buy, cook, make, choose, get 등	ask

Andy **told** me his address.
→ Andy **told** his address **to** me.

Austin **bought** me some postcards.
→ Austin **bought** some postcards **for** me.

2 목적격보어

• 목적격보어: 목적어에 관해 보충 설명하는 말로, 주로 명사, 형용사, 분사를 목적격보어로 쓰지만 다음 동사들은 목적격보어로 to부정사를 쓴다.

want 원하다	ask 요구하다	tell 말하다	order 명령하다
expect 기대하다	advise 충고하다	cause 야기하다	enable 가능하게 하다

Mr. Emerson thinks himself **a great judge**.
My parents want me **to study** abroad.

The news made me **happy**.
Laura expected me **to play** the guitar.

• 사역동사와 지각동사의 목적격보어

동사	사역동사(make, have, let)	지각동사(watch, hear, see, feel)
의미	…을 …하게 하다	…가 …하는 것을 감각으로 느끼다
목적격보어의 형태	동사원형	동사원형, 현재분사

Robert **let** me **use** his computer.

I **heard** someone **knocking** at the door.

1 보어, 목적어

A 보어

1 문장의 기본 요소: 주어와 동사가 있어야 문장이 만들어진다.

Fire burns.　　Birds sing.

Plus Grammar
문장 구성에 필요한 주어, 서술어, 목적어, 보어, 수식어 등을 문장 성분이라고 한다.

2 보어가 필요한 동사

• 동사 뒤에 주어에 관해 보충 설명하는 말이 있어야 하는 동사가 있다.

동사	be동사	become	turn, get
의미	…이다	…이[하게] 되다	…한 상태가 되다
보어	명사, 형용사		형용사

Time **is money.**　　The color **turns yellow.**

• 감각동사: 감각을 나타내는 동사 뒤에는 보어로 형용사를 쓴다.

look …해 보이다　feel …하게 느끼다　sound …하게 들리다
taste …한 맛이 나다　smell …한 냄새가 나다

You **look tired** today.　　The chicken soup **tastes delicious.**

cf. 감각동사 뒤에 명사가 오면 〈감각동사+like+명사〉의 형태로 쓴다.

Ben **looks like** a basketball player.
The jelly **tastes like** cheese.

B 목적어

1 목적어: 동사가 나타내는 동작의 대상이 필요한 동사를 타동사라고 하며, 동작의 대상이 되는 말을 목적어라고 한다. 명사 역할을 하는 말이 목적어로 쓰인다.

We must protect **nature.**　　Tom wants to buy **a new computer.**

Plus Grammar
주어, 목적어, 보어로는 명사 이외에도 명사 역할을 하는 여러 가지 어구가 쓰일 수 있다.
To learn a language is not easy. 〈to부정사〉
Listening to music makes me happy. 〈동명사〉
That he has lots of money is true. 〈명사절〉
I hurt **myself.** 〈재귀대명사〉
I don't know **how to work the machine.** 〈의문사+to부정사〉
Do you know **what he was going to do?** 〈의문사절〉

2 수여동사

• 받는 대상(간접목적어)과 주어지는 것(직접목적어)을 목적어로 취하여 〈수여동사+간접목적어+직접목적어〉로 쓴다.

We sent **Pam a text message.**

• 수여동사가 쓰인 문장에서 두 목적어의 자리를 바꿔 쓸 수도 있다. 이때 간접목적어 앞에는 전치사를 쓴다.

전치사	동사
to	bring, give, lend, send, show, teach, tell 등
for	buy, cook, make, choose, get 등
of	ask

Andy **told** me his address.

→ Andy **told** his address **to** me.

Grammar Practice >>

Answer p. 1

A1 짝지어진 문장에서 밑줄 친 부분의 문장 성분이 같은 것을 고르시오.

(1) ⓐ The room is a restroom.
　ⓑ The boy looks sad.

(2) ⓐ She is a famous designer.
　ⓑ The baby laughs happily.

(3) ⓐ The first class starts at 8 a.m.
　ⓑ He is my younger brother.

A2 밑줄 친 부분의 역할을 〈보기〉에서 고르시오.

보기
ⓐ 목적어　ⓑ 보어　ⓒ 수식어

(1) James is very friendly.
(2) The coffee smells good.
(3) The boys lay on the grass.
(4) This game is really boring.
(5) We enjoyed watching this show.
(6) My favorite numbers are 1 and 7.
(7) The ship will sail along the coast.

A3 두 문장이 같은 의미가 되도록 빈칸에 알맞은 말을 쓰시오.

(1) My mom smiles happily.
　= My mom looks ________.

(2) I ate the food, and it's similar to spaghetti.
　= I ate the food, and it tasted ________ spaghetti.

(3) I was angry because they were late.
　= I ________ angry because they were late.

B1 목적어에 밑줄을 그으시오.

(1) Ms. Smith teaches us English.
(2) Our hens lay eggs every day.
(3) The man enjoys reading books.
(4) Kevin wrote a long letter to me.
(5) Sally passed me the note in class.

B2 괄호 안에서 알맞은 것을 고르시오.

(1) Andy showed the photos (her, to her).
(2) The old earrings are (beautiful, beautifully).
(3) Our family went to the park (merry, merrily).
(4) My father bought a new computer (me, for me).
(5) The chef cooked delicious sandwiches (for us, to us).

B3 두 문장이 같은 의미가 되도록 빈칸에 알맞은 말을 쓰시오.

(1) James gives us useful information.
　= James gives useful information ________.

(2) Louis made this ribbon for Emily.
　= Louis made ________ this ribbon.

(3) Ann's uncle sent Ann a gift.
　= Ann's uncle sent ________ Ann.

(4) We didn't ask him many questions.
　= We didn't ask many ________ him.

(5) My father bought a bike for me.
　= My father bought ________.

교과서 어휘 burn 타다　tired 피곤한　protect 보호하다　address 주소　friendly 다정한　grass 잔디　boring 지루한　sail 항해하다　coast 해안　similar to …와 유사한　lay (알을) 낳다　earrings 귀걸이

2 목적격보어

C 목적어와 목적격보어

1 목적격보어: 목적어에 관해 서술하는 말로서, 목적격보어로는 명사, 형용사, 부정사, 분사 등을 쓴다.

Judy's mistakes made her friends angry. 〈her friends → angry〉
(her friends: 목적어, angry: 목적격보어)

Mr. Emerson thinks himself **a great judge.** 〈명사〉
The news made me **happy.** 〈형용사〉
I found your dog **running.** 〈분사〉

2 다음 동사들은 목적격보어로 to부정사를 쓴다.

want 원하다	ask 요구하다	tell 말하다	order 명령하다
expect 기대하다	advise 충고하다	cause 야기하다	enable 가능하게 하다

My parents **want** me **to study** abroad.
Laura **expected** me **to play** the guitar.

Plus Grammar

- **직접목적어와 목적격보어 구분**
  목적어 뒤의 내용이 목적어에 대한 서술이면 목적격보어이고, 다른 대상이면 직접목적어이다.
  I showed Bob **my bike** (≠ Bob). → 직접목적어
  We think Bob **smart** (= Bob). → 목적격보어
- 목적격보어로 쓰이는 말의 품사에 따라, 수식어, 또는 목적어가 함께 쓰일 수 있다.
  I don't think him a **good** boy. 〈목적격보어 수식〉
  I don't want you to tell **my secret.** 〈목적격보어의 목적어〉

D 사역동사의 목적격보어

'…하게 하다'라는 의미의 make, let, have 등을 사역동사라고 하며 목적격보어로 동사원형을 쓴다.
Robert **let** me **use** his computer.
My mom will **have** Tom **clean** his room.
cf. help(…가 …하는 것을 돕다)는 목적격보어로 동사원형이나 to부정사를 쓴다.
I **helped** Sam **(to) fix** the radio.

E 지각동사의 목적격보어

watch, hear, see, feel 등의 감각과 관련된 동사는 목적격보어로 동사원형 또는 현재분사를 쓴다.
Sora **felt** her heart **beat** when she saw Tony.
I **heard** someone **knocking** at the door.
cf. 지각동사, 사역동사의 목적격보어와 목적어의 관계가 수동이면 목적격보어로 과거분사를 쓴다.
I **had** the wall **painted.**
I **saw** the man **taken** to the hospital.

Grammar Practice >>

Answer p. 1

C1 주어진 단어들을 배열하여 문장을 완성하시오.

(1) Sumin ____________________.
(named, Pinky, her dog)

(2) You always ____________________.
(your room, clean, keep)

(3) Tom wanted ____________________.
(to repair, his dad, the bike)

(4) Justin ____________________ for three hours. (his brother, waiting, kept)

C2 목적격보어에 밑줄을 그으시오.

(1) They call their captain King.

(2) These flowers make this room cheerful.

(3) The doctor advised me to stop taking pills.

(4) Don't leave your baby crying.

D1 괄호 안에서 알맞은 것을 고르시오.

(1) His joke made everyone (laugh, to laugh, laughing).

(2) I helped him (collected, to collect, collecting) the bottles.

(3) We had our daughter (setting, set, to set) the table.

(4) My mom let me (stop, to stop, stopping) writing sentences in English.

D2 짝지어진 문장에서 밑줄 친 부분의 문장 성분이 같은 것을 고르시오.

(1) ⓐ I want <u>to join the music club</u>.
ⓑ Erin helped me <u>to meet Bill</u>.

(2) ⓐ We saw James put <u>a lot of letters</u> in the blue box.
ⓑ Mom made me <u>get</u> up at 6 o'clock every morning last year.

(3) ⓐ You should keep the windows <u>closed</u>.
ⓑ He made Peter <u>cut the grass</u>.

E1 밑줄 친 부분이 어법에 맞으면 ○표를 하고, 틀리면 알맞은 형태로 고쳐 쓰시오.

(1) We heard Sally cry <u>loudly</u>.

(2) Sam felt somebody <u>touched</u> him.

(3) Pamela heard someone <u>call</u> her name at the corner.

(4) I saw her <u>puts</u> sugar in her coffee.

E2 주어진 단어를 빈칸에 알맞은 형태로 쓰시오.

(1) They saw a man __________ delicious cakes. (bake)

(2) Sarah helped her brother __________ pictures. (draw)

(3) My sister never let me __________ her MP3 player. (use)

(4) Our teacher told us __________ many books. (read)

(5) The rainbow makes me __________ my hometown. (miss)

교과서 어휘 judge 판사 abroad 해외에서 fix 수리하다 beat 박동하다 knock 두드리다 repair 수리하다 captain 지도자, 주장 cheerful 활기찬 advise 조언하다 pill 알약 sentence 문장 hometown 고향

Grammar Test

01 우리말을 영어로 바르게 옮긴 것은?

나는 어머니께 카드를 만들어 드릴 것이다.

① I will make my mother a card.
② I will make a card my mother.
③ I will make a card to my mother.
④ I will make my mother to a card.
⑤ I will make for my mother a card.

02 문장의 형식이 나머지 넷과 다른 것은?

① You can call me Peter.
② You must keep your room clean.
③ I bought my younger sister a doll.
④ Too much stress makes you ill.
⑤ My father told me to do my homework.

03 밑줄 친 단어의 형태가 바르게 짝지어진 것은?

• Mr. Black let me reply to the question.
• I saw a beautiful lamp hang from the ceiling.

① reply – hang
② reply – to hang
③ to reply – to hang
④ replying – hang
⑤ replying – hanging

서술형 평가

04 두 문장을 한 문장으로 바꿔 쓸 때 빈칸에 알맞은 말을 쓰시오.

(1) I saw Minho. He was playing soccer.
= I saw Minho ______________.

(2) Tom watched Yuri. She was singing a song.
= Tom watched Yuri ______________.

[05~06] 빈칸에 알맞지 않은 것을 고르시오.

05

The carpenter looks ________ today.

① tired ② sad ③ angrily
④ pretty ⑤ happy

06

Mom ________ me to go swimming after school.

① told ② asked ③ made
④ wanted ⑤ advised

서술형 평가

07 주어진 단어들을 이용하여 우리말을 영어로 옮기시오.

Justin의 엄마는 그에게 닭고기 수프를 요리해 주셨다. (cook, chicken soup)

→ ______________________________

교과서 어휘 doll 인형 stress 스트레스, 압박감 ill 아픈 reply 대답하다 lamp 전등 ceiling 천장 carpenter 목수

Answer p. 1

08 빈칸에 들어갈 말이 바르게 짝지어진 것은?

A James, you look ________.
B Yes, my father bought a bag ________.

① sad – for me ② sadly – to me
③ happily – for me ④ happy – for me
⑤ happy – to me

서술형 평가

09 어법상 어색한 부분을 찾아 바르게 고쳐 쓰시오.

(1) This cloth feels smoothly.
__________ → __________

(2) He told Sora share the room with her sister.
__________ → __________

(3) Mom made me to take the English course.
__________ → __________

10 빈칸에 들어갈 말이 나머지와 넷과 다른 것은?

① Yuri showed her new hat ________ Bob.
② Sena sent a Christmas card ________ Helen.
③ Grandmother told an interesting story ________ us.
④ Ms. Kang teaches Korean culture ________ us.
⑤ Uncle Ken made a nice doghouse ________ me.

11 〈보기〉의 문장과 형식이 같은 것은?

보기
Just one movie made John a star.

① Time flies like an arrow.
② She handed the driver a map.
③ We should keep the earth clean.
④ Henry wrote this poem himself.
⑤ The leaves turned red and yellow.

12 어법상 어색한 것은?

① Sam feels very hungry.
② We felt the ground move.
③ I helped Yuri to buy a new CD.
④ They found the play very exciting.
⑤ These pictures make me thinking of my childhood.

서술형 평가

13 다음 글에서 어법상 어색한 부분을 찾아 바르게 고쳐 쓰시오.

Yesterday was (1) Ann's birthday. Her friend Jack sent her a beautiful card. Emily gave (2) a blue cap to her. Maria bought (3) a teddy bear her. Ann showed all these presents (4) to her classmates. She (5) looked happily.

__________ → __________
__________ → __________

교과서 어휘 share 공유하다 culture 문화 doghouse 개집 arrow 화살 map 지도 poem 시 leaf 나뭇잎 ground 땅 play 연극 childhood 어린 시절 cap 야구모자 present 선물

Reading

[1~2] 다음을 끊어 읽고 ☑, 해석을 쓰시오.

Dolls Around the World

I'm Sweepy. I'm from Germany and my job is to clean chimneys. During winter, chimney sweeps help people to keep warm and safe. So people think chimney sweeps bring them good luck. People even want chimney sweeps to be at their weddings! If you see me, it is your lucky day.

My name is Jose and these are my mariachi band members. We play folk music and always wear our sombreros, or big hats. In Mexico, people wear these hats to stay cool under the hot and strong sunlight. We mariachi players ⓐ<u>to, want, look, our sombreros</u> fancy. So we often decorate them with a lot of different materials. Which of our sombreros do you like best?

1 밑줄 친 ⓐ를 어순에 맞게 배열하시오.

2 위 글에서 언급되지 <u>않은</u> 것은?

① 굴뚝 청소부를 행운의 상징으로 여기기 시작한 때
② 사람들이 결혼식에 굴뚝 청소부를 초청하는 이유
③ 마리아치 악단이 주로 연주하는 음악
④ 멕시코 사람들이 솜브레로를 쓰는 목적
⑤ 마리아치 악단이 솜브레로를 장식하는 이유

교과서 어휘 **Germany** 독일 **chimney sweep** 굴뚝 청소부 **wedding** 결혼식 **mariachi** 마리아치(멕시코 전통 악사) **folk music** 민속 음악 **sombrero** 솜브레로(챙이 넓은 멕시코 모자) **sunlight** 햇볕 **fancy** 화려한, 멋진 **decorate** 장식하다 **material** 재료; 직물

Answer p. 1

3 Fantastic Zoo에서 하게 될 활동이 아닌 것은?

관광 안내

May I have you attention please? Welcome to the Fantastic Zoo. I'm Helen, your tour guide today. Here is the plan for our tour. First, we will go to the Bird World. A new peacock arrived last month. Enjoy his magnificent feathers. Next, we will take a mini train and go to the African Area. You can **see elephants taking** a nap. We will have lunch at the Sunflower Garden. On the way to the Sunflower Garden, we will drop by the Green Lake and watch hippos. After lunch, we will come back to the main gate. Do you have any questions?

① 공작새 관람　② 소형 열차 탑승　③ 코끼리 쇼 관람
④ 하마 관람　⑤ 점심 식사

4 Scott Wade에 관한 다음 글의 내용과 일치하지 않는 것은?

예술

What comes to your mind when you **see a car covered** with dust? Scott Wade had an interesting idea. He thought that it was a perfect canvas for a piece of art. He drew wonderful pictures on the dirty rear window of the car. He changed a dirty car into a moving art gallery. Because of his wonderful work and creativity, he is known as the "da Vinci of dust." At the bottom of the art, he wrote the time, not the date. That's because his artwork can be easily erased by rain or wind, so writing the date is meaningless.

① 먼지로 덮인 차를 그림 그릴 공간으로 여긴다.
② 먼지로 덮인 차의 창문에 그림을 그린다.
③ '먼지의 다빈치'라고 불린다.
④ 작품의 아랫부분에 자신의 이름을 남긴다.
⑤ 그림이 쉽게 지워지므로 작품에 날짜를 쓰지 않는다.

3 **peacock** 공작새 **magnificent** 참으로 아름다운 **feather** 깃털 **drop by** …에 들르다 **hippo** 하마
4 **come to one's mind** 생각이 떠오르다 **dust** 먼지 **rear** 뒤쪽의 **creativity** 창조성 **erase** 지우다 **meaningless** 무의미한

Expression

1 관심 있는 것 묻기 / 관심 말하기

관심 있는 것 묻기

- Are you interested in ...?
- What are you interested in?
- Do you find ... interesting?

관심 말하기

- I'm interested in ....
- I have an interest in ....
- ... interests me (a lot / greatly).
- I'm fascinated by ....
- I'm into ....

2 정보 묻기

구체적인 종류 묻기

- What kind of ... are you going to ...?
- What kind of ... do you ...?
- Which ... do you ...?

여가 활동 묻기

- What do you usually do in your free time?
- What do you like to do for fun?
- What's your hobby?

여가 활동 말하기

- I usually .... / I like to .... / I enjoy ....

Expression Test

Answer p. 2

1 빈칸에 알맞은 것은?

A ____________________
B I'm interested in gardening.

① What should I do?
② What are you doing?
③ What are you interested in?
④ What's your favorite animal?
⑤ Why are you interested in it?

서술형 평가

2 빈칸에 알맞은 말을 쓰시오.

A I'll be a movie director in the future.
B That's cool. What ________ ________ ________ are you going to make?
A I'd like to make a horror movie.

3 밑줄 친 부분과 바꿔 쓸 수 있는 것은?

A Are you interested in rock climbing?
B No. <u>I'm not interested in it.</u>

① I'm into it.
② I like it so much.
③ It's really interesting.
④ I have no interest in it.
⑤ I'm really interested in it.

서술형 평가

4 두 문장이 같은 의미가 되도록 빈칸에 알맞은 말을 쓰시오.

What is your hobby?
= What ________ ________ usually do in your ________ ________?

5 빈칸에 알맞은 것은?

A ____________________
B I listen to rap music.

① Why don't you listen to me?
② Why do you like it so much?
③ What kind of food do you like?
④ What would you like to do today?
⑤ What kind of music do you listen to?

6 자연스러운 대화가 되도록 (A)–(D)를 바르게 배열한 것은?

(A) I like to go skating.
(B) What do you usually do in your free time?
(C) I usually go inline skating and, in the winter, skate on the ice rink.
(D) Sounds interesting. Which skate do you mean, inline skating or ice skating?

① (B) – (C) – (A) – (D)
② (B) – (A) – (C) – (D)
③ (B) – (A) – (D) – (C)
④ (C) – (A) – (B) – (D)
⑤ (D) – (B) – (A) – (C)

서술형 평가

Answer p. 2

1 주어진 단어들을 이용하여 밑줄 친 우리말을 영어로 옮기시오.

A Jane, what do you do in your free time?
B (1) 나는 주로 책을 읽어. (usually, read)
A (2) 너는 어떤 종류의 책을 읽니? (kind of)
B I really like scary novels. Edgar Allan Poe is my favorite writer.
A Oh, I want to read his novels. Can you recommend me one?
B Sure, try "Black Cat."
A Thanks.

(1) ________________________________
(2) ________________________________

2 빈칸에 알맞은 말을 〈보기〉에서 골라 문장을 완성하시오. (형태 변화 가능)

보기

easily	take a rest
sleep	a lazy doll

(1) Some students think math __________.
(2) I call my sister __________.
(3) Long speech made me __________.
(4) Mom looks tired. I want her __________.

3 〈보기〉와 같이 문장을 바꿔 쓰시오.

보기
Dad tells us fun stories.
→ Dad tells fun stories to us.

(1) He wrote me a poem.
→ ________________________________

(2) I made the children kites.
→ ________________________________

(3) Can I ask you something?
→ ________________________________

4 그림을 보고, 주어진 단어들을 배열하여 문장을 완성하시오.

(1)

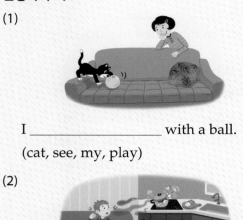

I ________________ with a ball.
(cat, see, my, play)

(2)

I ________________ in the kitchen.
(smell, something, burn)

5 목록을 보고, 주어진 단어들을 이용하여 글을 완성하시오. (형태 변화 가능)

내가 가장 아끼는 물건	
나무 책상	아빠가 내게 만들어 주신 것
골동품 탁자	이모가 프랑스에서 내게 보내 주신 것
노트북 컴퓨터	언니가 생일 선물로 내게 사 준 것

make, it, send, for, buy, this desk, to

These are the most precious things to me. First, the wooden desk is my favorite thing in the world. When I was five, my dad (1) ________ ________ ________ ________. Secondly, this antique table is also precious. Last year, my aunt (2) ________ ________ ________ ________ from France. The last thing is my laptop. My sister (3) ________ ________ ________ ________ for my birthday.

Final Test

Answer p. 2

난이도: 상 ★★★ 중 ★★ 하 ★

★
01 짝지어진 단어의 관계가 나머지 넷과 다른 것은?

① fix – repair ② bright – dark
③ reply – ask ④ clean – dirty
⑤ ill – healthy

★
02 단어의 성격이 나머지 넷과 다른 것은?

① captain ② judge
③ doll ④ designer
⑤ chimney sweep

★★
03 밑줄 친 부분과 바꿔 쓸 수 있는 것은?

A Do you like winter?
B Yes, I do. I'm interested in skiing.

① I'm tired of ② I'm good at
③ I'm really into ④ I have a plan for
⑤ I have a talent for

★★ 서술형 평가
04 그림을 보고, 주어진 단어들을 이용하여 빈칸에 알맞은 말을 쓰시오. (형태 변화 가능)

A What are you interested in?
B I'm ______________________.
(chess, interest, play)

★★
05 자연스러운 대화가 되도록 (A)–(D)를 바르게 배열한 것은?

(A) I'm interested in writing stories. What about you, Karen?
(B) Oh, that's cool.
(C) What are you interested in, Henry?
(D) I really like sports, especially table tennis. I want to be a table tennis player.

① (A) – (C) – (B) – (D)
② (B) – (A) – (D) – (C)
③ (C) – (A) – (D) – (B)
④ (D) – (B) – (C) – (A)
⑤ (D) – (C) – (B) – (A)

★★ 시험에 잘 나오는 문제
06 짝지어진 대화가 어색한 것은?

① A What do you have an interest in?
B I enjoy making candles.
② A What kind of sports do you like?
B I like playing rugby.
③ A Do you like watching TV?
B Yes, I do. I usually watch TV in my free time.
④ A Are you interested in drawing?
B Not really. I'm into drawing pictures.
⑤ A What do you usually do in your free time?
B I like to go shopping.

교과서 어휘 dark 어두운 chess 체스 table tennis 탁구 have an interest in …에 흥미를 가지다 candle 양초 rugby 럭비 picture 그림; 사진

Final Test

★★
07 밑줄 친 우리말을 영어로 바르게 옮긴 것은?

A 너는 무슨 종류의 운동을 좋아하니?
B I like ball games.

① How kind sports do you like?
② What kind sports do you like?
③ How kind of sports do you like?
④ What kind of sports do you like?
⑤ What kind of do you like sports?

★★ 시험에 잘 나오는 문제
08 빈칸에 알맞지 않은 것은?

A What do you like to do for fun?
B ________________

① I went shopping.
② I usually go fishing.
③ I like watching movies.
④ I like to read comic books.
⑤ My hobby is playing soccer.

★★★
09 문장 성분 표시가 알맞지 않은 것은?

① My favorite food (주어) was (동사) pizza (주격보어).
② Coffee (주어) keeps (동사) me (목적어) awake (목적격보어).
③ Mom (주어) made (동사) me (간접목적어) a carrot cake (직접목적어).
④ There (주어) are (동사) many flowers (주격보어) in the vase (부사구).
⑤ We (주어) know (동사) that he comes from London (목적어).

★
10 괄호 안에서 알맞은 것을 고르시오.

(1) The news made the teenagers (happy, happily).
(2) Let me (to introduce, introduce) myself to you.

★★
11 밑줄 친 부분이 목적어인 것은?

① He had Susan do the work.
② These apples look very good.
③ I found this novel interesting.
④ The parents named their baby Charlie.
⑤ Somebody sent me a strange e-mail.

★★ 서술형 평가
12 〈보기〉와 같이 문장을 바꿔 쓸 때 빈칸에 알맞은 말을 쓰시오.

보기
John will wash the dishes. (Ron)
→ Ron will have John wash the dishes.

(1) Bill will clean the room. (I)
→ I'll have Bill ________ the room.
(2) She saw the doctor. (Ted)
→ Ted had her ________ the doctor.

★★★ 시험에 잘 나오는 문제
13 밑줄 친 부분이 어법상 어색한 것은?

① Dad made me wash his car.
② They heard the baby crying.
③ I want Mary go shopping with me.
④ He saw his dog bark at the stranger.
⑤ We helped the farmers pick up the apples.

교과서 어휘 ball game 구기 종목 for fun 재미로 comic book 만화책 awake 깨어 있는 carrot 당근 teenager 청소년 novel 소설 strange 낯선, 이상한 (*n.* stranger 낯선 사람)

★★
14 두 문장을 한 문장으로 바꿔 쓸 때 빈칸에 알맞은 것은?

• Tom saw Jane.
• She was dancing to the music.
→ Tom saw ________ to the music.

① to dance Jane ② dancing Jane
③ Jane dances ④ Jane to dance
⑤ Jane dancing

[15~16] 빈칸에 알맞은 것을 고르시오.

★
15

My grandparents want me ________ a good computer programmer.

① be ② to be ③ being
④ to being ⑤ been

★★
16

Yuri ________ me water the plants.

① wanted ② told ③ made
④ asked ⑤ advised

★★ 서술형 평가
17 두 문장이 같은 의미가 되도록 빈칸에 알맞은 말을 쓰시오.

(1) Ann bought us a concert ticket.
= Ann bought a concert ticket ________ us.

(2) Roy usually tells me a joke.
= Roy usually tells a joke ________ me.

★★★
18 같은 형식의 문장을 〈보기〉에서 고르시오.

보기
ⓐ I heard you sing a song.
ⓑ Judy always has breakfast at 7:00.
ⓒ Picasso and Gogh were famous painters.

(1) Knowledge is power.
(2) We called the cat Kitty.
(3) My new shoes are very nice.
(4) You must keep your teeth clean.
(5) We can't eat any food in the fridge.
(6) I bought a notebook and two erasers.

★★ 서술형 평가
19 〈보기〉와 같이 문장을 바꿔 쓸 때 빈칸에 알맞은 말을 쓰시오.

보기
"Turn off the radio, Tom."
→ I told Tom to turn off the radio.

(1) "Take care of the dog, Bill."
→ ________________________

(2) "Boys, be quiet in the classroom."
→ ________________________

★★
20 〈보기〉와 문장의 형식이 같은 것은?

보기
I think Sora smart.

① The boy runs very quickly.
② I can't understand modern art.
③ Apples and peaches are delicious.
④ Peter sent me a Christmas present.
⑤ I saw him put the key on the table.

교과서 어휘 grandparent 조부모 water 물을 주다 joke 농담 painter 화가 knowledge 지식 fridge 냉장고 eraser 지우개 turn off 끄다 smart 똑똑한 quickly 재빠르게 peach 복숭아

Final Test

★★ 서술형 평가

21 어법상 <u>어색한</u> 부분을 찾아 바르게 고쳐 쓰시오.

A You look tiredly. What's wrong?
B I didn't sleep well last night. It was too hot.

__________ → __________

★★

22 밑줄 친 부분의 알맞은 형태로 바르게 짝지어진 것은?

• Good music will make you <u>feel</u> better.
• Mr. and Ms. Park saw their son <u>study</u> in his room.

① feel – study ② feel – to study
③ to feel – study ④ feeling – studying
⑤ feeling – to study

★★

23 밑줄 친 ⓐ–ⓓ 중 어법상 <u>어색한</u> 것은?

A Look ⓐ <u>at</u> the flower.
B Wow. It's very ⓑ <u>beautiful</u>.
A It smells ⓒ <u>sweetly</u>, ⓓ <u>too</u>.

① ⓐ ② ⓑ ③ ⓒ ④ ⓓ ⑤ 없음

★★ 서술형 평가

24 주어진 단어들을 바르게 배열하여 문장을 완성하시오.

(1) me, bought, a new backpack
→ Mom __________________.

(2) a birthday present, sent, his friend
→ He __________________.

★★

25 빈칸에 알맞은 것은?

Lantern Festival is a holiday celebrated in China and other Asian countries. It's on the last day of the Spring Festival. It celebrates the first full moon of the new lunar year. During the festival, houses are decorated with colorful lanterns, often with riddles written on them. If anyone answers the riddle correctly, the riddle maker ________ the solver a small gift.

① lends ② teaches ③ shows
④ gives ⑤ considers

★★

26 (A)–(C)의 순서로 알맞은 것은?

Are you curious about volcanoes? You can make a volcano at home. Get an empty plastic bottle. Cover the bottle with clay except the hole.

(A) Add two spoonfuls of baking soda to the liquid.
(B) Pour vinegar into the volcano slowly and wait for the eruption.
(C) Fill it with warm water.

Lava will slowly flow everywhere!

*eruption (화산의) 분화, 폭발 *lava 용암

① (A) – (B) – (C) ② (A) – (C) – (B)
③ (B) – (A) – (C) ④ (C) – (A) – (B)
⑤ (C) – (B) – (A)

교과서 어휘 lantern 등, 전등 celebrate 기념하다 lunar year 음력 riddle 수수께끼 correctly 정확하게 volcano 화산 clay 찰흙 a spoonful of 한 숟가락의 … liquid 액체

Answer p. 2

[27~28] 다음을 읽고, 물음에 답하시오.

Hello, Jinsu!

Thanks for replying to my e-mail so quickly. Also, thank you for saying that you can give me a ride from Incheon Airport to the hotel. I finally finished packing. I am so thrilled. I will take the Airbus A380 from Heathrow Airport and arrive at Incheon International Airport at 10:30 a.m. Let's meet in front of Arrival Gate 6 at 11:30. If there are any changes, I'll let you know. I'm looking forward to visiting Korea.

With love, *Lucy*

★★
27 Jinsu와 Lucy가 만날 장소로 알맞은 것은?

① hotel ② Airbus A380
③ Jinsu's house ④ Heathrow Airport
⑤ Incheon Airport

★★
28 밑줄 친 know의 형태로 알맞은 것은?

① knew ② know ③ to know
④ knowing ⑤ have known

[29~30] 다음을 읽고, 물음에 답하시오.

I'm Sarah Parrott from class 7. ⓐI'm looking for an antique hand mirror. I carved the initials of my name, SP on it. ⓑI think I left it on the hand dryer in the girl's restroom on the second floor. ⓒIt looks quite old and has scratches here and there. But it is precious to me because ⓓmy grandma gave me it. If anyone finds it, ⓔplease leave a comment here or text me. My phone number is 099-0094-9400.

★★
29 글쓴이가 찾는 물건에 대한 설명으로 알맞지 않은 것은?

① 오래되어 보인다.
② Sarah Parrott이 새겨져 있다.
③ 여기저기 흠집이 나 있다.
④ 할머니께서 주셨다.
⑤ 2층 화장실에 마지막으로 두었다.

★★
30 밑줄 친 ⓐ–ⓔ 중 어법상 어색한 것은?

① ⓐ ② ⓑ ③ ⓒ ④ ⓓ ⑤ ⓔ

교과서 어휘 **give ... a ride** …을 차로 태워 주다 **thrilled** 흥분되는 **antique** 골동품의 **mirror** 거울 **carve** 새기다 **initial** 이름의 머리글자 **scratch** 흠집 **precious** 귀중한 **leave a comment** 댓글을 남기다 **text** 문자 메시지를 보내다

>> Grammar

A 보어

1 동사 뒤에서 주어에 관해 보충 설명하는 말이 있어야 하는 동사가 있다.

동사	be동사	become	turn, get
의미	…이다	…이(하게) 되다	…한 상태가 되다
보어	명사, 형용사		형용사

Time **is money**. The color **turns yellow**.

2 **감각동사**: 감각을 나타내는 동사 뒤에는 보어로 형용사를 쓴다.

look …해 보이다	feel …하게 느끼다	sound …하게 들리다
taste …한 맛이 나다	smell …한 냄새가 나다	

You **look tired** today. The chicken soup **tastes delicious**.

B 목적어

1 **목적어**: 동작의 대상이 되는 말을 목적어라고 하며, 명사 역할을 하는 말이 목적어로 쓰인다.

We must protect **nature**. Tom wants to buy **a new computer**.

2 **수여동사**

〈수여동사+간접목적어+직접목적어〉의 어순으로 쓰며, 두 목적어의 자리를 바꿔 쓸 때 간접목적어 앞에는 전치사를 쓴다.

to	for	of
bring, give, lend, send, show, teach, tell 등	buy, cook, make, choose, get 등	ask

Andy **told** me his address.
→ Andy **told** his address **to** me.

Austin **bought** me some postcards.
→ Austin **bought** some postcards **for** me.

C 목적어와 목적격보어

목적격보어는 목적어에 관해 보충 설명하는 말로, 주로 명사, 형용사, 부정사, 분사를 목적격보어로 쓰며 다음 동사들은 목적격보어로 to부정사를 쓴다.

want 원하다	ask 요구하다	tell 말하다	order 명령하다
expect 기대하다	advise 충고하다	cause 야기하다	enable 가능하게 하다

Mr. Emerson thinks himself **a great judge**. The news made me **happy**.
My parents want me **to study** abroad. Laura expected me **to play** the guitar.

D 사역동사의 목적격보어

'…하게 하다'라는 의미의 사역동사 make, let, have는 목적격보어로 동사원형을 쓴다.

Robert **let** me **use** his computer. My mom will **have** Tom **clean** his room.

cf. help(…가 …하는 것을 돕다)는 목적격보어로 동사원형이나 to부정사를 쓴다.
I **helped** Sam **(to) fix** the radio.

E 지각동사의 목적격보어

watch, hear, see, feel 등의 감각과 관련된 동사는 목적격보어로 동사원형 또는 현재분사를 쓴다.

Sora **felt** her heart **beat** when she saw Tony.

I **heard** someone **knocking** at the door.

cf. 지각동사, 사역동사의 목적격보어와 목적어의 관계가 수동이면 목적격보어로 과거분사를 쓴다.
I **had** the wall **painted**. I **saw** the man **taken** to the hospital.

>> Expression

1 관심 있는 것 묻기 / 관심 말하기

관심 있는 것 묻기
- Are you interested in ...?
- What are you interested in?
- Do you find ... interesting?

관심 말하기
- I'm interested in ....
- I have an interest in ....
- ... interests me (a lot / greatly).
- I'm fascinated by ....
- I'm into ....

2 정보 묻기

구체적인 종류 묻기
- What kind of ... are you going to ...?
- What kind of ... do you ...?
- Which ... do you ...?

여가 활동 묻기
- What do you usually do in your free time?
- What do you like to do for fun?
- What's your hobby?

여가 활동 말하기
- I usually .... / I like to .... / I enjoy ....

Lesson 02

to부정사

Grammar Preview

1 to부정사

〈to+동사원형〉의 형태로 명사, 형용사, 부사의 역할을 하며, 동사처럼 목적어, 수식어구와 함께 쓰인다.

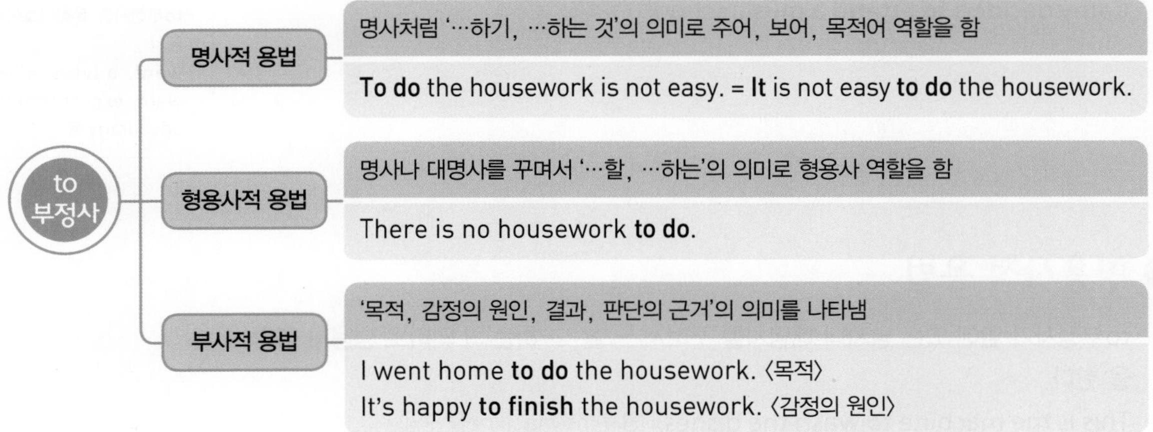

to 부정사
명사적 용법
명사처럼 '…하기, …하는 것'의 의미로 주어, 보어, 목적어 역할을 함
To do the housework is not easy. = It is not easy to do the housework.
형용사적 용법
명사나 대명사를 꾸며서 '…할, …하는'의 의미로 형용사 역할을 함
There is no housework to do.
부사적 용법
'목적, 감정의 원인, 결과, 판단의 근거'의 의미를 나타냄
I went home to do the housework. 〈목적〉
It's happy to finish the housework. 〈감정의 원인〉

2 to부정사의 활용

• to부정사가 나타내는 동작의 행위자를 to부정사의 의미상 주어라고 한다.

I'm happy to hear the news. 〈to hear의 주어 I〉

The movie is not easy **for me** to understand. 〈to understand의 주어 me〉

It was careless **of you** to break the plate. 〈to break의 주어 you〉

It's expensive **(for people)** to buy designer shoes. 〈to buy의 주어가 일반인이므로 생략〉

• 의문사+to부정사

what+to부정사	무엇을 …할지	when+to부정사	언제 …할지
where+to부정사	어디서(로) …할지	how+to부정사	어떻게 …할지
which+to부정사	어느 것을 …할지	who(m)+to부정사	누구를(에게) …할지

• to부정사의 관용 표현

형용사(부사)+enough+to부정사 = so ... that+주어+can(could) ... …할 만큼 충분히 …한(하게)

too+형용사(부사)+to부정사 = so ... that+주어+can't(couldn't) ... 너무 …해서 …할 수 없는

1 to부정사

A 명사적 용법

to부정사가 명사처럼 쓰여서 문장의 주어, 보어, 목적어 역할을 한다.

To do the housework is not easy. 〈주어〉
= **It** is not easy **to do** the housework. 〈가주어 it〉
My hobby is **to collect** postcards. 〈보어〉
Cathy decided **to attend** a music school. 〈목적어〉

Plus Grammar

- **to부정사를 목적어로 취하는 동사**
  want, wish, hope, decide, plan, expect, promise, fail, ask, agree, learn, refuse, need, choose 등
- **to부정사를 목적격보어로 취하는 동사**
  want, advise, allow, ask, warn, expect, order, cause, encourage 등

B 형용사적 용법

to부정사가 앞에 있는 명사나 대명사를 꾸며서 '…할, …하는'의 의미로 형용사 역할을 한다.

This is the machine **to wash** the dishes. 〈명사 the machine을 꾸밈〉
I have nothing **to eat.** 〈대명사 nothing을 꾸밈〉

cf. 형용사적 용법의 to부정사가 꾸미는 (대)명사가 to부정사 뒤에 쓰이는 전치사의 목적어이면, to부정사 뒤의 전치사를 생략할 수 없다.
My grandma needs an armchair **to sit on.**
I need a real friend **to talk with.**

C 부사적 용법

to부정사가 문장에서 부사 역할을 할 때는 목적, 감정의 원인, 결과, 판단의 근거를 나타낸다.

목적	…하기 위하여(=in order to / so as to)
감정의 원인	…해서, …하게 되어(주로 감정을 나타내는 sad, glad, frightened, happy, surprised 등의 형용사 다음에 쓰임)
결과	(…해서) …하다
판단의 근거	…하다니(추측을 표현)

I go to the gym **to lose** weight. 〈목적〉
I'm happy **to hear** our picnic plan. 〈감정의 원인〉
Sienna grew up **to be** a world-famous cook. 〈결과〉
Gary must be a soldier **to behave** like that. 〈판단의 근거〉

cf. to부정사가 앞에 쓰인 형용사를 꾸며 '…하기에'라는 뜻도 지닌다.
This word is difficult **to remember.**

Grammar Practice >>

Answer p. 4

A1 밑줄 친 부분의 역할을 <보기>에서 고르시오.

보기

ⓐ 주어 ⓑ 보어 ⓒ 목적어

(1) To see is to believe.
(2) I want to eat something.
(3) To laugh loudly makes you healthy.
(4) My hobby is to chat with my friends.
(5) To watch a sports game on TV is boring.
(6) Jim hopes to be a singer in the future.

A2 두 문장이 같은 의미가 되도록 빈칸에 알맞은 말을 쓰시오.

(1) To live without water is impossible.
= ________ is impossible ________ ________ without water.

(2) To learn to cook is very exciting.
= It is very ________ ________ ________ to cook.

(3) It is necessary to finish your work.
= ________ ________ ________ ________ is necessary.

B1 주어진 단어들을 배열하여 문장을 완성하시오.

(1) Here are the ____________________.
(to, answer, questions)

(2) Sam has some ____________________.
(with, play, to, friends)

(3) Jacob looks thirsty. Will you give him ____________________?
(to, something, drink)

(4) I have nothing ____________________.
(tell, you, it, to, about)

B2 우리말과 일치하도록 빈칸에 알맞은 말을 쓰시오.

(1) Owen은 그의 딸에게 들려줄 이야기가 많이 있다.
→ Owen has many stories ________ ________ his daughter.

(2) 나는 읽을 책을 몇 권 샀다.
→ I bought some books ________ ________.

(3) Olivia는 오늘 해야 할 일이 많다.
→ Olivia has many things ________ ________ today.

(4) 나는 편지를 쓸 종이가 한 장 필요하다.
→ I need a sheet of paper ________ ________ a letter ________.

C1 괄호 안에서 알맞은 것을 고르시오.

(1) I turned on my laptop (checked, to check) my e-mail account.
(2) Mina was pleased (to win, to won) the game.
(3) Mr. Archer arrived at his office (know, to know) it's Sunday.
(4) This story is difficult (to understood, to understand).

C2 밑줄 친 부분의 의미를 <보기>에서 고르시오.

보기

ⓐ 목적 ⓑ 판단의 근거
ⓒ 감정의 원인 ⓓ 결과

(1) I went to the library to finish the report.
(2) Ann was happy to get a new bike.
(3) Alan must be strong to carry the table.
(4) Jane got to Leo's home to find he's not there.

교과서 어휘 housework 집안일 attend 출석하다 armchair 안락의자 gym 체육관 world-famous 세계적으로 유명한
behave 행동하다(n. behavior 행동) loudly 큰 소리로 thirsty 목이 마른 carry 들다, 나르다

D to부정사의 의미상 주어

1 to부정사가 나타내는 동작의 행위자를 to부정사의 의미상 주어라고 한다.
I'm happy to hear the news. 〈to hear의 주어 I〉
Brenda hopes to become a president. 〈to become의 주어 Brenda〉

2 to부정사의 의미상 주어가 문장의 주어와 다르면, to부정사 앞에 〈for+목적격〉의 형태로 쓴다. to부정사의 의미상 주어가 특정인이 아니거나, 명확히 드러나는 경우에는 생략한다.
The movie is not easy **for me** to understand.
It's necessary **for professional players** to practice hard.
The movie is not easy **(for people)** to understand.
It's important **(for you)** to keep your receipt.

3 사람에 대한 평가나 사람의 성격을 나타내는 형용사와 함께 쓰이는 to부정사 앞에서는 의미상 주어를 〈of+목적격〉의 형태로 쓴다.
It was careless **of you** to break the plate.
It was stupid **of her** to waste a lot of money.

> **Plus Grammar**
> **사람에 대한 평가나 사람의 성격을 나타내는 형용사**
> brave, polite, foolish, careful, wise, kind, nice, rude 등

E to부정사의 관용 표현

1 **의문사+to부정사:** 주어, 보어, 목적어 역할을 하는데, 주로 목적어로 쓰이며, 〈의문사+주어+should+동사원형〉으로 바꿔 쓸 수 있다.

what+to부정사	무엇을 …할지	when+to부정사	언제 …할지
where+to부정사	어디서[로] …할지	how+to부정사	어떻게 …할지
which+to부정사	어느 것을 …할지	who(m)+to부정사	누구를[에게] …할지

Tell me **when to return** the book.
= Tell me **when I should return** the book.

2 enough to / too … to

형용사[부사]+enough+to부정사	**too+형용사[부사]+to부정사**
= so+형용사[부사]+that+주어+can …	= so+형용사[부사]+that+주어+can't …
…할 만큼 충분히 …한[하게]	너무 …해서 …할 수 없는

Ann is clever **enough to find** the answer.
= Ann is **so** clever **that** she **can find** the answer.
Harry is **too** young **to understand** the poem.
= Harry is **so** young **that** he **can't understand** the poem.

> **Plus Grammar**
> enough가 명사를 꾸밀 때는 명사 앞이나 뒤에 쓴다. 형용사나 부사를 꾸밀 때는 그 뒤에 쓴다.
> Max has **enough money** to buy the diamond ring. (Max는 다이아몬드 반지를 살 만큼 충분한 돈이 있다.)
> Amy is **diligent enough** to help her mother in the morning. (Amy는 아침에 엄마를 도울 만큼 충분히 부지런하다.)

Grammar Practice >>

Answer p. 4

D1 to부정사의 의미상 주어에 밑줄을 그으시오.

(1) It was foolish of you to buy that skirt.

(2) My dad told me to clean the room.

(3) It's dangerous for children to play in the street.

(4) It is kind of her to give a lot of money to the poor.

D2 우리말과 일치하도록 빈칸에 알맞은 말을 쓰시오.

(1) 네가 제시간에 오는 것은 중요하다.

→ It is important ________ ________ to be on time.

(2) Gina가 게임에서 이기는 것은 힘들다.

→ It is hard ________ ________ to win the game.

(3) 내 강아지를 돌봐 주다니 너는 참 착하다.

→ It is nice ________ ________ to take care of my dog.

(4) 그 마을을 찾는 것이 내게는 어려웠다.

→ It was difficult ________ ________ to find the village.

D3 주어진 단어들을 이용하여 빈칸에 알맞은 말을 쓰시오.

(1) It was ________________ to throw away useful things. (careless, Sally)

(2) It's ________________ to say bad words. (rude, him)

(3) It's ________________ to win the lottery. (impossible, Tommy)

(4) It was ________________ to think so. (silly, her)

E1 괄호 안에서 알맞은 것을 고르시오.

(1) The boy is (so, too) young to enter the theater.

(2) I know where (take, to take) the ladder.

(3) This room is (so, too) large that all of us can stay there.

(4) The movie is (great enough, enough great) to win the prize.

(5) Please let me know (how, what) to make pizza.

(6) Stanley is too lazy (to finish, finish) the work by tomorrow.

(7) I don't know (what, where) to get off the bus.

E2 두 문장이 같은 의미가 되도록 빈칸에 알맞은 말을 쓰시오.

(1) Let me know when to leave.

= Let me know when I ________ leave.

(2) Emilia is so tall that she can touch the ceiling.

= Emilia is tall ________ to touch the ceiling.

(3) Elizabeth was too happy to sleep.

= Elizabeth was so happy that she ________ sleep.

(4) I'm clever enough to solve the puzzle.

= I'm ________ clever that I ________ solve the puzzle.

(5) Can you tell me where I should stay?

= Can you tell me where ________ ________?

교과서 어휘 president 대통령 careless 부주의한 plate 접시 stupid 어리석은 on time 제시간에 useful 유용한 rude 무례한 lottery 복권 silly 어리석은 ladder 사다리 get off 내리다 ceiling 천장

Grammar Test

[01~02] 빈칸에 알맞은 것을 고르시오.

01

_______ in this river is very dangerous.

① Swim ② Swam ③ Swim to
④ To swim ⑤ To swimming

02

There isn't a chair _______.

① to sit ② sit ③ sitting
④ sit on ⑤ to sit on

03 밑줄 친 부분의 형태로 바르게 짝지어진 것은?

• The bed is too heavy move.
• Do you know where put this table?

① move – put ② move – to put
③ moving – put ④ to move – putting
⑤ to move – to put

서술형 평가

04 빈칸에 알맞은 말을 쓰시오.

• It's necessary _______ you to read the book.
• It was very kind _______ Lucy to show the foreigner the way.

05 밑줄 친 부분의 쓰임이 나머지와 다른 것은?

① I was very glad to see you.
② Robert must be wise to say so.
③ Matilda grew up to be a nurse.
④ Sarah went to Canada to learn English.
⑤ Ian promised to help me with the work.

06 빈칸에 알맞지 않은 것은?

It was _______ of Joe to buy the MP3 player for his sister.

① foolish ② wise ③ careless
④ nice ⑤ impossible

서술형 평가

07 어법상 어색한 부분을 찾아 문장을 고쳐 쓰시오.

It was very wise for you to say so.

→ _______________________

08 두 문장의 의미가 같도록 할 때 빈칸에 알맞은 것은?

I don't know when I should sell my house.
= I don't know _________ my house.

① when selling ② when to sell
③ to when sell ④ to sell when
⑤ when to selling

교과서 어휘 river 강 move 옮기다 necessary 필요한, 필수의 foreigner 외국인 wise 현명한 nurse 간호사 promise 약속하다

Answer p. 4

서술형 평가

09 우리말과 일치하도록 빈칸에 알맞은 말을 쓰시오.

Ethan은 혼자서 여행할 수 있을 만큼 충분히 나이가 들었다.

→ Ethan is ________ ________ ________ travel by himself.

[10~11] 주어진 문장과 의미가 같은 것을 고르시오.

10

Tom is very smart. So he can find the answer.

① Tom is too smart to find the answer.
② Tom is smart enough to find the answer.
③ Tom is enough smart to find the answer.
④ Tom is so smart that he can't find the answer.
⑤ Tom is not smart but he can find the answer.

11

The bread was too dry for me to eat.

① The bread was so dry that I can eat it.
② The bread wasn't dry that I can't eat it.
③ The bread was so dry that I could eat it.
④ The bread wasn't dry that I couldn't eat it.
⑤ The bread was so dry that I couldn't eat it.

12 〈보기〉의 밑줄 친 부분과 쓰임이 같은 것은?

보기
Sue went to the market <u>to buy</u> some apples.

① English is difficult <u>to learn</u>.
② Please give me a hat <u>to wear</u>.
③ Molly doesn't want <u>to go</u> on a boat trip.
④ Adam was surprised <u>to see</u> the fantastic scene.
⑤ Nora will take a camera <u>to take</u> some pictures.

서술형 평가

13 두 문장을 〈보기〉와 같이 한 문장으로 바꿔 쓰시오.

보기
Anna ran very fast. She wanted to win the race.
→ Anna ran very fast to win the race.

I went to the bakery. I wanted to buy some bread.

→ ________________________________

14 두 문장의 의미가 같도록 할 때 빈칸에 들어갈 말이 바르게 짝지어진 것은?

Milo is tall enough to hit his head on the ceiling.
= Milo is ________ tall that he ________ hit his head on the ceiling.

① so – could ② too – could
③ too – couldn't ④ so – can
⑤ so – can't

교과서 어휘 by oneself 혼자서 smart 똑똑한 dry 마른, 건조한 market 시장 hat 모자 fantastic 환상적인 scene 장면

Reading

[1~2] 다음을 끊어 읽고 ☑, 해석을 쓰시오.

My Tech-Free Trip Story

Last summer, I had a new and different experience: a family trip to Barcelona without a smartphone. Our first day was ⓐ nice. On the way to our guesthouse around Plaza Reial, we got lost. Dad was busy looking at the map and asking for directions with a few Spanish words. ⓑ Even though our guesthouse was right next to the Plaza, it took us about two hours to get there. Next day, we had seafood fried rice at a small local restaurant. The dish was ⓒ amazing. I really wanted to take pictures of the food and post them on my blog. But without my phone, I just decided to enjoy the moment. During the remaining days, we ⓓ relied more and more on the locals. We were able to meet and talk with various people there. Also, our family talked a lot with each other all the time and everywhere. Before the trip, I was (A) so dependent on my smartphone that I couldn't do anything without it. But now I see that I can enjoy the moment ⓔ without it.

1 밑줄 친 ⓐ–ⓔ 중 문맥상 의미가 어색한 것은?

① ⓐ ② ⓑ ③ ⓒ ④ ⓓ ⑤ ⓔ

2 밑줄 친 (A)를 주어진 단어들을 이용하여 바꿔 쓰시오.

______________________ (too, to)

교과서 어휘 experience 경험, 체험 on the way to …로 가는 길에 plaza 광장 get lost 길을 잃다 map 지도 ask for directions 길을 묻다 local 지역의, 현지의; 현지인 post 게시하다 remaining 남아 있는 rely on …에 의지하다 various 다양한 dependent 의지하는

Answer p. 4

3 밑줄 친 ⓐ–ⓔ 중 글 전체의 흐름상 어색한 것은?

심리

Have you ever experienced getting in line **to buy** some "limited edition" baseball caps or clothes? ⓐ Then, you might have FOMO. ⓑ The word stands for Fear of Missing Out. If you think you won't be able to get a product because it's selling quickly, ⓒ you're not likely to rush **to buy** it. Therefore, ⓓ many companies use FOMO a lot in marketing. Apple, for example, uses this strategy ⓔ when it releases a limited number of phones **to make** people want **to buy** them.

① ⓐ ② ⓑ ③ ⓒ ④ ⓓ ⑤ ⓔ

4 밑줄 친 mysterious machine에 관한 다음 글의 내용과 일치하지 않는 것은?

일화

A mysterious machine arrived at the Franklin Institute Science Museum. It looked like a young boy, but no one knew anything about it. Curators put the old parts together and set motors in motion. Then, the machine came to life. It opened its eyes, held a pen in hand with amazing movements and wrote poetry. The machine wrote these words in French: "Written by the Automaton of Maillardet." This machine was made by Henri Maillardet, a Swiss clockmaker. In the eighteenth century, clockmakers often invented machines like this **to show off** their skill.

*automaton 로봇 같은 사람

① 소년처럼 생겼다. ② 살아 있는 것처럼 움직였다. ③ 손으로 펜을 쥐고 시를 썼다.
④ 프랑스어를 쓸 줄 알았다. ⑤ 18세기 큐레이터들이 만들었다.

3 **limited edition** 한정판 **stand for** …을 의미하다 **rush** 급히 움직이다 **strategy** 전략 **release** 공개하다
4 **curator** 큐레이터 **part** 부품 **put together** 조립하다 **set ... in motion** …에 시동을 걸다 **come to life** 살아 움직이다 **show off** 자랑하다

Expression

1 길 묻고 답하기

길 묻기

- Where is ...?
- Can(Could) you show me the way to ...?
- Can(Could) you tell me where ... is?
- How do(can) I get to ...?
- I'm looking for ....

길 안내하기

- Go straight for three blocks.
- Turn left(right) at the second corner.
- It's across(next to) the bank.
- You can't miss it.
- Sorry. I'm new(a stranger) here, too.

소요 시간 묻고 답하기

- How long does(will) it take to go to ...?
- (Maybe) It takes(will take) about ....

2 능력 여부 묻기 / 능력 표현하기

능력 여부 묻기

- Are you good at ...?
- Do you know how to ...?
- Can you (tell me how to) ...?

능력 표현하기

- I'm good at ....
- I can ....
- I know how to ....
- I'm able to ....

Expression Test

Answer p. 5

1 빈칸에 알맞지 않은 것은?

A Do you know how to fix this radio?
B Sorry, but ____________.
You can ask Minsu. He is good at it.

① I can't fix a radio
② I don't know how to fix it
③ I can tell you how to fix it
④ I'm not good at fixing things
⑤ I don't know about the machine well

2 밑줄 친 부분과 바꿔 쓸 수 없는 것은?

A Excuse me. Where is the nearest bank?
B Turn right at the second corner. It's on your left.

① How do I get to
② How can I get to
③ How far is it from here to
④ Could you tell me the way to
⑤ Can you show me the way to

3 짝지어진 대화가 어색한 것은?

① A Are you good at driving?
B That's good for me.
② A How long will it take to get there?
B It'll take about 30 minutes.
③ A Can you tell me where the bakery is?
B Sorry, but I don't know.
④ A How can I go to the museum?
B You can take a shuttle bus over there.
⑤ A Go straight for two blocks. You can see it on your left.
B Thank you.

서술형 평가

4 우리말과 일치하도록 빈칸에 알맞은 말을 쓰시오.

A ________ ________ I get ________ the subway station?
(지하철역에 어떻게 가죠?)
B Go straight for two blocks.

5 밑줄 친 부분과 바꿔 쓸 수 있는 것은?

A Can you tell me how to fly drones?
B Sure. I'm good at drones. I can tell you how.

① How about flying drones?
② Why don't you fly drones?
③ Are you going to fly drones?
④ How did you learn to fly drones?
⑤ Do you know how to fly drones?

서술형 평가

6 그림을 보고, 빈칸에 알맞은 말을 쓰시오.

A Can you tell me the way to the bookstore?
B Go straight for ________ ________ and turn left. It's ________ to the bakery.
A Thanks.

서술형 평가

Answer p. 5

1 주어진 단어들을 이용하여 밑줄 친 우리말을 영어로 옮기시오.

A Jake, (1) 너 수리점이 어디에 있는지 아니? (know, where, the repair shop)
B Yeah, it's on Pearson Street.
A Can you tell me how to get there from school?
B Yeah, take the bus no. 7 and get off at Green Park. (2) 그것은 공원 건너편에 있어. (across, the park)
A Thanks a lot.

(1) ______________________________
(2) ______________________________

2 두 문장이 같은 의미가 되도록 빈칸에 알맞은 말을 넣어 문장을 완성하시오.

(1) The tea is too hot for me to drink.
= The tea is so ____________.

(2) The pizza was too big for me to eat alone.
= The pizza was so ____________.

3 표를 보고, 빈칸에 알맞은 말을 쓰시오.

Where	What to do
Lucy's Table	have breakfast
Green Park	take some pictures
Grand Theater	watch the musical *Lion King*

Today is Joy's last day in New York. Joy has many things to do today. She will go to Lucy's Table (1) ____________ ____________. Next, she will go to Green Park (2) ____________. At night, she will go to (3) ____________ ____________.

4 그림을 보고, 주어진 단어들을 이용하여 그림 속 인물의 말을 완성하시오.

(1)

I need ____________.
(a pen, write)

(2)

I want ____________.
(some dessert, eat)

5 엄마의 메모를 보고, 〈보기〉와 같이 문장을 완성하시오.

Dear John,
I'm going out. Eat the sandwiches in the refrigerator. Do your homework. Turn off lights when you go out. I'll be back by 8 o'clock.
Mom

보기
Mom told me to eat the sandwiches in the refrigerator.

(1) Mom wanted me ____________.
(2) Mom asked ____________ when I go out.

Final Test

Answer p. 5

난이도: 상 ★★★ 중 ★★ 하 ★

★

01 짝지어진 단어의 관계가 나머지 넷과 다른 것은?

① true – false ② loud – noisy
③ wise – smart ④ move – carry
⑤ rely – depend

★★ 서술형 평가

02 빈칸에 알맞은 단어를 〈보기〉에서 골라 쓰시오.

보기: chat scene direction

(1) Which ________ should I go to get to the log cabin?
(2) I ________ with my friends on the phone every night.
(3) The police arrived at the ________ of the accident.

★★ 시험에 잘 나오는 문제

03 빈칸에 알맞지 않은 것은?

A Excuse me. ____________________
B Go straight one block and turn right. It's on your left.

① How do I get to the park?
② How can I get to the park?
③ How do you go to the park?
④ Could you tell me the way to the park?
⑤ Could you tell me how to get to the park?

★★ 서술형 평가

04 〈보기〉에서 알맞은 말을 골라 대화를 완성하시오.

보기: much make long take

A How ________ does it ________ to go to the library?
B It takes about ten minutes to the library.

★★

05 빈칸에 알맞은 것은?

A ____________________
B Sure, what is it?
A I need to move this box, but it's so heavy.

① Can I help you?
② May I help you?
③ Can you help me?
④ How may I help you?
⑤ What can I do for you?

★★ 서술형 평가

06 자연스러운 대화가 되도록 A의 말에 이어질 (A)–(C)의 순서를 바르게 배열하시오.

A Is there a post office around here?
(A) Great. How do I get there?
(B) Yes, there's one near here.
(C) Go straight two blocks and turn right. It's on your left.

________ → ________ → ________

교과서 어휘 **false** 거짓의 **get to** …에 도착하다 **chat with** …와 이야기를 나누다 **accident** 사고 **heavy** 무거운 **post office** 우체국

Final Test

★ 시험에 잘 나오는 문제

07 밑줄 친 부분과 바꿔 쓸 수 있는 것은?

A Do you know how to order pizza on the Internet?
B Yes, it's easy.

① Can you ② Where can I
③ Why don't we ④ Do you mind if I
⑤ Would you like to

★★ 서술형 평가

08 주어진 단어들을 배열하여 대화를 완성하시오.

A Will you go swimming with me?
B Sorry, but I can't. ____________
(swim, to, able, I, not, am)

★★

09 〈보기〉의 밑줄 친 부분과 쓰임이 같은 것은?

보기
I have something to tell you.

① I'm glad to see this beautiful sight.
② Alex grew up to be a famous painter.
③ People want to watch his concert.
④ We hurried to catch the train to Busan.
⑤ Neil Armstrong was the first man to walk on the moon.

★★ 서술형 평가

10 주어진 단어들을 바르게 배열하여 문장을 완성하시오.

I'm hungry. Is there ________ ________ ________? (to, anything, eat)

[11~12] 빈칸에 알맞은 것을 고르시오.

★

11

His dream is ________ a famous singer.

① be ② became ③ to being
④ to be ⑤ become

★★

12

We went to the gym ____________.

① to catch a train
② to have dinner
③ to play badminton
④ to get some stamps
⑤ to buy some bread

★★ 서술형 평가

13 두 문장을 한 문장으로 바꿔 쓸 때 빈칸에 알맞은 말을 쓰시오.

(1) Anderson saved money. He wanted to buy a new cell phone.
→ Anderson saved money ________ ________ a new cell phone.

(2) Anna will go to Paris. She wants to shop for designer clothes.
→ Anna will go to Paris ________ ________ for designer clothes.

교과서 어휘 order 주문하다 sight 풍경 hurry 서두르다 moon 달 gym 체육관 save (돈을) 모으다 designer 유명 디자이너가 만든

Answer p. 5

★
14 빈칸에 알맞지 않은 것은?

It is ________ for him to understand this book.

① possible ② difficult ③ easy
④ silly ⑤ important

★★ 서술형 평가
15 어법상 어색한 부분을 찾아 문장을 고쳐 쓰시오.

(1) It was kind for him to visit me when I was ill.
→ ________________________

(2) Dad taught me how playing chess.
→ ________________________

★★
16 우리말을 영어로 바르게 옮긴 것은?

Tom은 너무 피곤해서 파티에 올 수 없었다.

① Tom was tired to come to the party.
② Tom is too tired to come to the party.
③ Tom wasn't tired to come to the party.
④ Tom was too tired to come to the party.
⑤ Tom is too tired not to come to the party.

★★ 서술형 평가
17 우리말과 일치하도록 빈칸에 알맞은 말을 쓰시오.

나는 무엇을 먹을지 결정하지 못했다.
→ I didn't decide ________ ________ ________.

★★ 시험에 잘 나오는 문제
18 밑줄 친 It(it)의 쓰임이 나머지와 다른 것은?

① It is too cold to play outside.
② It is important to obey the safety rules.
③ It is dangerous for her to swim in this river.
④ Is it difficult for Tom to win the boxing match?
⑤ It's a great pleasure to meet a close friend after a long time.

★★ 서술형 평가
19 빈칸에 각각 알맞은 전치사를 쓰시오.

• It is impossible ________ Minho to speak French.
• It was foolish ________ you to be late for the important interview.

★★
20 빈칸에 알맞은 것은?

A Judy is so kind! She took me to the library yesterday.
B I think so, too. She is ____________ do that.

① kind enough to
② kind to enough
③ enough kind to
④ to kind enough
⑤ not enough kind to

교과서 어휘 **ill** 병에 걸린, 아픈 **decide** 결정하다 **outside** 밖에서 **obey** 따르다, 순종하다 **safety rule** 안전 수칙 **match** 경기, 시합 **close** 친한 **interview** 인터뷰, 면접

Final Test

★★
21 밑줄 친 부분의 쓰임이 나머지와 다른 것은?

① I'm happy to meet you again.
② Jake grew up to be a scientist.
③ They liked to hear the ghost story.
④ Amy phoned to invite me to a party.
⑤ I went to the playground to play hide and seek.

[22~23] 밑줄 친 부분을 알맞은 형태로 바꿔 쓰시오.

★
22

I went to the library borrow some books.

→ ____________

★★
23

He encouraged me try again.

→ ____________

★★★
24 어법상 옳은 것은?

① I was too busy contact players.
② I don't know what saying about it.
③ To go out late at night is dangerous.
④ Sally is enough smart to know the answer.
⑤ They needed money in order buying food.

★★
25 다음 글의 내용과 일치하지 않는 것은?

My name is Antonia and I like performing with exotic musical instruments. I learned to play bagpipe three years ago from my Irish friend. Dad taught me how to play harp. I'm also an excellent djembe player. I taught myself by watching videos online. I'm applying for a Teen Talent Show audition to show off my skills. I hope you all enjoy my performance.

① Antonia는 이국적인 악기에 관심이 많다.
② Antonia는 백파이프를 연주할 수 있다.
③ Antonia는 아버지에게 하프 연주법을 배웠다.
④ Antonia는 친구로부터 젬베 연주법을 배웠다.
⑤ Antonia는 오디션에 참가한다.

★
26 다음 글의 종류로 알맞은 것은?

Do you think two people who have nothing in common can fall in love? Last weekend my son and I watched the movie *Me Before You* and we loved the story. In the movie, a woman fell in love with a man who decided to end his life. If you want a moving story full of humor, this movie is perfect for you. You can laugh, cry and smile throughout this masterpiece.

① a diary
② a movie script
③ a news article
④ a movie review
⑤ an advertisement

교과서 어휘 hide and seek 숨바꼭질 contact 연락하다 exotic 이국적인 instrument 악기 online 인터넷으로 apply for …에 지원하다 performance 공연 fall in love 사랑에 빠지다 moving 감동적인 masterpiece 걸작, 명작

Answer p. 5

[27~28] 다음을 읽고, 물음에 답하시오.

Dear Anna,

Welcome to the city of love, Vienna!

My apartment is small but it will be cozy enough ___(A)___ you ___(B)___ stay for two days. The food in the refrigerator is all for you. There are eggs, milk, jam and butter. Pasta and bread are on the shelf in the kitchen. If you need anything, there is a convenience store on Goldberg Street, next to the flower shop. Make yourself at home. If you have any questions, e-mail me. Enjoy your stay!

With love, *Stella*

★
27 위 글의 Stella의 아파트에 없는 것은?

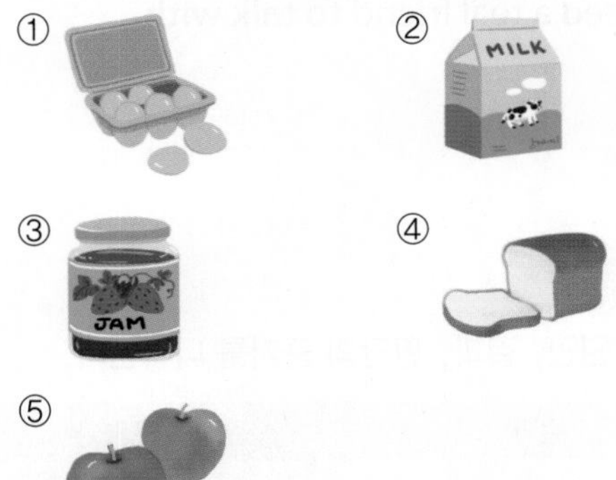

★★
28 빈칸 (A)와 (B)에 들어갈 말이 바르게 짝지어진 것은?

① to – of ② by – to ③ for – to
④ to – for ⑤ of – for

[29~30] 다음을 읽고, 물음에 답하시오.

____________________ One possible theory is that this tradition began in ancient Greece. The Greeks would make round cakes to honor Artemis, the goddess of the moon. They lit candles on the cake ⓐto represent the glow of the moon, and they believed the smoke from the candles carried people's prayers to the gods in the skies. Some scholars believe the tradition actually started in Germany. The Germans placed candles on the cake to represent "the light of life."

★★
29 빈칸에 알맞은 것은?

① Have you ever been to Germany?
② What do you do on your birthday?
③ Why do people like birthday candles?
④ What did the Greeks eat on birthday?
⑤ Where did the tradition of birthday candles come from?

★★
30 밑줄 친 ⓐ와 쓰임이 같은 것은?

① We don't have time to watch TV.
② To believe in yourself is important.
③ My sister went to Paris to study art.
④ Rose was surprised to see such a big parade.
⑤ My brother wishes to win the soccer match.

교과서 어휘 cozy 아늑한 shelf 선반 convenience store 편의점 make oneself at home 느긋하게 쉬다 theory 이론 ancient 고대의 honor 기리다 represent 상징하다, 나타내다 glow 불꽃 smoke 연기 scholar 학자

>> Grammar

A 명사적 용법

to부정사가 명사처럼 쓰여서 문장의 주어, 보어, 목적어 역할을 한다.

주어	**To do** the housework is not easy. = **It**'s not easy **to do** the housework. 〈가주어 it〉
보어	My hobby is **to collect** postcards.
목적어	Cathy decided **to attend** a music school.

B 형용사적 용법

to부정사가 앞에 있는 명사나 대명사를 꾸며서 '…할, …하는'의 의미로 형용사 역할을 한다.

This is the machine **to wash** the dishes.
My grandma needs an armchair **to sit on**.
I have nothing **to eat**.
I need a real friend **to talk with**.

C 부사적 용법

to부정사가 문장에서 부사 역할을 할 때는 목적, 감정의 원인, 결과, 판단의 근거를 나타낸다.

목적	감정의 원인	결과	판단의 근거
…하기 위하여	…해서, …하게 되어	(…해서) …하다	…하다니

I go to the gym **to lose** weight. 〈목적〉
I'm happy **to hear** our picnic plan. 〈감정의 원인〉
Sienna grew up **to be** a world-famous cook. 〈결과〉
Gary must be a soldier **to behave** like that. 〈판단의 근거〉

D to부정사의 의미상 주어

to부정사가 나타내는 동작의 행위자를 to부정사의 의미상 주어라고 한다.

I'm happy to hear the news.
The movie is not easy **for me** to understand.
It was careless **of you** to break the plate.
The movie is not easy **(for people)** to understand.

E to부정사의 관용 표현

1 의문사+to부정사

what+to부정사	무엇을 …할지	when+to부정사	언제 …할지
where+to부정사	어디서(로) …할지	how+to부정사	어떻게 …할지
which+to부정사	어느 것을 …할지	who(m)+to부정사	누구를(에게) …할지

2 enough to / too … to

형용사(부사)+enough+to부정사 …할 만큼 충분히 …한(하게)
= so+형용사(부사)+that+주어+can …
too+형용사(부사)+to부정사 너무 …해서 …할 수 없는
= so+형용사(부사)+that+주어+can't …

Ann is clever **enough to find** the answer.
= Ann is **so** clever **that** she **can find** the answer.
Harry is **too** young **to understand** the poem.
= Harry is **so** young **that** he **can't understand** the poem.

Expression

1 길 묻고 답하기

길 묻기
- Where is ...?
- Can(Could) you show me the way to ...?
- Can(Could) you tell me where ... is?
- How do(can) I get to ...?
- I'm looking for ....

길 안내하기
- Go straight for three blocks.
- Turn left(right) at the second corner.
- It's across(next to) the bank.
- You can't miss it.
- Sorry. I'm new(a stranger) here, too.

소요 시간 묻고 답하기
- How long does(will) it take to go to ...?
- (Maybe) It takes(will take) about ....

2 능력 여부 묻기 / 능력 표현하기

능력 여부 묻기
- Are you good at ...?
- Do you know how to ...?
- Can you (tell me how to) ...?

능력 표현하기
- I'm good at ....
- I can ....
- I know how to ....
- I'm able to ....

Lesson 03

동명사

Grammar Preview

1 동명사

• 동명사: 〈동사원형+ing〉의 형태로 명사 역할(주어, 보어, 목적어)을 한다.

Cutting onions can make you cry. 〈주어〉

My hobby is **traveling** alone. 〈주격보어〉

My dad enjoys **wearing** the straw hat. 〈동사의 목적어〉

Sean is afraid of **missing** this chance. 〈전치사의 목적어〉

• 동명사의 관용 표현

go -ing …하러 가다	be used to -ing …하는 데 익숙하다
on -ing …하자마자	cannot help -ing …하지 않을 수 없다
feel like -ing …하고 싶다	have difficulty -ing …하는 데 어려움이 있다
be good at -ing …을 잘하다	look forward to -ing …하기를 고대(기대)하다
be busy -ing …하느라 바쁘다	keep(stop) ... from -ing …가 …하지 못하게 하다
keep (on) -ing 계속해서 …하다	How(What) about -ing …하는 게 어때?

2 동명사, to부정사, 현재분사

• 동명사와 to부정사를 목적어로 쓰는 동사

동사+동명사	finish, enjoy, give up, mind, quit, practice, avoid 등
동사+to부정사	want, choose, learn, promise, hope, decide, plan, expect, ask 등
동사+동명사[to부정사]	like, love, hate, start, continue, begin 등 〈뜻이 동일함〉 remember, forget, regret 〈동명사 → 과거에 대한 내용 / to부정사 → 미래에 대한 내용〉

• 동명사와 현재분사

	역할	예문
동명사	명사(주어, 목적어, 보어)	Terry's hobby is **walking** along the river. 〈걷기: 보어 역할〉 **waiting** room 〈동명사+명사〉
현재분사	형용사(보어, 수식어)	Terry is **walking** along the river. 〈걷고 있는: 보어 역할〉 **waiting** people 〈waiting이 people을 꾸밈〉

1 동명사

A 동명사

1 동명사

형태	동사원형+ing
의미	동사가 명사처럼 주어, 보어, 목적어 역할을 하는 경우, 동명사의 형태로 써서 '…하기, …하는 것'의 의미로 쓰임
특징	명사 역할을 하지만, 동사가 변형한 것이어서 동사처럼 목적어, 수식어구를 취할 수 있음

2 동명사의 역할: 명사 역할을 하여 주어, 보어, 목적어로 쓰인다.

Cutting onions can make you cry. 〈주어〉

My hobby is **traveling** alone. 〈주격보어〉

My dad enjoys **wearing** the straw hat. 〈동사의 목적어〉

Sean is afraid of **missing** this chance. 〈전치사의 목적어〉

cf. 동명사의 부정은 동명사 바로 앞에 not(never)을 쓴다.

Ryan complained of **not having** time to play.

Plus Grammar

동명사를 목적어로 취하는 동사

avoid, consider, enjoy, finish, give up, mind, stop, suggest, quit 등

B 동명사의 관용 표현

go -ing …하러 가다

on -ing …하자마자

without -ing …하지 않고

feel like -ing …하고 싶다

be busy -ing …하느라 바쁘다

have difficulty -ing …하는 데 어려움이 있다

keep(stop) … from -ing …가 …하지 못하게 하다

look forward to -ing …하기를 고대(기대)하다

be good at -ing …을 잘하다

keep (on) -ing 계속해서 …하다

be used to -ing …하는 데 익숙하다

How(What) about -ing? …하는 게 어때?

cannot help -ing …하지 않을 수 없다

The storm **kept(stopped)** me **from going** there.

I **could not help laughing** at the sight.

I'**m used to getting** up early.

On seeing the thief, the brave woman chased him.

→ **As soon as she saw** the thief, the brave woman chased him.

How about going to the supermarket after lunch?

→ **Why don't you go** to the supermarket after lunch?

Grammar Practice >>

Answer p. 7

A1 빈칸에 들어갈 말을 〈보기〉에서 골라 알맞은 형태로 쓰시오.

보기
make answer do take

(1) Thank you for ________ me laugh.
(2) I finished ________ my homework.
(3) Yuri avoids ________ my questions.
(4) Harry should consider ________ my advice.

A2 밑줄 친 부분의 문장 성분을 〈보기〉에서 고르시오.

보기
ⓐ 주어 ⓑ 보어 ⓒ 목적어

(1) Playing basketball is fun.
(2) Isabel likes eating meat.
(3) My plan is helping the poor.
(4) My dream is becoming the president.
(5) Speaking English well requires a lot of practice.
(6) Amara's favorite activity is drawing a picture.
(7) Climbing the mountain is good for health.
(8) James went to sleep without saying "Good night."
(9) Mr. Kim enjoys listening to classical music.
(10) I'm interested in playing tennis with my classmate.

B1 밑줄 친 부분을 알맞은 형태로 쓰시오.

(1) How about try this recipe? → ________
(2) On hear the news, Jack started crying. → ________
(3) Hana can read the book without use a dictionary. → ________
(4) Angela doesn't feel like take a cello lesson today. → ________
(5) I had difficulty find the entrance to the subway. → ________

B2 우리말과 일치하도록 주어진 단어들을 이용하여 빈칸에 알맞은 말을 쓰시오.

(1) David와 Alice는 낚시하러 가는 것을 좋아한다.
→ David and Alice like to ________ ________. (fish)
(2) 우리 부모님은 곧 네 소식을 듣기를 고대하신다.
→ My parents are ________ ________ ________ ________ from you soon. (forward, hear)
(3) Jonathan은 저녁을 준비하느라 바쁘다.
→ Jonathan ________ ________ ________ dinner. (prepare)

B3 주어진 단어들을 배열하여 문장을 완성하시오. (형태 변화 가능)

(1) ______________ me to your party. (invite, thank, for, you)
(2) Yuri ______________ Chinese food. (make, is, at, good)
(3) I ______________ to London. (like, travel, feel)

교과서 어휘 onion 양파 alone 혼자 straw 밀짚 miss 놓치다 complain of …에 관해 불평하다 storm 폭풍 sight 광경 thief 도둑 chase 쫓다 meat 고기 activity 활동 recipe 조리법 dictionary 사전 entrance 입구

2 동명사, to부정사, 현재분사

C 동명사와 to부정사

1 동명사와 to부정사는 명사의 역할을 할 수 있다는 점이 같다. 하지만, to부정사는 전치사의 목적어로 쓰이지 않는다.

His favorite activity is **playing**(**to play**) basketball.

Larry is interested in **watching** concerts. 〈to watch는 쓸 수 없음〉

2 동사에 따른 목적어의 형태

• 동명사와 to부정사를 목적어로 쓰는 동사

동사+동명사	동사+to부정사	동사+동명사(to부정사)
finish, stop, enjoy, give up, mind, quit, practice, avoid 등	want, choose, learn, promise, hope, decide, plan, expect, ask 등	like, love, hate, start, continue, begin 등

Elena **enjoys sitting** outside in the sunshine.

Eric **wanted to accept** her proposal.

I **like taking**(**to take**) photographs on holidays.

• remember, forget, regret: 목적어로 동명사를 쓰면 과거에 대한 내용, to부정사를 쓰면 미래에 대한 내용을 나타낸다.

Joe remembers **seeing** Alan before. 〈과거〉

Joe remembers **to see** Alan tomorrow. 〈미래〉

cf. stop+동명사: …하기를 멈추다 / stop+to부정사: …하기 위해 멈추다

I stopped **listening** to the music. 〈stop: 타동사〉

I stopped **to listen** to the music. 〈stop: 자동사〉

Plus Grammar

try+동명사: …을 시도하다
try+to부정사: …하려고 애쓰다
Austin tried scuba-diving in the sea. (스쿠버다이빙을 시도하다)
Austin tried to scuba-dive in the sea. (스쿠버다이빙을 하려고 애쓰다)

D 동명사와 현재분사

동명사는 명사 역할을 하여 주어, 목적어, 보어로 쓰이고, 현재분사는 형용사 역할을 하여, 명사를 꾸미거나 주어, 목적어의 보어로 쓰인다.

Terry's hobby is **walking** along the river. 〈동명사: 걷기〉

Terry is **walking** along the river. 〈현재분사: 걷고 있는〉

cf. 명사 앞에 쓰일 때, 동명사는 뒤의 명사의 목적이나 용도를 나타내는 또 다른 명사의 역할을 하며, 현재분사는 뒤의 명사를 꾸미는 형용사 역할을 한다.

The **waiting** room is full of **waiting** people.

동명사+명사
= room for waiting

현재분사+명사
= people who is waiting

Plus Grammar

현재분사에 목적어나 수식어구가 붙는 경우, 뒤에서 명사를 꾸민다.
There is a soldier **wearing a uniform**.

Grammar Practice >>

Answer p. 7

C1 괄호 안에서 알맞은 것을 고르시오.

(1) They all want (to go, going) on a vacation.

(2) I enjoy (to watch, watching) horror movies.

(3) Don't forget (to switch, switching) off the light when you leave.

(4) I decided (to keep, keeping) a diary.

(5) Sarah plans (visiting, to visit) Canada.

(6) Would you mind (close, closing) the window?

(7) Kane hopes (to lose, losing) weight for his health.

(8) Yuna gave up (coming, to come) to school on foot.

(9) Grace avoids (to make, making) any promise.

(10) I asked (to see, seeing) the manager.

C2 어법상 어색한 부분을 찾아 바르게 고치시오.

(1) Do you mind to open the door?

_______________ → _______________

(2) John finished to fold laundry.

_______________ → _______________

(3) I planned studying abroad.

_______________ → _______________

(4) Iris gave up to watch TV at night.

_______________ → _______________

(5) Sally remembers to visit the park last weekend.

_______________ → _______________

D1 밑줄 친 부분의 역할을 〈보기〉에서 고르시오.

보기
ⓐ 현재분사 ⓑ 동명사

(1) They were sitting on the bench then.

(2) I saw a singing girl on the street.

(3) My cat likes touching me on the arm.

(4) Exercising regularly is important.

(5) Harry is taking a bath now.

(6) I'll buy you dancing shoes.

(7) Bryan is working in the office.

(8) I enjoy sunbathing on the beach.

(9) My brother and I saw the flying plane.

(10) My dad is preparing my breakfast.

D2 밑줄 친 부분에 주의하여 문장을 우리말로 옮기시오.

(1) Ms. Potter is drawing a funny cartoon character.

→ _______________

(2) Listening to music makes me feel better.

→ _______________

(3) Let's go to see the dancing girl.

→ _______________

(4) The running girl is my sister.

→ _______________

(5) You'll need a sleeping bag.

→ _______________

(6) I want to buy a new washing machine.

→ _______________

(7) Swimming in the river at night is dangerous.

→ _______________

교과서 어휘 sunshine 햇볕 accept 받아들이다 proposal 제안 waiting room 대기실 vacation 휴가 horror movie 공포 영화 switch off …을 끄다 lose weight 체중을 감량하다 on foot 걸어서 sunbathe 일광욕을 하다 washing machine 세탁기

Grammar Test

서술형 평가

[01~02] 밑줄 친 부분을 알맞은 형태로 고쳐 쓰시오.

01 My little sister is afraid of <u>skate</u>.

→ ________

02 I remember <u>go</u> to see a movie with Alice last night.

→ ________

03 밑줄 친 부분의 쓰임이 나머지 넷과 다른 것은?

① His job is <u>teaching</u> us music.
② My hobby is <u>collecting</u> pretty dolls.
③ Did you finish <u>cleaning</u> your room?
④ Nora is <u>watching</u> a soccer game now.
⑤ <u>Making</u> the right choice is important.

04 밑줄 친 부분의 형태가 바르게 짝지어진 것은?

- I finished <u>make</u> a house for my dog.
- My mother decided <u>buy</u> the kimchi refrigerator.

① make – buy ② making – buying
③ to make – to buy ④ making – to buy
⑤ to make – buying

05 문장을 바꿔 쓸 때 빈칸에 들어갈 말이 바르게 짝지어진 것은?

- Why don't you leave earlier?
 → How about ________ earlier?
- As soon as Mark reached Seoul, he ate something.
 → ________ Seoul, Mark ate something.

① leave – To reach
② leaving – To reach
③ to leave – To reach
④ leaving – On reaching
⑤ to leave – On reaching

06 빈칸에 공통으로 들어갈 말로 알맞지 <u>않은</u> 것은?

- Kelly ________ playing table tennis with Sam.
- Kelly ________ to play cards with Sam.

① starts ② begins ③ likes
④ loves ⑤ avoids

서술형 평가

07 어법상 <u>어색한</u> 문장을 찾아 고쳐 쓰시오.

A What is your hobby?
B I like playing the drums. I practice to play the drums almost every day.

→ ________

교과서 어휘 be afraid of …을 두려워하다 choice 선택 refrigerator 냉장고 reach …에 도착하다 table tennis 탁구 almost 거의

Answer p. 7

08 빈칸에 알맞은 것은?

A I ________________ my bike today.
B Really? Let's go together.

① feel like ride ② feel like to ride
③ feel like riding ④ feel like to riding
⑤ feel like rode

서술형 평가

09 그림을 보고, 주어진 단어들을 이용하여 빈칸에 알맞은 말을 쓰시오.

Jack should lose weight, so he ________ ________ ________ a hamburger. (give, eat)

10 어법상 어색한 것은?

① My hobby is reading a novel.
② Who is the girl write a letter?
③ They are having lunch at the cafeteria.
④ The crying boy is my younger brother.
⑤ Look at the sleeping dog under the table.

서술형 평가

11 주어진 대화와 일치하도록 빈칸에 알맞은 말을 넣어 문장을 완성하시오.

Jisu Did you call Mina?
Minho No, I totally forgot. I'll call her tomorrow.

→ Minho forgot ________________.

12 우리말을 영어로 잘못 옮긴 것은?

① 파티를 여는 게 어때?
→ How about having a party?
② 나는 그 경기를 보기를 기대하고 있다.
→ I'm looking forward to seeing the game.
③ 그는 그 소식을 듣자마자 창백해졌다.
→ To hearing the news, he turned pale.
④ 그녀는 시험을 준비하느라 바쁘다.
→ She is busy preparing for the exam.
⑤ 나는 이곳에서 일하는 데 어려움이 있다.
→ I have difficulty working here.

서술형 평가

13 밑줄 친 부분에 주의하여 문장을 우리말로 옮기시오.

(1) Tyler remembered to visit Tom's house and went there hastily.
→ ________________

(2) Bobby forgot buying earphones and bought ones again.
→ ________________

교과서 어휘 novel 소설 cafeteria 식당 call 전화하다 pale 창백한 hastily 급하게 earphones 이어폰

Reading

[1~2] 다음을 끊어 읽고 ☑, 해석을 쓰시오.

Seconds from Winning

At the go-kart race track, many people ⓐ are cheering excitedly. Max has five more laps to go. He sees the race's leader, Simon's kart ahead, just out of Max's reach and he presses harder on the gas pedal. Max really wants to win the race because the winner gets to meet the world famous racer L. J. Richards. Max sees the official ⓑ waving a white flag. It means the last lap. Max is right behind Simon. The finish line ⓒ is getting closer. "I can do it!" Max says loudly. He can feel his heart ⓓ beating hard. The karts rush into the finish line. Who is the winner?

Max's eyes are filled with tears as he finds out that he came in second. "No need for tears, kid," says a man's voice. The man ⓔ is standing in front of him is L. J. Richards! "Thank you, but I'm not the winner," says Max. "Even though you didn't win the race, you did your ________. That's the thing that counts!" says L. J. Richards.

1 밑줄 친 ⓐ–ⓔ 중 어법상 어색한 것은?

① ⓐ ② ⓑ ③ ⓒ ④ ⓓ ⑤ ⓔ

2 빈칸에 알맞은 것은?

① worst ② exercise ③ best ④ time ⑤ business

교과서 어휘 **lap** 한 바퀴 **out of one's reach** …의 손이 닿지 않는 곳에 **gas pedal** 가속 페달 **official** 심판 **wave** …을 흔들다 **beat** (심장이) 고동치다 **rush** 돌진하다 **come in second** 2등을 차지하다 **count** 중요하다

Answer p. 7

3 다음 글의 내용과 일치하는 것은?

인물

Alex Scott was a regular kid. Unfortunately, in 1997, Alex was diagnosed with childhood cancer. When Alex was four, she came up with a plan of **making** a lemonade stand in front of her house. She donated all the money that she earned to childhood cancer research. Word spread and she raised two thousand dollars. By **selling** lemonade every year she raised over one million dollars and built awareness for childhood cancer. After Alex died, her parents set up Alex's Lemonade Stand Foundation for childhood cancer.

① Alex는 14세에 소아암 진단을 받았다.
② Alex의 부모님은 집 앞에 레모네이드 판매대를 설치했다.
③ Alex는 레모네이드를 판매하여 총 200달러를 모금했다.
④ Alex는 소아암에 대한 인식을 높이는 데 기여했다.
⑤ Alex는 Alex's Lemonade Stand Foundation을 설립했다.

4 밑줄 친 부분이 가리키는 것으로 알맞은 것은?

인물

When Bessie Coleman was a child, **flying** in an airplane was still a dream. But when Bessie became a young woman, her brothers told her **exciting** stories about the pilots they saw during World War I. Bessie had an adventurous spirit. She decided to become a pilot. At that time, however, no flight schools accepted women or people of color. Instead of **giving** up <u>her dream</u>, Bessie earned money and taught herself French. Finally, she was accepted to a flight school in France and became the first African American female pilot.

① to learn French ② to be a pilot ③ to take a plane
④ to be a president ⑤ to fight in the war

3 **diagnose** 진단하다 **childhood cancer** 소아암 **stand** 가판대 **spread** 퍼지다 **raise** (돈을) 모으다 **awareness** 의식
4 **pilot** 조종사 **adventurous** 모험적인 **flight school** 비행 학교 **people of color** 유색 인종

Expression

1 상기시켜 주기

상기시켜 주기

- Don't forget to .... / Remember to ....
- Be sure to .... / Make sure to ....
- Make sure (that) ....
- Keep in mind (that) ....

상기시키는 말에 답하기

- (Don't forget to ....) Okay, I won't.
- (Remember to ....) Okay, I will.

2 설명 요청하기 / 열거하기

설명 요청하기

- What do you mean (by that)?
- What does that mean?
- What is that supposed to mean?
- Could you explain ...?

설명하기

- It means (that) .... / I mean (that) ....

열거하기

- First, ... Second, ... Third, ...
- First of all, ... Next, ... Finally, ...

Expression Test

Answer p. 8

1 의도하는 바가 나머지와 다른 것은?

① What do you mean?
② What does that mean?
③ What do you mean by that?
④ What do you think of that?
⑤ What is that supposed to mean?

서술형 평가

2 자연스러운 대화가 되도록 A의 말에 이어질 (A)–(C)를 바르게 배열하시오.

A Eric, are you feeling better?
(A) That's good. But remember to take the medicine.
(B) Okay, I will.
(C) Yes, Mom.

________ → ________ → ________

3 밑줄 친 부분과 바꿔 쓸 수 있는 것은?

A Mom, you told me to buy cheese, tomatoes, and milk, right?
B Right. Don't forget to check the date on the milk bottle before buying it.
A Don't worry, Mom.

① You cannot
② Make sure to
③ You must not
④ You should not
⑤ Don't remember to

서술형 평가

4 두 문장이 같은 의미가 되도록 빈칸에 알맞은 말을 쓰시오.

Make sure you put on your helmet when you ride a bike.
= Don't ________________ put on your helmet when you ride a bike.

5 빈칸에 알맞은 것은?

A Rebecca is a walking dictionary.
B ________________
A It means she has a lot of knowledge.

① What do you know?
② What does she like?
③ What's your favorite fruit?
④ What do you mean by that?
⑤ How often do you meet her?

6 밑줄 친 ⓐ–ⓔ 중 대화의 흐름상 어색한 것은?

A Lisa, I have to go to the hospital now. ⓐ Can you tell me how to get there?
B Okay. ⓑ First, go straight two blocks this way. ⓒ Finally, turn right at the corner. ⓓ Then, you'll see the gym. ⓔ The hospital is between the gym and the bookstore.
A Thanks.

① ⓐ ② ⓑ ③ ⓒ ④ ⓓ ⑤ ⓔ

서술형 평가

Answer p. 8

1 주어진 단어들을 이용하여 밑줄 친 우리말을 영어로 옮기시오.

A Do you have any special plans tomorrow?
B No, but I'm going to be a couch potato all day.
A A couch potato? (1) 무슨 뜻이니? (mean)
B I'll sit on a couch and watch TV all day long eating potato chips.
A I see. I'm going to watch baseball so I was thinking of inviting you.
B No thanks. I just want to rest. By the way, (2) 우산 가져가는 것을 잊지 마. (forget, bring, an umbrella) It's going to rain tomorrow.

(1) ______________________
(2) ______________________

2 그림을 보고, 주어진 단어들을 배열하여 문장을 완성하시오.

(1)

______________________ for the first time. (playing, I, tried, the guitar)

(2)

Jason ______________________.
(swimming, in, enjoys, the sea)

3 빈칸에 알맞은 말을 〈보기〉에서 골라 알맞은 형태로 쓰시오.

보기
cook ride wait

(1) ________ a skateboard in the rain is dangerous.
(2) My grandma is good at ________ fish.
(3) Would you mind ________ for a while?

4 우리말과 일치하도록 주어진 단어들을 이용하여 문장을 완성하시오.

(1) 그 영화는 볼만했다. (worth, watch)
→ The movie was ______________.
(2) 나는 직장을 그만두고 싶다. (feel, quit)
→ I ______________ my job.
(3) 당신을 곧 보기를 고대합니다. (forward, see)
→ I ______________ you soon.

5 주어진 단어를 알맞은 형태로 바꿔 쓰시오.

I've decided (1) ________(do) many things for my health. First, I'm planning (2) ________(exercise) every morning. Second, I will stop (3) ________(eat) snacks to lose weight. Lastly, I will try not (4) ________(skip) a meal. I believe that these things will be good for my health.

Final Test

Answer p. 8

난이도: 상 ★★★ 중 ★★ 하 ★

★

01 짝지어진 단어의 관계가 나머지와 다른 것은?

① cry – laugh ② accept – refuse
③ lend – borrow ④ require – need
⑤ forget – remember

★★

02 주어진 설명에 해당하는 단어로 알맞은 것은?

to put your hand or finger on somebody or something

① hit ② touch ③ exercise
④ choose ⑤ volunteer

★★★ 서술형 평가

03 빈칸에 공통으로 들어갈 알맞은 말을 쓰시오.

• On seeing our teacher come in, we all ________ up.
• The people living upstairs are so noisy. I can't ________ it.
• There are magazines and newspapers on the ________.

★★

04 밑줄 친 부분과 바꿔 쓸 수 있는 것은?

A What should I bring to the sports day?
B Don't forget to wear a class shirt on the sports day.

① Let me ② Be sure to
③ Keep in mind ④ I'd love to
⑤ I'm suppose to

★★ 서술형 평가

05 자연스러운 대화가 되도록 A의 말에 이어질 (A)–(D)를 바르게 배열하시오.

A Lucas, can you take care of my dog?
(A) Yes. You should not leave him alone.
(B) Sure. Is there anything I should know?
(C) Okay, anything else?
(D) Well, make sure to give him enough food.

________ → ________ → ________ → ________

★★ 시험에 잘 나오는 문제

06 짝지어진 대화가 어색한 것은?

① A Don't forget to be on time.
B Okay, I will. See you then.
② A What do you mean by that?
B It means Lucy loves you.
③ A Do you know how to make a hotdog?
B Of course. First, boil the sausages.
④ A Remember to get your own lunch.
B I see. Thanks.
⑤ A Can you show me the way to the post office?
B Sure. First, go straight one block and then turn right.

★★ 서술형 평가

07 우리말과 일치하도록 빈칸에 알맞은 말을 쓰시오.

A The interview was a piece of cake.
B What do ____________________?
(그게 무슨 뜻이니?)
A I mean it's very easy.

교과서 어휘 refuse 거절하다 require 요청하다 exercise 운동하다 volunteer 자원봉사하다 boil 끓이다 a piece of cake 식은 죽 먹기

Final Test

★★
08 빈칸에 알맞지 않은 것은?

A It'll rain tomorrow. ___________
B Okay.

① Be sure to take your umbrella.
② Make sure to take your umbrella.
③ Remember to take your umbrella.
④ Don't forget to take your umbrella.
⑤ You don't have to take your umbrella.

★
09 밑줄 친 부분 중 의미상 어색한 것은?

A ① Do you know how to make ramyeon?
B ② First, boil some water. ③ Third, put the ramyeon and soup mix in the boiling water. ④ Finally, boil it ⑤ for a few minutes.

① ② ③ ④ ⑤

★★
10 짝지어진 문장의 의미가 서로 다른 것은?

① Ann loves dancing.
= Ann loves to dance.
② I forgot sending the e-mail.
= I forgot to send the e-mail.
③ My dream is studying art in college.
= My dream is to study art in college.
④ Suddenly it started raining.
= Suddenly it started to rain.
⑤ Being a good scientist is difficult.
= To be a good scientist is difficult.

★★
11 빈칸에 들어갈 말이 바르게 짝지어진 것은?

• ________ old coins is my hobby.
• Thank you for ________ the door for me.

① To collect – open
② To collect – to open
③ Collecting – to open
④ Collecting – opening
⑤ Collect – opening

서술형 평가
★
12 두 문장이 같은 의미가 되도록 빈칸에 알맞은 말을 쓰시오.

To draw a dinosaur is not easy.
= __________ a dinosaur is not easy.

[13~14] 빈칸에 알맞은 것을 고르시오.

★★
13
Please stop ________ so many sweets. Or you'll gain weight.

① eat ② to eat ③ ate
④ eating ⑤ to eating

★★
14
Mr. Kim is really busy ________ handicapped people.

① help ② to help
③ helped ④ to helping
⑤ helping

교과서 어휘 umbrella 우산 art 예술, 미술 scientist 과학자 coin 동전 dinosaur 공룡 sweet 단것 gain weight 살이 찌다 handicapped 장애가 있는

Answer p. 8

★ 서술형 평가

15 우리말과 일치하도록 빈칸에 알맞은 말을 쓰시오.

나는 바이올린을 배우기 시작했다.

→ I started __________ the violin.

★★

16 어법상 옳은 것은?

① I look forward to meet you.
② Take a walk is good for health.
③ Jason planned washing the cars.
④ He felt like to cry at the sad news.
⑤ Would you mind closing the window?

★★ 시험에 잘 나오는 문제

17 빈칸에 공통으로 들어갈 말로 알맞지 않은 것은?

• Felix ________ writing with color pencils.
• Helen ________ to draw pictures of many kinds of animals.

① loves ② starts ③ enjoys
④ begins ⑤ likes

★★ 서술형 평가

18 어법상 어색한 부분을 찾아 고쳐 쓰시오.

I remember to send Jane a letter last weekend.

______________ → ______________

★

19 빈칸에 알맞은 것은?

A I'm really ______________ to Disneyland.
B Me too.

① looking forward go
② looking forward going
③ looking forward to go
④ looking forward went
⑤ looking forward to going

★★ 서술형 평가

20 우리말과 일치하도록 주어진 단어를 이용하여 문장을 완성하시오.

(1) 드라마 동아리에 가입하는 게 어때? (join)
→ How about ________ a drama club?
(2) 우리집을 찾는 데 어려움이 있었니? (find)
→ Did you have any difficulty ________ my house?

★★

21 밑줄 친 단어의 형태가 바르게 짝지어진 것은?

• They plan <u>reduce</u> the fat in their food.
• I enjoy <u>see</u> an animation when I'm free.

① reduce – see
② reduce – seeing
③ reducing – to see
④ to reduce – to see
⑤ to reduce – seeing

교과서 어휘 **take a walk** 산책하다 **sad** 슬픈 **send** 보내다 **join** 가입하다, 합류하다 **reduce** 줄이다 **fat** 지방 **free** 한가한

Final Test

★★ 서술형 평가

22 밑줄 친 부분에 주의하여 주어진 문장을 우리말로 옮기시오.

(1) You should not forget to buy some salt and pepper.

→ ______________________

(2) You forgot buying some salt and pepper.

→ ______________________

★★ 시험에 잘 나오는 문제

23 밑줄 친 부분의 쓰임이 나머지 넷과 다른 것은?

① I don't mind turning off the heater.
② Luna is good at speaking Chinese.
③ My favorite activity is playing tennis.
④ What were the children doing in the park?
⑤ Reading humorous stories makes me happy.

★★★ 서술형 평가

24 어법상 어색한 문장을 찾아 다시 쓰시오.

A What will you do this Saturday?
B I want to play baseball with my friends.
A Do you like playing baseball?
B Yes, I do. Then what will you do this Saturday?
A I'll go to shopping with my mother.

____

→ ______________________

★★

25 주어진 문장이 들어가기에 알맞은 곳은?

However, we still need dust.

Seeing dust in the air is not easy. (①) It's very tiny. Nobody likes dust. (②) We wash, wipe and mop to clean the dust. (③) A lot of dust makes us sick these days. (④) Dust in the air blocks the sun's strong rays and protects our eyes. (⑤) Without it, we can't see rain and snow.

★★★

26 다음 글의 내용을 요약할 때, 빈칸 (A)와 (B)에 들어갈 말이 바르게 짝지어진 것은?

A famous composer, Dvorak, loved the sound of trains. Listening to the sound of the trains became his favorite hobby. He liked trains so much that he even moved to a house near a train station. He could tell the kind of trains only by listening to the sounds. His love for trains affected his classical music, "New World Symphony."

Dvorak loved the ___(A)___ of the trains and it affected his ___(B)___.

① smell – love ② shape – book
③ sound – music ④ color – illness
⑤ picture – movie

교과서 어휘 pepper 후추 heater 난방기 humorous 재미있는 mop 대걸레로 닦다 block 차단하다 ray 광선, 빛살 protect 보호하다 composer 작곡가 tell 구분하다 affect 영향을 미치다

Answer p. 8

[27~28] 다음을 읽고, 물음에 답하시오.

Have you ever ⓐ bought used items on the Internet? Then, you have experienced the sharing economy. The sharing economy is built on the idea that ⓑ share certain goods, services, and skills is more efficient. It is ⓒ efficient because it can reduce costs for available goods, services, and time. For instance, if you only need ⓓ to use a screw driver once a year, then it is better for you ⓔ to pay 10 dollars and rent one from a neighbor than ____________________.

★★★
27 밑줄 친 ⓐ-ⓔ 중 어법상 어색한 것은?

① ⓐ ② ⓑ ③ ⓒ ④ ⓓ ⑤ ⓔ

★★★
28 빈칸에 알맞은 것은?

① to borrow it
② to share it with others
③ to buy one of your own
④ to donate a lot of money
⑤ to resell it on the Internet

[29~30] 다음을 읽고, 물음에 답하시오.

A 16-year-old girl Jessica Watson sailed on a yacht on October 18th, 2009. Many people worried about her traveling around the world on a small yacht. But she enjoyed challenging herself. Nothing could stop her. She headed northeast through South Pacific and crossed Atlantic Ocean to South Africa. During the journey, her yacht turned over several times and she met huge storms. Even then, she didn't give up. After seven months, she came back to Australia safely.

*turn over 뒤집히다

★★
29 Jessica Watson에 관한 위 글의 내용과 일치하지 않는 것은?

① 2009년 10월 18일 세계 일주를 시작했다.
② 요트를 타고 세계 일주를 했다.
③ 여행 동안 요트가 여러 번 뒤집어졌다.
④ 부상을 당해 세계 일주를 포기해야 했다.
⑤ 7개월 후 호주로 돌아왔다.

★★
30 밑줄 친 부분과 쓰임이 같은 것은?

① My hobby is collecting coins.
② The worker is using a shovel.
③ Waiting in a long line is boring.
④ My cat's favorite activity is sleeping.
⑤ My sister likes meeting new people.

교과서 어휘 **experience** 경험하다 **sharing economy** 공유 경제 **certain** 특정한 **goods** 상품, 제품 **efficient** 효율적인 **cost** 비용 **available** 이용 가능한 **sail** 항해하다 **challenge** 도전하다 **head** …로 향하다

>> Grammar

A 동명사

형태	동사원형+ing
의미	동사가 명사처럼 주어, 보어, 목적어 역할을 하는 경우, 동명사의 형태로 써서 '…하기, …하는 것'의 의미로 쓰임
특징	명사 역할을 하지만, 동사가 변형한 것이어서 동사처럼 목적어, 수식어구를 취할 수 있음

Cutting onions can make you cry. 〈주어〉
My hobby is **traveling** alone. 〈주격보어〉
My dad enjoys **wearing** the straw hat. 〈동사의 목적어〉
Sean is afraid of **missing** this chance. 〈전치사의 목적어〉

B 동명사의 관용 표현

go -ing …하러 가다
on -ing …하자마자
without -ing …하지 않고
feel like -ing …하고 싶다
be busy -ing …하느라 바쁘다
have difficulty -ing …하는 데 어려움이 있다
keep(stop) ... from -ing …가 …하지 못하게 하다
look forward to -ing …하기를 고대(기대)하다
be good at -ing …을 잘하다
keep (on) -ing 계속해서 …하다
be used to -ing …하는 데 익숙하다
How(What) about -ing? …하는 게 어때?
cannot help -ing …하지 않을 수 없다

The storm **kept(stopped)** me **from going** there.
I **could not help laughing** at the sight.
I'**m used to getting** up early.
On seeing the thief, the brave woman chased him.
How about going to the supermarket after lunch?

C 동명사와 to부정사

• 동명사와 to부정사를 목적어로 쓰는 동사

동사+동명사	동사+to부정사	동사+동명사(to부정사)
finish, stop, enjoy, give up, mind, quit, practice, avoid 등	want, choose, learn, promise, hope, decide, plan, expect, ask 등	like, love, hate, start, continue, begin 등

Elena **enjoys sitting** outside in the sunshine.

Eric **wanted to accept** her proposal.

I **like taking(to take)** photographs on holidays.

• remember, forget, regret: 목적어로 동명사를 쓰면 과거에 대한 내용, to부정사를 쓰면 미래에 대한 내용을 나타낸다.

Joe remembers **seeing** Alan before. 〈과거〉

Joe remembers **to see** Alan tomorrow. 〈미래〉

D 동명사와 현재분사

	역할	예
동명사	명사(주어, 목적어, 보어)	Terry's hobby is **walking** along the river. **waiting** room
현재분사	형용사(보어, 수식어)	Terry is **walking** along the river. **waiting** people

>> Expression

1 상기시켜 주기

상기시켜 주기
- Don't forget to .... / Remember to ....
- Be sure to .... / Make sure to ....
- Make sure (that) ....
- Keep in mind (that) ....

상기시키는 말에 답하기
- (Don't forget to ....) Okay, I won't.
- (Remember to ....) Okay, I will.

2 설명 요청하기 / 열거하기

설명 요청하기
- What do you mean (by that)?
- What does that mean?
- What is that supposed to mean?
- Could you explain ...?

설명하기
- It means (that) .... / I mean (that) ....

열거하기
- First, ... Second, ... Third, ...
- First of all, ... Next, ... Finally, ...

Lesson 04

분사, 수동태

1 분사

• 형용사처럼 다른 명사를 꾸미거나 주어, 목적어의 보어 역할을 한다. 분사가 목적어나 부사(구)와 함께 구를 이뤄 명사를 꾸미면 명사 뒤에 쓴다.

	형태	의미
현재분사	동사원형+ing	능동(…하는) / 진행(…하고 있는, …하면서)
과거분사	동사원형+ed	수동(…되는, … 당하는) / 완료(…된, …한)

The **studying** boy is my son.
The boy **playing** tennis is my son.
My name was **called** by someone.
I heard my name **called** by someone.

• 형용사처럼 쓰이는 분사

exciting 흥분하게 하는
excited 흥분한
confusing 혼란하게 하는
confused 혼란스러운
surprising 놀라게 하는
surprised 놀란
tiring 지치게 하는
tired 지친
interesting 관심을 끄는
interested 관심을 가진
disappointing 실망시키는
disappointed 실망한
satisfying 만족시키는
satisfied 만족한
boring 지루하게 만드는
bored 지루한

2 수동태

• 수동태 문장

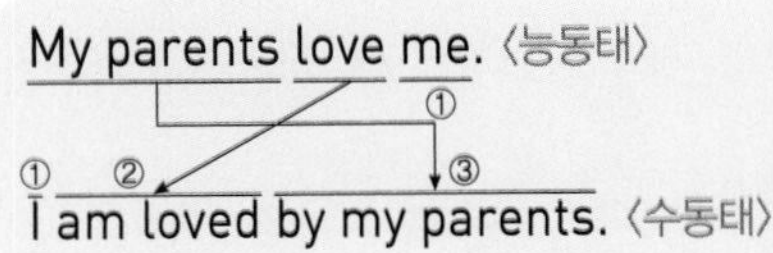

① 능동태 문장의 목적어를 수동태 문장의 주어로 쓴다.
② 능동태 동사 → 수동태 동사 〈be동사+과거분사〉
③ 능동태 문장의 주어 → 수동태 문장 끝에 〈by+목적격〉으로

• 수동태의 동사 형태

과거 수동태	was(were)+과거분사	진행 수동태	be동사+being+과거분사
미래 수동태	will be+과거분사	조동사 수동태	조동사+be+과거분사

• by 이외의 전치사를 쓰는 수동태 표현

be filled with …으로 가득하다
be satisfied with …에 만족하다
be interested in …에 관심이 있다
be covered with …으로 덮이다
be surprised at …에 놀라다
be disappointed with …에 실망하다

1 분사

Grammar

A 분사의 형태와 의미

동사를 변형하여 형용사처럼 쓰며 현재분사(-ing)와 과거분사(-ed)가 있다.

	형태	의미
현재분사	동사원형+ing	능동(…하는) / 진행(…하고 있는, …하면서)
과거분사	동사원형+ed	수동(…되는, … 당하는) / 완료(…된, …한)

Look! Leaves are **falling.** 〈진행〉

smoke **polluting** the sky 〈능동〉

Fallen leaves are beautiful. 〈완료〉

the river **polluted** with oil 〈수동〉

Plus Grammar

동사를 현재분사로 만드는 방법은 동명사를 만드는 방법과 같고, 과거분사의 형태는 대부분 과거형과 같으나, 불규칙적으로 변하기도 한다.

원형	과거형	과거분사
go	went	gone
break	broke	broken

B 분사의 역할

분사는 형용사처럼 명사를 꾸미거나 주어, 목적어의 보어 역할을 한다. 분사가 목적어나 부사(구)와 함께 구를 이뤄 명사를 꾸미면 명사 뒤에 쓴다.

The **studying** boy is my son. 〈분사+명사〉

The boy **playing** tennis is my son. 〈명사+분사구〉

My name was **called** by someone. 〈주격보어〉

I heard my name **called** by someone. 〈목적격보어〉

cf. 동명사와 현재분사

동명사	현재분사
명사(주어, 목적어, 보어)	형용사(보어, 수식어)
Swimming is fun. 〈수영하기: 명사〉 **swimming** pool 〈명사+명사〉	Terry is **swimming.** 〈수영하고 있는: 형용사〉 **swimming** boy 〈형용사+명사〉

Plus Grammar

분사는 동사의 일부로 쓰여 진행시제, 완료시제, 수동태를 만든다.

- 현재진행시제(현재분사)
  Kelly **is playing** golf with her friends.
- 현재완료시제(과거분사)
  Jina **has played** the cello for an hour.
- 수동태(과거분사)
  The goal **was scored** by Mr. Jackson.

C 형용사처럼 쓰이는 분사

동사(…하게 만들다)	현재분사(…하게 만드는)	과거분사(…하는 / …한)
excite(흥분하게 하다)	exciting(흥분하게 하는)	excited(흥분한)
interest(관심을 끌다)	interesting(관심을 끄는)	interested(관심을 가진)
confuse(혼란하게 하다)	confusing(혼란하게 하는)	confused(혼란스러운)
disappoint(실망시키다)	disappointing(실망시키는)	disappointed(실망한)
surprise(놀라게 하다)	surprising(놀라게 하는)	surprised(놀란)
satisfy(만족시키다)	satisfying(만족시키는)	satisfied(만족한)
tire(지치게 하다)	tiring(지치게 하는)	tired(지친)
bore(지루하게 하다)	boring(지루하게 만드는)	bored(지루한)

The result **interested** me. 〈동사〉

The result was **interesting.** 〈현재분사〉

I was **interested** in the result. 〈과거분사〉

Grammar Practice >>

Answer p. 10

A1 괄호 안에서 알맞은 것을 고르시오.

(1) Lois loves the man (playing, played) the guitar now.
(2) The man (talking, talked) to Anna is my son.
(3) The pen (leaving, left) in the box is mine.
(4) The ring (making, made) by Mr. Tavarez is expensive.
(5) There was a big truck (parking, parked) in front of the building.

A2 밑줄 친 부분을 어법에 맞게 고쳐 쓰시오.

(1) Betty had her bike <u>repair</u>.
(2) The puppy <u>follow</u> me is mine.
(3) The customer looked very <u>satisfy</u>.
(4) I moved the <u>break</u> cup to the kitchen.
(5) What is the language <u>speak</u> in Korea?

B1 밑줄 친 부분의 역할을 〈보기〉에서 고르시오.

보기
ⓐ 수식어 ⓑ 주격보어 ⓒ 목적격보어

(1) There is a flight <u>leaving</u> at noon.
(2) Austin wanted all the letters <u>sent</u>.
(3) The boy <u>talking</u> on his phone is Kyle.
(4) I saw Helen <u>walking</u> down the street.
(5) Mr. Choi is <u>interested</u> in singing a song.
(6) Ashley looked very <u>worried</u> about something.
(7) It is difficult for Joan to read a book <u>written</u> in Latin.

B2 밑줄 친 부분의 역할을 〈보기〉에서 고르시오.

보기
ⓐ 동명사 ⓑ 현재분사

(1) All <u>living</u> things need water.
(2) Mr. Tyler is in the <u>waiting</u> room.
(3) A <u>rolling</u> stone gathers no moss.
(4) Jessica's job is <u>teaching</u> mathematics.
(5) <u>Smoking</u> is not allowed in the building.
(6) I read the <u>surprising</u> news on the phone.
(7) I moved my son <u>sleeping</u> on the sofa to his room.

C1 주어진 단어를 빈칸에 알맞은 형태로 쓰시오.

(1) It's an ________ horror movie. (excite)
(2) We were ________ at the great painting. (amaze)
(3) I was ________ to hear of Margaret's death. (shock)
(4) My trip to Greenland was pretty ________. (satisfy)
(5) I'm so ________ that I can't understand your words. (confuse)

C2 주어진 문장들이 일치하도록 빈칸에 알맞은 말을 쓰시오.

(1) Glen's sudden question confused me.
= I was ________ by Glen's sudden question.
= Glen's sudden question was ________.
(2) The final match excited Koreans.
= Koreans were ________ at the final match.
= The final match was ________.

교과서 어휘 smoke 연기 pollute 오염시키다 pool 수영장 leave 남기다 park 주차하다 customer 손님 waiting room 대기실 gather 모으다 moss 이끼 allow 허락하다 sudden 갑작스러운 match 경기

D 능동태와 수동태

1 수동태 문장

My parents love me. 〈능동태: 주어가 동작의 주체가 되는 문장〉

I am loved by my parents. 〈수동태: 주어가 동작의 대상이 되는 문장〉

① 능동태 문장의 목적어를 수동태 문장의 주어로 쓴다.

② 능동태 문장의 동사를 〈be동사+과거분사〉로 바꿔 수동태의 동사로 쓴다.

③ 능동태 문장의 주어를 〈by+목적격〉 형태로 수동태 문장의 끝에 쓴다.

Walter **makes the model car.** 〈능동태〉

→ **The model car is made** by Walter. 〈수동태〉

Plus Grammar

- 수동태 문장을 만들 때 주어나 목적어가 인칭대명사인 경우, 격과 수에 맞게 변형하며, be동사도 주어의 수와 능동태 문장의 시제에 맞춘다.
  They help us.
  → We are helped by them.
- have(가지다), meet(만나다), resemble(닮다) 등의 동사는 수동태로 쓰지 않는다.

2 수동태의 부정문과 의문문

수동태의 부정문	주어+be동사+**not**+과거분사 ….
수동태의 의문문	**be동사+주어+과거분사** …? – Yes, 주어+be동사. / No, 주어+be동사+not.

The model car **is not made** by Walter. 〈수동태의 부정문〉

Is the model car **made** by Walter? 〈수동태의 의문문〉

– Yes, it is. / No, it isn't.

Plus Grammar

수동태의 의문사 의문문

〈의문사+be동사+주어+과거분사 …?〉 / 〈의문사 주어+be동사+과거분사 …?〉

When did he build his house?

→ When was his house built (by him)?

What did Roger build?

→ What was built by Roger?

E 수동태의 동사 형태

과거 수동태	was(were)+과거분사	진행 수동태	be동사+being+과거분사
미래 수동태	will be+과거분사	조동사 수동태	조동사+be+과거분사

The model car **is being made** by Walter. 〈진행 수동태〉

The model car **must be made** by Walter. 〈조동사 수동태〉

F 주의해야 할 수동태

1 〈by+목적격〉 생략: 수동태의 행위자가 일반인(we, you, they, people 등)이거나, 불분명하거나, 밝힐 필요가 없는 경우 생략한다.

English is spoken in Australia (by Australians).

2 by 이외의 전치사를 쓰는 수동태 표현

be filled with …으로 가득하다	be interested in …에 관심이 있다
be surprised at …에 놀라다	be satisfied with …에 만족하다
be covered with …으로 덮이다	be disappointed with …에 실망하다

The basket **was filled with** baseballs.

Cynthia **is interested in** dancing.

Plus Grammar

구별해서 알아야 할 수동태 표현

- be made of(…로 만들어지다 – 물리적 변화)
- be made from(…로 만들어지다 – 화학적 변화)
- be known to(…에게 알려지다)
- be known by(…에 의해 알려지다)
- be known for(…로 유명하다)
- be known as(…라고 알려지다)

Grammar Practice >>

Answer p. 10

D1 괄호 안에서 알맞은 것을 고르시오.

(1) The singer (loves, is loved) by many girls.

(2) Columbus (discovered, was discovered) America.

(3) All the bananas (ate, were eaten) by him.

(4) (Did, Were) these shoes (make, made) by Tom last year?

(5) (Does, Is) English (teach, taught) by Mr. Green?

D2 주어진 문장을 바꿔 쓸 때 빈칸에 알맞은 말을 쓰시오.

(1) The mayor didn't open the new school.

→ The new school ________ ________ ________ the mayor.

(2) The nice kite wasn't made by my father.

→ My father ________ ________ the nice kite.

(3) My brother didn't bake the cookies.

→ The cookies ________ ________ ________ my brother.

E1 주어진 문장을 바꿔 쓸 때 빈칸에 알맞은 말을 쓰시오.

(1) Ms. Cooper will teach music to us.

→ Music ____________________ to us by Ms. Cooper.

(2) They are correcting some mistakes.

→ Some mistakes ____________________ by them.

E2 우리말과 일치하도록 주어진 단어들을 이용하여 빈칸에 알맞은 말을 쓰시오.

(1) 그 방은 유리에 의해 즉시 청소되어야 한다.

→ The room ____________________ at once by Yuri. (must, clean)

(2) 많은 공원들이 그들에 의해 도시에 지어질 것이다.

→ Many parks ____________________ in the city by them. (will, build)

(3) 선물은 내 친구들에 의해 숨겨질지도 모른다.

→ The presents ____________________ by my friends. (may, hide)

F1 생략할 수 있는 부분에 밑줄을 그으시오.

(1) Many cars are made in Korea by people.

(2) My ruler and pencil case were stolen by someone.

(3) Salt is sold at that store by them.

(4) My truck was broken by somebody.

F2 우리말과 일치하도록 〈보기〉의 단어를 이용하여 빈칸에 알맞은 말을 쓰시오.

보기
surprise   satisfy   cover

(1) 엄마는 내일 그 소식에 만족하실 것이다.

→ Mom ____________________ the news tomorrow.

(2) 그들은 나의 이른 귀가에 놀랐다.

→ They ____________________ my returning home early.

(3) 그 거리는 많은 낙엽으로 덮여 있었다.

→ The street ____________________ many fallen leaves.

교과서 어휘 **model** 모형의 **basket** 바구니 **discover** 발견하다 **mayor** 시장 **kite** 연 **hide** 숨기다 **ruler** 자 **salt** 소금 **fallen leaves** 낙엽

Grammar Test

[01~03] 우리말과 일치하도록 할 때 빈칸에 알맞은 것을 고르시오.

01

The cats ________ water are my new pets. (물을 마시고 있는 고양이들은 나의 새 애완동물이다.)

① drink ② drinks ③ drank
④ drunk ⑤ drinking

02

________ cars are blocking the road. (부서진 차들이 도로를 막고 있다.)

① Break ② Breaks ③ Broke
④ Broken ⑤ Breaking

03

The tall man ________ a yellow shirt is Russel. (노란색 셔츠를 입은 키 큰 남자는 Russel이다.)

① wear ② wears ③ worn
④ wearing ⑤ was worn

서술형 평가

04 분사를 이용하여 두 문장을 한 문장으로 바꿔 쓸 때 빈칸에 알맞은 말을 쓰시오.

The girl is Dave's sister. She is playing the violin.
→ The girl ________________ is Dave's sister.

05 빈칸에 들어갈 말이 바르게 짝지어진 것은?

- He was satisfied ________ the dinner.
- Suho is interested ________ making model planes.

① at – by ② with – by ③ by – in
④ in – with ⑤ with – in

06 밑줄 친 부분의 쓰임이 같은 것끼리 짝지어진 것은?

ⓐ Cathy's dream is climbing Mt. Everest.
ⓑ I once liked his smiling face.
ⓒ Dad is singing in the shower.
ⓓ You need to carry a walking stick for the elderly man.
ⓔ It's exciting to live in a foreign country.

① ⓐ, ⓑ ② ⓐ, ⓑ, ⓓ ③ ⓑ, ⓒ, ⓓ
④ ⓑ, ⓒ, ⓔ ⑤ ⓒ, ⓓ, ⓔ

07 어법상 어색한 것은?

① Breakfast is served at 9 by the waiter.
② Was this fantastic movie direct by Spielberg?
③ *The Last Leaf* was written by O. Henry.
④ Those stamps aren't sold in the supermarket.
⑤ The presents are being wrapped by the twins.

교과서 어휘 **pet** 애완동물 **block** 막다 **climb** 등반하다 **walking stick** 지팡이 **elderly** 연로한 **direct** (영화를) 감독하다 **wrap** 포장하다 **twin** 쌍둥이

Answer p. 10

[08~09] 밑줄 친 부분이 어법상 어색한 것을 고르시오.

08 ① Felix always feels tiring after work.
② The cartoon was not interesting.
③ The soccer game was very exciting.
④ Clara was shocked at the news of the accident.
⑤ Alice was bored with reading the same book.

09 ① Look at those shouting people.
② Jade heard her name calling.
③ The barking dog looks scary.
④ We enjoyed the exciting musical.
⑤ Leo gave me a book written in English.

서술형 평가

10 〈보기〉의 말을 이용하여 Hanmi Hall을 설명하는 문장을 완성하시오.

Hanmi Hall

• 1967년 준공 • 현재 진선 재단 소유
• 미술 센터로 이용 • 모던 아트 작품 전시

보기: own build use

Hanmi Hall ____________ in 1967. Now, this hall ____________ the Jinsun Foundation and it ____________ as an art center for modern art.

[11~12] 주어진 문장을 수동태 문장으로 바꿔 쓸 때 빈칸에 알맞은 것을 고르시오.

11 Mom washed colored clothes separately.
→ Colored clothes ____________ separately by Mom.

① are washed ② were washed
③ were be washed ④ have washed
⑤ have been washed

12 We should spend less money on clothes.
→ Less money ____________ on clothes.

① should spent
② should be spend
③ should be spent
④ should been spend
⑤ should been spent

서술형 평가

13 밑줄 친 문장을 수동태로 바꿔 쓰시오.

A I think Jessy is very smart.
B Why do you think so?
A She solved math questions very easily.

→ ____________

교과서 어휘 cartoon 만화 shout 소리 지르다 scary 무서운 own 소유하다 modern 현대의 separately 분리하여 spend 소비하다 easily 쉽게

Reading

[1~2] 다음을 끊어 읽고 ☑, 해석을 쓰시오.

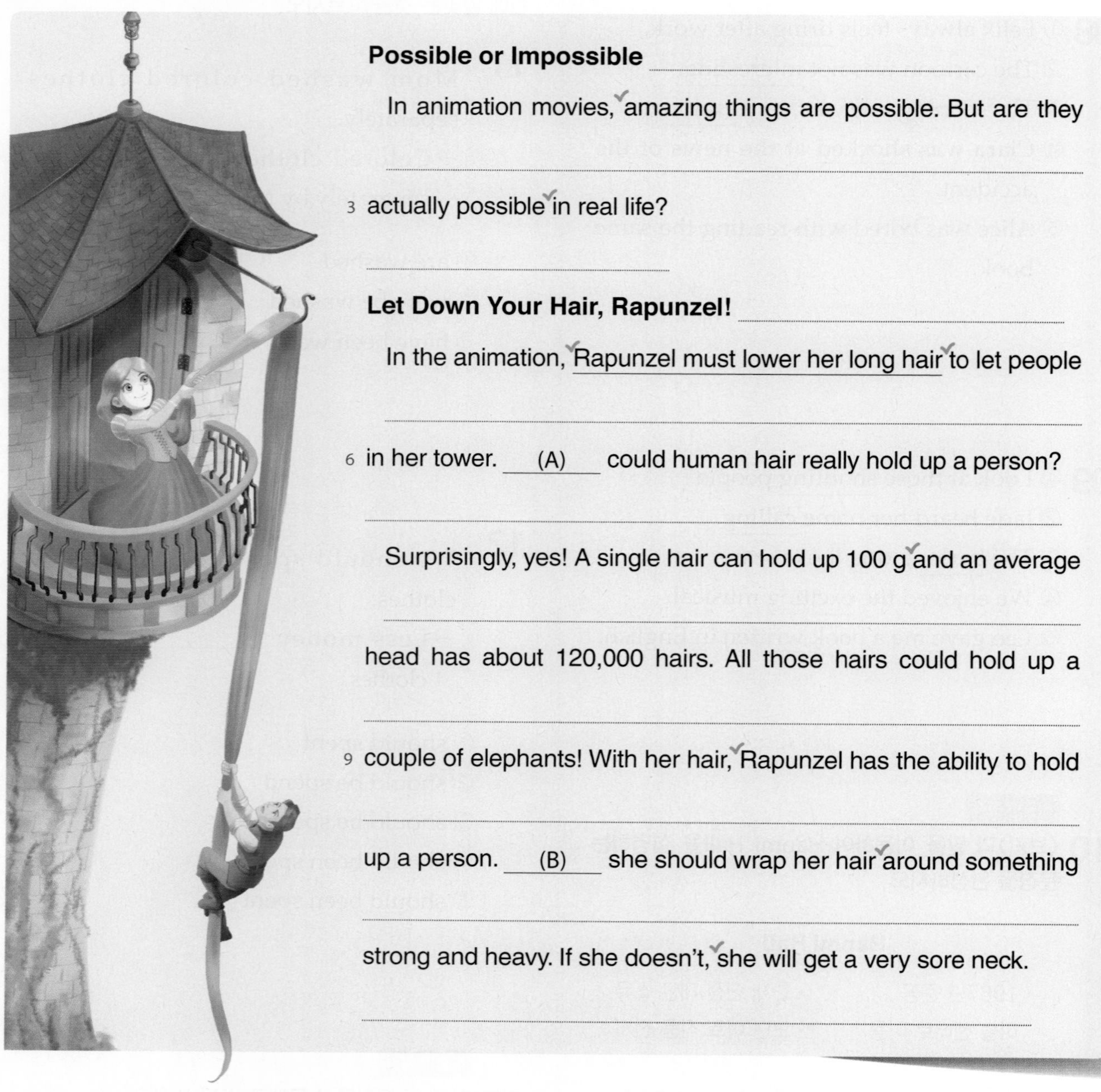

Possible or Impossible

In animation movies, amazing things are possible. But are they actually possible in real life?

Let Down Your Hair, Rapunzel!

In the animation, Rapunzel must lower her long hair to let people in her tower. ___(A)___ could human hair really hold up a person? Surprisingly, yes! A single hair can hold up 100 g and an average head has about 120,000 hairs. All those hairs could hold up a couple of elephants! With her hair, Rapunzel has the ability to hold up a person. ___(B)___ she should wrap her hair around something strong and heavy. If she doesn't, she will get a very sore neck.

1 밑줄 친 문장을 수동태 문장으로 바꿔 쓰시오.

____

2 빈칸 (A), (B)에 공통으로 들어갈 알맞은 말을 위 글에서 찾아 쓰시오.

____

교과서 어휘 **possible** 가능한(↔ impossible) **let down** 내리다 **lower** 내리다, 낮추다 **hold up** 들다, 지탱하다 **surprisingly** 놀랍게도 **average** 평균의 **a couple of** 두 개의 **sore** 아픈, 쑤시는 **neck** 목

Answer p. 10

3 다음 글을 읽고 답할 수 없는 것은?

행사 안내

The 9th annual flea market to help *Safe Home for Children* **is scheduled** for Saturday and Sunday, June 2 and 3, at Green Park. *Safe Home for Children* **was founded** in 1985 to help children **left** behind by war. These days the organization helps children in war refugee camps. The sale starts at 10 a.m. Anyone can sell and buy items in the flea market. Those **wishing** to sell items should contact Rena Danes in advance to rent space and a tent. Free snack bars will be available during lunch time.

*refugee camp 난민촌

① What does *Safe Home for Children* do?
② When does the annual flea market start?
③ Where can people meet Rena Danes?
④ What should people do to sell items?
⑤ When can people use snack bars?

4 다음 글의 내용과 일치하지 않는 것은?

세계 문화

Boxing Day is a holiday **celebrated** on the day after Christmas Day. It originated in the UK and now it **is celebrated** in a number of countries like Australia and Canada. No one knows for sure when Boxing Day started. Some believe it was centuries ago. Masters used to give their servants the presents in boxes to reward their hard work during Christmas. These days, it is now a day of relaxation and shopping. Shopping malls **are filled with** people who came to shop for the Boxing Day sales.

① Boxing Day는 크리스마스 바로 다음 날이다.
② Boxing Day는 호주와 캐나다 등 여러 나라에서 기념된다.
③ 수 세기 전에 크리스마스에 하인들이 주인들에게 선물을 바쳤다.
④ 요즘 Boxing Day에는 사람들이 쉬고 쇼핑을 한다.
⑤ 요즘 Boxing Day에는 쇼핑몰에서 세일을 한다.

3 **annual** 연례의 **found** 설립하다 **leave behind** 남기다 **organization** 기관 **in advance** 미리 **available** 이용 가능한
4 **celebrate** 기념하다 **originate** 유래하다 **a number of** 많은 **servant** 하인 **reward** 보상하다 **relaxation** 휴식

Expression

1 제안하기 / 제안에 답하기

제안하기

- How about -ing ...?
- Why don't we(you) ...?
- You'd better ....
- (I think) You should ....
- I suggest (that) we ....
- Let's ....

도움 제안하기

- Can I help you?
- Let me help you.
- Can I give you a hand?
- Do you need help?

제안에 답하기

- Yes! / Okay! / Sure! / All right! / No problem.
- (That) Sounds good.
- Sorry ..., but ....
- No, thank you.
- I'm afraid I can't ....
- Maybe next time.

2 희망, 기대 표현하기

희망, 기대 표현하기

- I hope ....
- I can't wait to(for) ....
- I'm looking forward to ....

Expression Test

Answer p. 11

1 밑줄 친 부분의 의도로 알맞은 것은?

A Which class are you going to take?
B I'm going to take the taekwondo class. <u>I can't wait!</u>

① 충고하기 ② 놀람 표현하기
③ 분노 표현하기 ④ 유감 표현하기
⑤ 기대 표현하기

서술형 평가

2 빈칸에 알맞은 말을 쓰시오.

A ________ about going to the art gallery?
B Sounds good. I like to see the great paintings.

3 자연스러운 대화가 되도록 A의 말에 이어질 (A)-(C)를 바르게 배열한 것은?

A Our field trip is next Monday, right?
(A) That's great.
(B) Yes. I'm looking forward to it. But where are we going?
(C) We're going to the Music Museum.

① (A) – (C) – (B)
② (B) – (A) – (C)
③ (B) – (C) – (A)
④ (C) – (A) – (B)
⑤ (C) – (B) – (A)

4 의도하는 바가 나머지 넷과 <u>다른</u> 것은?

① Let's jog after dinner.
② Shall we jog after dinner?
③ Are you going to jog after dinner?
④ Why don't we jog after dinner?
⑤ How about jogging after dinner?

5 빈칸에 알맞은 것은?

A Shall we have dinner tonight?
B I'd love to, but ________________.

① I'm very tired today
② I like Korean food
③ I want to meet you
④ I'm looking forward to it
⑤ I'd like to go to the Italian restaurant

6 밑줄 친 부분과 바꿔 쓸 수 있는 것은?

A You know what? Ruth will visit Korea this summer vacation.
B Really? <u>I'm really looking forward to meeting her.</u>

① I'm going to meet her.
② I can't wait to meet her.
③ Make sure you meet her.
④ I won't be able to meet her.
⑤ I don't feel like meeting her.

서술형 평가

Answer p. 11

1 밑줄 친 단어들을 바르게 배열하여 대화를 완성하시오.

A Mike, Do you know how to book a hotel at the lowest price?
B Sure. I booked a hotel for my family trip last month.
A Great. My family is also planning to stay in Busan next month but I can't find a hotel with a reasonable price.
B Well, (1) help, me, let, you. I use this app to search the prices. Just put the date and hit the search button.
A Oh, thank you. (2) trip, looking, to, I'm, family, forward, my to Busan.

(1) ______________________________
(2) ______________________________

2 주어진 단어를 이용하여 빈칸에 알맞은 말을 쓰시오.

(1)
A Where did you take this picture?
B The picture ________ ________ in Paris. (take)

(2)
A Who sent this package?
B ________ ________ ________ by my aunt, Jane. (send)

3 어법상 어색한 부분을 찾아 고쳐 쓰시오.

Yesterday was the little boy's birthday. His parents were thrown a surprise party for him. The exciting boy loved the party and enjoyed the food.

(1) ______________ → ______________
(2) ______________ → ______________

4 분사를 이용하여 주어진 단어들로 그림을 묘사하는 문장을 완성하시오.

(1)

The girl ______________________ is my sister. (carry, books, library)

(2)

The man ______________________ is my uncle. (fix, break, fence)

5 그림을 보고, 〈보기〉의 단어들을 이용하여 빈칸에 알맞은 말을 쓰시오. (형태 변화 가능)

보기
surprise　　invite　　sit

Alice in Wonderland

I followed a rabbit to Wonderland. I (1) ________ ________ to Mad Hatter's tea party. Everything was strange. The person (2) ________ in the middle of the table was the Mad Hatter. I (3) ________ ________ to see a mouse pour tea into my cup.

Final Test

Answer p. 11

난이도: 상 ★★★ 중 ★★ 하 ★

★★
01 영영풀이에 해당하는 것은?

to cover something by putting something such as paper or cloth round it

① hold ② wrap ③ lower
④ park ⑤ correct

★★
02 영영풀이를 완성할 때 빈칸에 알맞은 것은?

ability: the physical or mental power or ________ needed to do something

① road ② couple ③ skill
④ hope ⑤ help

★★
03 밑줄 친 부분과 바꿔 쓸 수 있는 것은?

<u>Let Down</u> Your Hair, Rapunzel!

① Lower ② Hold ③ Comb
④ Cut ⑤ Show

★★ 서술형 평가
04 주어진 단어를 이용하여 빈칸에 알맞은 말을 쓰시오.

A I'm ________________ Mina's birthday party. (look)
B When is it?
A It's this weekend. I can't wait!

★★ 서술형 평가
05 우리말과 일치하도록 빈칸에 알맞은 말을 쓰시오.

A I ________ ________ ________ ride a bike on Jeju. (나는 제주도에서 자전거 타는 것을 매우 기대해.)
B That's great. Jeju is the best place to ride a bike.

★★
06 빈칸에 알맞은 것은?

A ________________
B How much is the watch?
A It's 30 dollars.

① I'll take it.
② Oh, I like it.
③ May I help you?
④ What's the price of it?
⑤ I'm looking for a watch.

★★ 서술형 평가
07 자연스러운 대화가 되도록 (A)-(C)를 바르게 배열하시오.

(A) Yes, I'm planning to volunteer at a day-care center for children.
(B) I'm looking forward to this Monday.
(C) Why? Do you have any special plans?

________ → ________ → ________

교과서 어휘 cover 덮다 physical 육체적인 mental 정신적인 comb 빗질하다 price 가격 day-care center 탁아소

Final Test

★★ 시험에 잘 나오는 문제

08 짝지어진 대화가 어색한 것은?

① A How about eating hamburgers for lunch?
  B Sounds good.
② A Why don't we go skating on Friday?
  B Why not?
③ A Shall we make a doghouse this Saturday?
  B Sorry, I can't.
④ A I think you should look on the bright side.
  B You're right. That's not a good idea.
⑤ A Let's take part in the cleanup campaign.
  B That's fine with me.

★★

09 빈칸에 알맞지 않은 것은?

A What about going to the concert this weekend?
B ________ I have an exam next week. I have to study for it.

① No, thank you. ② Maybe next time.
③ Sorry, but I can't. ④ That sounds good.
⑤ I'm afraid I can't.

★★ 서술형 평가

10 밑줄 친 단어들을 알맞은 형태로 쓰시오.

• Maradona (a) score the first goal in the last game.
• The first goal (b) score by Maradona in the last game.

(a) ________ (b) ________

[11~13] 빈칸에 들어갈 말이 바르게 짝지어진 것을 고르시오.

★★

11

• I'm ________ in making robots.
• Making robots is ________.

① interest – interest
② interesting – interesting
③ interesting – interested
④ interested – interesting
⑤ interested – interested

★★

12

• The girl ________ a black dress is my cousin.
• I can't find the bag ________ in Italy.

① wears – buys
② wearing – buying
③ wearing – bought
④ worn – buying
⑤ worn – bought

★★★

13

• ________ the roses grown by my mother?
• A lot of vegetables should ________ by children.

① Were – eat
② Were – be ate
③ Did – eaten
④ Did – be eaten
⑤ Were – be eaten

교과서 어휘 look on the bright side 긍정적으로 생각하다 take part in …에 참가하다 score 득점하다 cousin 사촌 rose 장미 vegetable 채소

Answer p. 11

[14~15] 빈칸에 알맞은 것을 고르시오.

★★
14

This short story ____________ by Edgar Allen Poe.

① writes ② wrote
③ is writing ④ was written
⑤ were written

★★
15

The box ____________ by my brother.

① is carrying ② is being carry
③ is been carried ④ is being carried
⑤ is been carrying

★★★ 서술형 평가
16 주어진 문장을 능동태 문장으로 바꿔 쓰시오.

He was sent out of the classroom by the teacher.
→ ____________

시험에 잘 나오는 문제
★★
17 어법상 어색한 것은?

① Sunglasses were used to hide their eyes.
② His glasses didn't broken by Sera.
③ Greece will be visited by many tourists this summer.
④ We were surprised at the news so much.
⑤ Are English and French used in Quebec?

★ 서술형 평가
18 빈칸에 공통으로 들어갈 알맞은 말을 쓰시오.

• My bike is covered ________ dust.
• Bryan was pleased ________ the toy car.

____

★★
19 밑줄 친 부분을 생략할 수 있는 것은?

① The princess was loved by the king.
② Mike was killed in the war by someone.
③ The problem was solved by Julian.
④ Mickey Mouse was made by Walt Disney.
⑤ My report card was sent to my parents by my teacher.

★★
20 밑줄 친 부분의 쓰임이 나머지와 다른 것은?

① The sleeping baby is so cute.
② He bought a new sleeping bag.
③ Don't touch the sleeping dog.
④ There is a sleeping cat under the table.
⑤ The sleeping boy next to you is my cousin.

★★
21 밑줄 친 부분이 어법상 어색한 것은?

① The car is parked in the park.
② The dog was fed by my dad.
③ The dress is being worn by Ann.
④ This kite was made at my friend.
⑤ Anna is being questioned now by the police.

교과서 어휘 send 보내다 tourist 여행객 French 프랑스어 dust 먼지 princess 공주 report card 성적표 cute 귀여운 feed 먹이다 question 묻다, 질문하다

Final Test

★★
22 주어진 문장을 수동태로 바꾼 것으로 알맞은 것은?

> Oscar is downloading music files from the Internet.

① Oscar is being downloading music files from the Internet.
② The Internet is being downloading music files from Oscar.
③ Music files are downloading from the Internet by Oscar.
④ Music files are being downloaded from the Internet by Oscar.
⑤ Music files are been downloading from the Internet by Oscar.

★★★
23 우리말과 일치하도록 주어진 단어들을 배열할 때 다섯 번째 오는 것은?

> 나는 프랑스에서 만들어진 셔츠를 샀다.
> (shirt, a, I, France, in, made, bought)

① in ② shirt ③ made
④ bought ⑤ France

★★★
24 어법상 올바른 것끼리 짝지어진 것은?

> ⓐ She is talked with her teacher.
> ⓑ The case still remains unsolved.
> ⓒ I would like some boiling eggs.
> ⓓ I saw an amazed sight on my way here.
> ⓔ We have to recycle used paper.

① ⓐ, ⓔ ② ⓑ, ⓒ ③ ⓑ, ⓓ
④ ⓑ, ⓔ ⑤ ⓒ, ⓔ

★★
25 빈칸에 알맞은 것은?

> There was an animation movie about a scientist who invents a machine that prints out hundreds of foods into the sky. Imagine a sky filled with hotdogs and chickens. Actually, this is ________. The 3D printers can now print out food. With the edible ink, a 3D printer can print out a fresh hamburger. Are you worried about its taste? Don't worry. It tastes wonderful.

① crazy ② fiction
③ possible ④ meaningless
⑤ unthinkable

★★
26 빈칸에 알맞은 것은?

> In the old days, people didn't use money to buy or sell things. Instead, they exchanged things. Later, people started to use unusual things as money. For example, people in a tiny island called Yap used big chunks of rock as money. In some Asian countries, tea was used as money. Ancient Roman soldiers were paid with salt. We could tell that ______________ if people in a society promise to use it as money.

① nothing could be money
② anything could be money
③ only salt could be money
④ money isn't that important
⑤ only unusual things could be money

교과서 어휘 download 내려받다 case 사건 sight 광경 hundreds of 수백의 imagine 상상하다 edible 먹을 수 있는 fiction 지어낸 이야기; 소설 meaningless 의미 없는 unthinkable 생각할 수 없는 exchange 교환하다 unusual 특이한 chunk 덩어리

[27~28] 다음을 읽고, 물음에 답하시오.

On Career Day, my class visited a broadcasting station. There, I sat at the desk where anchors announce the news. There were two screens (A) [hung/hanging] in front. I read aloud the news script (B) [written/writing] on the screen. On the other screen, I could see myself (C) [shown/showing] on TV. I looked like a real news anchor. After that, we went to the cafeteria and had lunch. Luckily, I saw my favorite anchor drinking coffee. It was a memorable day.

★

27 글쓴이의 심정으로 알맞은 것은?

① sad ② bored ③ worried
④ terrified ⑤ excited

★★★

28 (A)-(C)에서 어법에 맞는 말이 바르게 짝지어진 것은?

	(A)	(B)	(C)
①	hung	writing	shown
②	hanging	writing	showing
③	hung	written	showing
④	hanging	written	shown
⑤	hanging	written	showing

[29~30] 다음을 읽고, 물음에 답하시오.

In rural India, ⓐthere is not enough resources for schools and students. Most students ⓑhave not proper desks. The nonprofit organization Aarambh came up with a creative solution called Help Desk. It ⓒis make carton paper. It is a kind of "upcycling." The cardboard desk can ⓓworn as a school bag but when it ⓔfold in a special way, it changes into a desk. It costs only 20 rupees to produce.

*rupee 인도의 화폐 단위

★★

29 위 글의 내용과 일치하지 않는 것은?

① 인도의 시골에는 자원이 풍부하지 않다.
② Help Desk는 비영리 기관 Aarambh가 만들었다.
③ Help Desk는 일종의 업사이클이다.
④ Help Desk는 옷으로도 활용할 수 있다.
⑤ Help Desk 한 개의 제작비는 20루피이다.

★★

30 밑줄 친 ⓐ-ⓔ를 어법에 맞게 고친 것은?

① ⓐ → there was
② ⓑ → didn't have
③ ⓒ → is made of
④ ⓓ → wear
⑤ ⓔ → folded

교과서 어휘 career 직업, 경력 broadcasting station 방송국 anchor 앵커 memorable 기억할 만한 terrified 겁에 질린 rural 시골의 resource 자원 proper 적절한 nonprofit 비영리의 carton 상자 fold 접다 produce 생산하다

>> Grammar

A 분사의 형태와 의미

	형태	의미
현재분사	동사원형+ing	능동(…하는) / 진행(…하고 있는, …하면서)
과거분사	동사원형+ed	수동(…되는, … 당하는) / 완료(…된, …한)

B 분사의 역할

분사는 형용사처럼 명사를 꾸미거나 주어, 목적어의 보어 역할을 한다. 분사가 목적어나 부사(구)와 함께 구를 이뤄 명사를 꾸미면 명사 뒤에 쓴다.

The **studying** boy is my son.
My name was **called** by someone.

The boy **playing** tennis is my son.
I heard my name **called** by someone.

C 형용사처럼 쓰이는 분사

exciting 흥분하게 하는 excited 흥분한	confusing 혼란하게 하는 confused 혼란스러운	surprising 놀라게 하는 surprised 놀란	tiring 지치게 하는 tired 지친
interesting 관심을 끄는 interested 관심을 가진	disappointing 실망시키는 disappointed 실망한	satisfying 만족시키는 satisfied 만족한	boring 지루하게 만드는 bored 지루한

D 능동태와 수동태

1 수동태 문장

My parents love me. 〈능동태: 주어가 동작의 주체가 되는 문장〉

①　②　③

I am loved by my parents. 〈수동태: 주어가 동작의 대상이 되는 문장〉

① 능동태 문장의 목적어를 수동태 문장의 주어로 쓴다.
② 능동태 문장의 동사를 〈be동사+과거분사〉로 바꿔 수동태의 동사로 쓴다.
③ 능동태 문장의 주어를 〈by+목적격〉 형태로 수동태 문장의 끝에 쓴다.

2 수동태의 부정문과 의문문

수동태의 부정문	주어+be동사+**not**+과거분사 ….
수동태의 의문문	**be동사**+**주어**+**과거분사** …? – Yes, 주어+be동사. / No, 주어+be동사+not.

E 수동태의 동사 형태

과거 수동태	was(were)+과거분사	진행 수동태	be동사+being+과거분사
미래 수동태	will be+과거분사	조동사 수동태	조동사+be+과거분사

F 주의해야 할 수동태

1 **〈by+목적격〉 생략**: 수동태의 행위자가 일반인(we, you, they, people 등)이거나, 불분명하거나, 밝힐 필요가 없는 경우 생략한다.
English is spoken in Australia (by Australians).

2 by 이외의 전치사를 쓰는 수동태 표현

be filled with …으로 가득하다
be surprised at …에 놀라다
be covered with …으로 덮이다
be interested in …에 관심이 있다
be satisfied with …에 만족하다
be disappointed with …에 실망하다

>> Expression

1 제안하기 / 제안에 답하기

제안하기
- How about -ing ...?
- Why don't we(you) ...?
- You'd better ....
- (I think) You should ....
- I suggest (that) we ....
- Let's ....

도움 제안하기
- Can I help you?
- Let me help you.
- Can I give you a hand?
- Do you need help?

제안에 답하기
- Yes! / Okay! / Sure! / All right! / No problem.
- (That) Sounds good.
- Sorry ..., but ....
- No, thank you.
- I'm afraid I can't ....
- Maybe next time.

2 희망, 기대 표현하기

- I hope ....
- I can't wait to(for) ....
- I'm looking forward to ....

Lesson 05

조동사

Grammar Preview

1 조동사 (1)

can / could		긍정문	부정문	의문문
형태		can+동사원형	cannot(can't)+동사원형	Can+주어+동사원형 …?
의미	능력	…할 수 있다	…할 수 없다	…할 수 있나요?
	허락	…해도 좋다		…해도 되나요? (= may)

may / might		긍정문	부정문	의문문
형태		may+동사원형	may not+동사원형	May+주어+동사원형 …?
의미	추측	…할지도 모른다	…하지 않을지도 모른다	–
	허락	…해도 좋다	…하면 안 된다	…해도 되나요?

2 조동사 (2)

must	의무	강한 추측
긍정문	…해야 한다 (must(have to)+동사원형)	…임에 틀림없다 (must+동사원형)
부정문	…하면 안 된다 (must not+동사원형) …할 필요 없다 (don't have to+동사원형)	…일 리 없다 (cannot+동사원형)
의문문	…해야 하나요? (Must+주어+동사원형 …? = Do(es)+주어+have to …?)	–

should	긍정문	부정문	의문문
형태	should+동사원형	should not+동사원형	Should+주어+동사원형 …?
의무, 당연	…해야 한다 (= ought to)	…하면 안 된다 (= ought not to)	…해야 하나요?

had better	긍정문	부정문
형태	had better+동사원형 (…하는 게 좋겠다)	had better not+동사원형 (…하지 않는 게 좋겠다)

used to+동사원형	과거의 규칙적인 습관	과거의 상태
의미	…하곤 했다	(예전에) …했었다 (지금은 아니다)

1 조동사 (1)

Grammar

A can / could

	긍정문	부정문	의문문
형태	can+동사원형	cannot(can't)+동사원형	Can+주어+동사원형 …?
능력	…할 수 있다	…할 수 없다	…할 수 있나요?
허락	…해도 좋다		…해도 되나요? (= may)

Our team **can win** the game easily. 〈능력〉

= Our team **is able to win** the game easily.

You **can have** one of my toys. 〈허락〉

Carol **could visit** the museum during the trip. 〈= was able to〉

Can you **speak** Japanese? — Yes, I can. / No, I can't.

Can I **talk** with you for a moment? 〈= may〉

Plus Grammar

- **be able to**
  '…할 수 있다'라는 뜻의 can과 바꿔 쓸 수 있다.
  Ann **can** ride a bike.
  = Ann **is able to** ride a bike.
- 조동사 두 개를 연달아 쓸 수 없다.
  He *will can* play soccer. (×)
  → He **will be able to** play soccer.
- **요청의 can**
  Can you wait a minute, please? (잠깐 기다려 주시겠어요?)
  – Yes, of course. / Certainly.
  – Sorry, I can't. / I'd like to, but I don't have time.

B may / might

1 추측

	긍정문	부정문
형태	may+동사원형	may not+동사원형
의미	…할지도 모른다	…하지 않을지도 모른다

My sister **may be** talking on the phone.

Sally **may not go** downtown.

Mr. Davis **might be** sick now. 〈과거형 might: 약한 추측〉

You **might not know** of Sandra.

2 허락

	긍정문	부정문	의문문
형태	may+동사원형	may not+동사원형	May+주어+동사원형 …?
의미	…해도 좋다	…하면 안 된다	…해도 되나요?

You **may have** candies after lunch.

You **may not have** chocolate.

May I **play** computer games? — Yes, you may. / No, you may not.

Plus Grammar

허락의 can과 may
can은 일상에서, may는 공적 발언 상황에서 쓴다.
Can I use your umbrella, please? 〈일상 대화〉
May I have your attention, please? 〈안내 방송〉

Grammar Practice >>

Answer p. 13

A1 괄호 안에서 알맞은 것을 고르시오.

(1) Ann can (bake, bakes) cookies.

(2) Can I (take, took) one of these?

(3) Ivy (can, could) play soccer last year.

(4) I was (be able to, able to) sing well.

(5) We both (are, were) able to visit there then.

(6) We'll (be able to, can) visit many places in Korea soon.

(7) Jessica can't (answers, answer) this question.

A2 빈칸에 알맞은 말을 쓰시오.

(1) A Can I go out tonight?
B No, ________ ________.

(2) A ________ you able to play baseball last weekend?
B No, I ________.

(3) A ________ I open the window?
B Of course.

B1 우리말과 일치하도록 주어진 단어들을 배열하여 문장을 완성하시오.

(1) 당신이 제 자리에 앉으셔도 됩니다.
(my seat, have, may, you)
→ ________________________

(2) Lydia는 배고플지도 모른다.
(be, Lydia, hungry, may)
→ ________________________

(3) 제가 이 쿠키들을 먹어도 되나요?
(I, have, may, these cookies)
→ ________________________

B2 괄호 안에서 알맞은 것을 고르시오.

(1) May I (turn, turning) on the music?

(2) Jacob (not may, may not) return to his home.

(3) Tom may (studying, be studying) in his room.

(4) May I (join, joins) in your conversation?

(5) It might (rain not, not rain) this afternoon.

(6) You may (lose, lost) it if you aren't careful.

(7) You might (made, make) mistakes on the test.

(8) Tom may (is, be) smart, but he is not kind.

B3 어법상 어색한 부분을 찾아 문장을 다시 쓰시오.

(1) Stella may be not in the garden.
→ ________________________

(2) It sound may strange, but it's true.
→ ________________________

(3) You not may use my computer.
→ ________________________

(4) Daisy may not staying at home this weekend.
→ ________________________

교과서 어휘 easily 쉽게 downtown 시내에 bake 굽다 soon 곧 return 돌아오다 conversation 대화 make a mistake 실수하다 sound …처럼 들리다 strange 이상한

C must

	의무	강한 추측
긍정문	…해야 한다 (must[have to]+동사원형)	…임에 틀림없다 (must+동사원형)
부정문	…하면 안 된다 (must not+동사원형) …할 필요 없다 (don't have to+동사원형)	…일 리 없다 (cannot+동사원형)
의문문	…해야 하나요? (Must+주어+동사원형 …? = Do(es)+주어+have to …?)	–

You **must treat** your pets nicely.
Brian **had to wait** for his mom. 〈must의 과거형〉
You **don't have to read** the book.
The letter **must be** from Eric.
Mr. Anderson **can't[cannot] betray** us.

Plus Grammar
- **추측의 확실성 정도**
  must > may > might > can
  Jack **must** be tired. (피곤한 것이 틀림없다)
  Jack **can** be tired. (피곤할 수도 있다)
- don't have to = need not
  = don't need to

D should

	긍정문	부정문	의문문
형태	should+동사원형	should not+동사원형	Should+주어+동사원형 …?
의무 당연	…해야 한다 (= ought to)	…하면 안 된다 (= ought not to)	…해야 하나요?

The young **should respect** the elderly.
We **should not make** the same mistake again.

Plus Grammar
should가 충고의 의미를 나타낼 때, had better로 바꿔 쓸 수 있다.
You look so sick. You **should [had better]** take a rest.

E had better / used to

1 had better

	긍정문	부정문
형태	had better+동사원형	had better not+동사원형
충고	…하는 게 좋겠다	…하지 않는 게 좋겠다

You **had better take** care of that puppy.
You'**d better take** some medicine.
You **had better not go** alone.

2 used to

- 과거의 규칙적인 습관: '…하곤 했다'의 뜻으로 과거에 반복적으로 행했던, 습관적 행동을 나타내며, 습관적이지 않은 경우 would로 쓸 수 있다.
  I **used to watch** cartoons on Sunday mornings.
- 과거의 상태: '(예전에) …했었다'의 뜻으로 과거에 한때 지속된 상태를 나타낸다.
  There **used to be** an old building in the town.

Grammar Practice >>

Answer p. 13

C1 〈보기〉에서 밑줄 친 부분의 의미를 고르시오.

보기
ⓐ 추측 ⓑ 의무

(1) That girl must be Hana.
(2) I'm afraid I must say goodbye.
(3) They must listen to the teacher.
(4) It must be somewhere in my room.
(5) You must buy a ticket to enter the concert hall.
(6) This tower must be more than 300 years old.

C2 두 문장이 같은 의미가 되도록 빈칸에 알맞은 말을 쓰시오.

(1) Naomi must show us the receipt.
= Naomi ________ ________ show us the receipt.
(2) I don't have to walk in the rain now.
= I ________ ________ walk in the rain now.
(3) Joe need not stop playing cards.
= Joe ________ ________ ________ stop playing cards.

D1 should를 이용하여 빈칸에 알맞은 말을 쓰시오.

(1) You look so tired. You ________ have some rest.
(2) You have to keep your room clean, so you ________ throw your clothes everywhere.
(3) This library is very quiet. You ________ make any noise in the library.

E1 괄호 안에서 알맞은 것을 고르시오.

(1) You (had, have) better practice harder.
(2) Jade (uses, used) to be very shy.
(3) There used to (be, being) a small bakery in this town.
(4) You'd better (finish, to finish) your homework first.
(5) You had (better not, not better) have an apple before you sleep.

E2 우리말과 일치하도록 빈칸에 알맞은 말을 쓰시오.

(1) 그들은 동물 가죽으로 자신의 옷을 만들곤 했다.
→ They ________ ________ make their clothes from animal skins.
(2) 너는 지금 집에 가는 것이 좋겠다.
→ You ________ ________ go home right now.
(3) 너는 그녀에게 그 소식을 말하지 않는 것이 좋겠다.
→ You ________ ________ ________ tell the news to her.

E3 어법상 어색한 부분을 찾아 고쳐 쓰시오.

(1) I used to coaches the baseball team.
________ → ________
(2) You had better tells him the truth.
________ → ________
(3) You had not better go out at night.
________ → ________

교과서 어휘 treat 다루다 betray 배신하다 respect 존중하다 elderly 연로한 puppy 강아지 medicine 약 alone 혼자
somewhere 어딘가에 tower 탑 receipt 영수증 shy 수줍은 skin 피부, 가죽 coach 지도하다

Grammar Test

01 〈보기〉의 밑줄 친 부분과 쓰임이 같은 것은?

보기
Sam walked all day. He must be tired.

① He must not tell a lie.
② Must I take him there?
③ Jane must be Tom's aunt.
④ We must be quiet in the library.
⑤ You must not cross the street here.

서술형 평가

02 어법상 어색한 부분을 찾아 바르게 고쳐 쓰시오.

A You are late for school again.
B I'm sorry. I went to bed late yesterday.
A You'd not better go to bed late at night.

_______________ → _______________

03 짝지어진 문장의 의미가 서로 다른 것은?

① No parking here.
 = You must not park here.
② May I speak to Anna?
 = Can I speak to Anna?
③ Larry can play the cello.
 = Larry is able to play the cello.
④ You have to bring your book.
 = You must bring your book.
⑤ You'd better play outside.
 = You shouldn't play outside.

04 밑줄 친 부분을 바르게 바꿔 쓴 것은?

A Can Tony ride a horse?
B No, he can't. But he can ride a horse soon. He is learning it now.

① has to ② is able to
③ is going to ④ was able to
⑤ will be able to

서술형 평가

05 두 문장이 같은 의미가 되도록 빈칸에 알맞은 말을 쓰시오.

(1) We must go home before dinner.
 = We _______ _______ go home before dinner.
(2) Can you stand on one foot?
 = _______ you _______ to stand on one foot?
(3) You should tidy your room before you go out.
 = You _______ _______ tidy your room before you go out.

06 빈칸에 들어갈 말이 바르게 짝지어진 것은?

• Tom was late for the party. We _______ wait for him for an hour.
• Sam studied English hard. So he _______ pass the test and he was proud of himself.

① must – can ② has to – could
③ had to – can ④ have to – can
⑤ had to – could

교과서 어휘 cross 건너다 bring 가져오다 ride 타다 horse 말 tidy 정리하다 pass 통과하다, 합격하다 be proud of …을 자랑스러워하다

Answer p. 13

서술형 평가

07 괄호 안의 지시에 맞게 빈칸에 알맞은 말을 쓰시오.

A Mom, can I play here?
B No, you can't. Look at that sign. You ________ not play here. (금지)

08 빈칸에 알맞지 않은 것은?

A I think I am overweight.
B You ________ get some exercise.

① should ② need to ③ would
④ ought to ⑤ had better

09 밑줄 친 부분과 바꿔 쓸 수 없는 것은?

A My girlfriend is mad at me. What should I do?
B I think you should buy her some flowers and apologize to her.

① must ② have to
③ had better ④ ought to
⑤ need not

10 빈칸에 알맞은 것은?

A ________ I use your computer?
B I'm afraid you can't. I'm checking my e-mail.

① Must ② Need ③ Have
④ Can ⑤ Had better

11 어법상 어색한 것은?

① Carol had to sweep the floor.
② I couldn't understand the meaning.
③ Oliver used to living in India in his childhood.
④ You'd better visit your mom this Sunday.
⑤ When Matt was angry, he would walk out of the room.

서술형 평가

12 우리말과 일치하도록 빈칸에 알맞은 말을 쓰시오.

(1) 그는 동호회 모임에 참석하지 않았다. 그는 아플지도 모른다.
→ He didn't come to our club meeting. He ________ ________ ________.

(2) 오늘은 일요일이다. 미나는 오늘 학교에 갈 필요가 없다.
→ Today is Sunday. Mina ________ ________ ________ go to school today.

13 우리말을 영어로 바르게 옮긴 것은?

틀림없이 너는 무척 기쁘겠다.

① You will be very pleased.
② You can be very pleased.
③ You must be very pleased.
④ You might be very pleased.
⑤ You have to be very pleased.

교과서 어휘 sign 표지판 overweight 과체중인 get exercise 운동하다 check 확인하다 sweep 쓸다 floor 바닥 pleased 기쁜

Reading

[1~2] 다음을 끊어 읽고 ☑, 해석을 쓰시오.

STAY TUNED: FOR MY STORY

RAP it OUT

Hey, I'm MC Joy. Do you want to write your own rap? You can rap about anything because everything can be a story for a rap. I get ideas ___(A)___ I'm on the bus, in the shower, or in my bed. I write down my ideas and use them when I write my rap. There are no rules for writing raps. You can start today!

Fantastic Pets

Welcome to Fantastic Pets! Having a pet is great. Today I'm going to introduce my pet hedgehog, Polly. When I first got Polly, she was very scared. I couldn't hold her because she raised her spikes. I placed my T-shirt in her cage and she got used to my smell. ___(B)___, I <u>was able to</u> hold her in my hands. Now, Polly is my best friend and always makes me happy.

1 빈칸 (A)와 (B)에 들어갈 말이 바르게 짝지어진 것은?

① when – Finally ② if – Most of all ③ when – However
④ because – Finally ⑤ because – However

2 밑줄 친 부분을 한 단어로 바꿔 쓰시오.

____

교과서 어휘 rap 랩 write down 적다 rule 규칙 fantastic 기이한, 환상적인 hedgehog 고슴도치 scared 두려움을 느끼는 spike 뾰족한 것, 가시 place 두다, 놓다 get used to …에 익숙해지다

Answer p. 13

3 글의 흐름으로 보아, 주어진 문장이 들어가기에 알맞은 곳은?

IT 문화

An influencer posts a picture of a cool baseball cap on social media. Then, many followers see it and buy that baseball cap. (①) Fashion influencers create fashion trends. (②) These days, about 40 percent of the world's population uses social media every day. These people look up to influencers on social media and follow them when they make a decision. (③) Celebrities, bloggers, famous writers, and politicians **can** be influencers. (④) Therefore, social media users **should** have critical thoughts on what they read on social media. (⑤)

*influencer (소셜 미디어에서 폴로어가 많아) 영향력이 있는 사람, 인플루언서

They can guide and misguide us at the same time.

① ② ③ ④ ⑤

4 다음 글의 내용과 일치하지 않는 것은?

한국 문화

The traditional house in Jeju **used to** have a special gate, jeongnang. It was made of long and thick logs placed at the entrance of a house. Jeongnang consists of three logs. The house owner is at home when all three logs are down. If all three logs are in position, there is no one at home. Two logs in position means the owner won't come back for a long time. Then, villagers **would** stop by the house and take care of cows and pigs there. If only one log is in position, then it means the owner would come back soon.

① 정낭은 제주도의 전통적인 대문을 의미한다.
② 정낭은 세 개의 통나무로 이루어져 있다.
③ 통나무가 모두 내려가 있으면, 집주인이 집에 있다는 것이다.
④ 집주인이 집을 비운 상태라면 집에 들어가면 안 된다.
⑤ 한 개의 통나무만 제자리에 있으면, 집주인이 곧 돌아온다는 것이다.

3 **population** 인구 **look up to** …을 우러러보다 **celebrity** 유명인 **politician** 정치인 **critical** 비판적인
4 **traditional** 전통적인 **gate** 문 **log** 통나무 **consist of** …으로 구성되다 **in position** 제자리에 **villager** 마을 주민

Expression

1 묘사하기

인물의 특징 묻기

- What is ... like?
- How can you describe ...?
- What kind of person(man/woman) is ...?

인물의 특징 묘사하기

- He(She) is ....
- He(She) does ....

인물의 외모 묻기

- What do(es) ... look like?
- How do(es) ... look?

인물의 외모 묘사하기

- He(She) is ....
- He(She) has ....
- He(She) is wearing ....

2 상황에 대해 묻기 / 격려하기

상황에 대해 묻기

- What's wrong?
- What's the matter?
- Why are you sad(disappointed)?

격려하기

- Cheer up!
- Don't give up!
- Take it easy!
- Don't worry!

Expression Test

Answer p. 14

서술형 평가

1 우리말과 일치하도록 빈칸에 알맞은 말을 쓰시오.

A Who's the lady in the picture?
B She is my math teacher.
A ________ ________ she ________?
(그녀는 어떤 분이니?)
B She is very kind to students.
She always helps us.

[2~3] 밑줄 친 부분과 바꿔 쓸 수 있는 것을 고르시오.

2

A I have a sister. Her name is Alice.
B What does she look like?
A She is short and thin. She has beautiful blue eyes.

① Who is Alice?
② Do you like Alice?
③ What does she like?
④ How does she look?
⑤ What does she watch?

3

A You have a long face. What's wrong?
B I failed my English test.
A You'll do better next time.

① Why don't you exercise?
② What are you going to do?
③ What do you mean by that?
④ What are you talking about?
⑤ Why are you so disappointed?

4 짝지어진 대화가 어색한 것은?

① A Who is Bobby?
B He is smart.
② A How old is Laura?
B She is only 14 years old.
③ A Who's your best friend?
B My best friend is Roger.
④ A Who's the girl over there?
B That's Mina, my classmate.
⑤ A What is your older sister like?
B She is very lazy.

5 빈칸에 알맞은 것은?

A What's wrong?
B I didn't do well on the math test.
A ________________ You'll do better next time.

① I'm sure.
② Cheer up!
③ That's right.
④ Sounds good!
⑤ Don't be shy.

서술형 평가

6 자연스러운 대화가 되도록 A의 말에 이어질 (A)–(C)를 바르게 배열하시오.

A How many brothers and sisters do you have?
(A) What does your sister look like?
(B) I have two brothers and one sister.
(C) She's very pretty. She has short hair.

________ → ________ → ________

서술형 평가

Answer p. 14

1 빈칸에 알맞은 말을 〈보기〉에서 골라 쓰시오.

보기
You're right.
You'll do fine.
What do you mean?
What's the matter?

A You look so down.
(1) ______________________
B I'm worried about the school play tomorrow.
A I saw you practice very hard. You seemed perfect.
B Yeah, but I get nervous when I'm in front of people.
A Don't worry.
(2) ______________________
B Thanks, Sarah. I'll do my best.

2 그림을 보고, 주어진 표현과 조동사 must를 이용하여 문장을 완성하시오.

(1)

You ______________________ in the lab. (eat or drink)

(2)

You ______________________ in this room. (turn off, your cell phone)

3 두 문장이 같은 의미가 되도록 빈칸에 알맞은 말을 쓰시오.

(1) Matilda can speak three languages.
= Matilda ____________ speak three languages.

(2) You must come back before midnight.
= You ____________ come back before midnight.

4 주어진 단어들을 배열하여 문장을 완성하시오.

(1) A Can I have some more ice cream?
B You ____________ too much ice cream. (eat, better, had, not)

(2) A Hello? Can I speak to Mark?
B Sorry. He ____________, but he went back to his hometown. (to, us, with, live, used)

5 빈칸에 알맞은 말을 〈보기〉에서 골라 쓰시오.

보기
used to　should　have to　may

I have a big problem. I am a boxer and I used to eat a lot. But these days, I lost my appetite. I (1) __________ like sweets, but now I don't eat ice cream or candies. Now I'm so skinny. I (2) __________ gain weight for the big match next month. If I don't put on weight, I (3) __________ not be able to fight. What (4) __________ I do?

Final Test

Answer p. 14

난이도: 상 ★★★ 중 ★★ 하 ★

★★
01 다음 영영풀이에 해당하는 것은?

> to have a good opinion of someone's character or ideas

① arrive ② respect ③ treat
④ react ⑤ lend

★★
02 빈칸에 알맞은 것은?

> • Don't ________ any noise in the library.
> • Everybody can ________ a mistake.

① bake ② make ③ take
④ get ⑤ have

★
03 의도하는 바가 나머지와 다른 것은?

① Cheer up! ② Don't worry!
③ Don't give up! ④ Take it easy!
⑤ Never do that again.

★★
04 밑줄 친 부분과 바꿔 쓸 수 있는 것은?

> A <u>What is Yuri like?</u>
> B She is honest and cheerful.

① Whom does Yuri like?
② What does Yuri look like?
③ Which person does Yuri like?
④ What kind of person is Yuri?
⑤ What kind of woman does Yuri like?

★★
05 짝지어진 대화가 어색한 것은?

① A How do you like this camera?
B I like it. It's not heavy.
② A Where is your brother?
B Over there. He's wearing blue jeans.
③ A Who is that tall boy over there?
B You mean the boy with a red T-shirt?
④ A What do you think of fast food?
B I think it's not good for your health.
⑤ A What is Oscar looking for?
B He is wearing sunglasses and a cap.

서술형 평가
★★
06 그림을 보고, 빈칸에 알맞은 말을 쓰시오.

> A What does your sister look like?
> B She ________ ________ glasses.

★
07 빈칸에 들어갈 말이 바르게 짝지어진 것은?

> A Who is that boy over there?
> B Oh, he is Scott, my classmate.
> A Really? ________ is he ________?
> B He's very kind and generous.

① What – as ② Who – like
③ What – like ④ Who – as
⑤ How – like

교과서 어휘 opinion 의견 character 성격 cheerful 명랑한 heavy 무거운 kind 친절한 generous 관대한

Final Test

★★ 서술형 평가

08 주어진 단어를 이용하여 밑줄 친 부분과 바꿔 쓸 수 있는 말을 쓰시오.

like　　what　　look

A　Who's Phillip? <u>How does he look?</u>
B　He's tall. He has long black hair.

____

★★

09 우리말을 영어로 잘못 옮긴 것은?

① 그들 중 몇 명은 그를 좋아하지 않을지도 모른다.
→ Some of them must not like him.
② Asher는 젊었을 때 여행을 많이 다니곤 했다.
→ Asher used to travel a lot when he was young.
③ 너는 이 수프를 먹지 않는 편이 좋다.
→ You'd better not eat this soup.
④ 너는 이 책을 살 필요가 없었다.
→ You didn't have to buy this book.
⑤ 그 암탉은 속에 황금알이 많이 있는 것이 틀림없다.
→ The hen must have a lot of golden eggs in it.

★★ 서술형 평가

10 두 문장이 같은 의미가 되도록 빈칸에 알맞은 말을 쓰시오.

Archer lived alone in the past, but he doesn't live alone anymore.

→ Archer ________ ________ live alone.

[11~12] 빈칸에 들어갈 말이 바르게 짝지어진 것을 고르시오.

★★

11

• You ________ fasten your seat belt. This plane will take off soon.
• We ________ live next to the airport so we couldn't sleep well at night.

① might – would　② must – had better
③ would – must　④ used to – must
⑤ must – used to

★★

12

• The windows were very dirty. I ________ clean them.
• Sarah ________ play the violin a few years ago.

① must – can　② must – do
③ have to – could　④ had to – could
⑤ had to – can

★★ 서술형 평가

13 두 문장이 같은 의미가 되도록 빈칸에 알맞은 말을 쓰시오.

(1) Tom could buy a new bike last month.
= Tom ________ ________ ________ buy a new bike last month.

(2) Alice should take exercise every day.
= Alice ________ ________ take exercise every day.

(3) You look so sick. You had better take some medicine.
= You look so sick. You ________ take some medicine.

교과서 어휘 travel 여행하다　hen 암탉　golden 금으로 된　not ... anymore 더 이상 …이 아닌　fasten 매다, 채우다　take off 이륙하다

★★
14 밑줄 친 부분의 의미가 같으면 S, 다르면 D를 쓰시오.

(1) ________ (a) It may snow tomorrow.
(b) You may use my umbrella.

(2) ________ (a) Sarah can read and write English.
(b) You can go now.

(3) ________ (a) I must help Mom do the dishes.
(b) You must be silent in the library.

★★ 서술형 평가
15 문장에서 어법상 어색한 부분을 찾아 바르게 고치시오.

(1)
Last year, I used to getting up early because I had to go to school by seven o'clock.

__________ → __________

(2)
That boy has to be Jerry. They said he was tall with bright red hair.

__________ → __________

★★
16 빈칸에 알맞은 것은?

There used to be a theater in that town, but ______________ now.

① I don't watch it
② I want to visit it
③ I like it very much
④ the theater isn't there
⑤ they are building a school

★★
17 어법상 어색한 것은?

① You'd not better go there.
② You should speak more loudly.
③ Samuel used to have really long hair.
④ We shouldn't listen to bad people.
⑤ I used to read many books when I was a child.

★ 서술형 평가
18 우리말과 일치하도록 빈칸에 알맞은 말을 쓰시오.

너는 늦지 않는 편이 좋겠다.

→ You ________ ________ ________ be late.

★
19 빈칸에 알맞은 것은?

It's cold today. You'd ________ a coat when you go out.

① wore ② worn ③ to wear
④ wearing ⑤ better wear

★★
20 주어진 문장을 지시대로 바꿔 쓴 것 중 어색한 것은?

① I can listen to music. (과거형)
→ I could listen to music.
② You must do the work at once. (과거형)
→ You had to do the work at once.
③ You ought to read the book. (부정문)
→ You ought not to read the book.
④ I can go to the gym after school. (미래형)
→ I'll be able to go to the gym after school.
⑤ I had to buy the hat yesterday. (부정문)
→ I had not to buy the hat yesterday.

교과서 어휘 umbrella 우산 do the dishes 설거지하다 silent 조용한 loudly 시끄럽게 at once 즉시 gym 체육관 hat 모자

Final Test

★★ 서술형 평가

21 빈칸에 알맞은 말을 쓰시오.

A Could you drive a car last year?
B No, ________ ________. But I can drive one now.

★

22 빈칸에 알맞은 것은?

A Do you like candies?
B Not now. But when I was a child, I ________ eat them almost every day.

① should ② can ③ had better
④ have to ⑤ used to

★★

23 빈칸에 공통으로 들어갈 말로 알맞은 것은?

• Emily and James ________ to take care of their little sister last weekend.
• You ________ better buy things carefully.

① had ② may ③ could
④ should ⑤ have

★★ 서술형 평가

24 밑줄 친 단어를 알맞은 조동사와 함께 쓰시오.

(a) People have to wait six months to meet Dr. Everett. She be a very good dentist.
(b) I don't remember the boy well, but he be Ann's brother.

(a) ________ (b) ________

★★

25 그림에서 다음 글의 내용과 일치하지 않는 것은?

We will start at a standing pose. Firstly, shift your weight to your right foot. Bend your left knee and raise your left foot. Clasp your left ankle with your right hand then put it in the inner right thigh. Now you're standing only with your right foot. Keep the balance gently. Lastly, press your palms together in prayer position at your chest. Can you guess the name of the pose? This is a tree pose.

[26~27] 다음을 읽고, 물음에 답하시오.

I used ⓐto having long hair so I bought this hair dryer ⓑto save time in the morning. It is strong and dries up my hair fast in five minutes. I bought it two years ago and it is still in a good condition. I recently had my hair cut and I really don't use the dryer ⓒas often as I did before. I want ⓓto sell it for 30 dollars. You can ⓔeither pick it up at my place or I could send it by delivery service. Contact 210-4567, Julie Benz.

교과서 어휘 pose 자세 shift 옮기다, 이동하다 bend 구부리다 clasp 움켜쥐다 inner 안쪽의 thigh 허벅다리 balance 균형 palm 손바닥 prayer 기도 chest 가슴 dry up 말리다 delivery service 배달 서비스

Answer p. 14

★★
26 글쓴이가 팔려는 물건에 관한 설명으로 옳지 않은 것은?

① 글쓴이가 2년 전에 구입했다.
② 머리를 5분 안에 빠르게 말려 준다.
③ 드라이어 기능에 이상이 없다.
④ 글쓴이는 30달러에 팔기를 원한다.
⑤ 배송 서비스를 이용해야 구매할 수 있다.

★★
27 밑줄 친 ⓐ–ⓔ 중 어법상 어색한 것은?

① ⓐ ② ⓑ ③ ⓒ ④ ⓓ ⑤ ⓔ

★★
28 대화 직후 Tom이 할 행동으로 알맞은 것은?

Tom Can I get some information on skate lessons?
Clerk Sure. Are you a beginner?
Tom Yes, I am.
Clerk Good. We offer the one-day basic course. You'll be able to skate right after the lesson.
Tom All right. When does it start?
Clerk At 3 p.m. today. Please fill out the form first to take the lesson. One more thing. You must wear a helmet.
Tom Okay. I brought my helmet.
Clerk Good. After you complete the form, please put it in the box.

① to clean the floor
② to fill out the form
③ to rent a helmet
④ to take the skate lesson
⑤ to teach him how to skate

[29~30] 다음을 읽고, 물음에 답하시오.

I moved around from city to city for a long time. I'm not traveling but working. It's been two weeks since I started looking for a perfect place for a haunted house. Can you guess what kind of job I have? I am a location manager. I look for places for a movie or a TV drama. To be a location manager, you have to travel a lot and develop a good eye for places and mood. Taking pictures and making notes of the places help a lot, too.

★★
29 글쓴이가 할 일로 알맞은 것은?

① 영화의 배경 음악 작곡
② 뮤지컬 무대 장치 설계
③ 드라마 촬영 장소 제안
④ 배우들의 외국어 대사 번역
⑤ 영화 출연 배우에게 의상 제안

★
30 밑줄 친 부분과 바꿔 쓸 수 있는 것은?

① do ② may ③ must
④ can ⑤ shall

교과서 어휘 one-day 하루의, 당일의 fill out 작성하다 form 양식 haunted house 귀신 나오는 집, 흉가 location manager 야외 촬영 관리자 eye 안목, 시각 mood 분위기 make notes of …을 메모하다

>> Grammar

A can / could

		긍정문	부정문	의문문
형태		can+동사원형	cannot(can't)+동사원형	Can+주어+동사원형 …?
의미	능력	…할 수 있다	…할 수 없다	…할 수 있나요?
	허락	…해도 좋다		…해도 되나요? (= may)

B may / might

1 추측

	긍정문	부정문
형태	may+동사원형	may not+동사원형
의미	…할지도 모른다	…하지 않을지도 모른다

2 허락

	긍정문	부정문	의문문
형태	may+동사원형	may not+동사원형	May+주어+동사원형 …?
의미	…해도 좋다	…하면 안 된다	…해도 되나요?

C must

	의무	강한 추측
긍정문	…해야 한다 (must(have to)+동사원형)	…임에 틀림없다 (must+동사원형)
부정문	…하면 안 된다 (must not+동사원형) …할 필요 없다 (don't have to+동사원형)	…일 리 없다 (cannot+동사원형)
의문문	…해야 하나요? (Must+주어+동사원형 …? = Do(es)+주어+have to …?)	–

D should

	긍정문	부정문	의문문
형태	should+동사원형	should not+동사원형	Should+주어+동사원형 …?
의무 당연	…해야 한다 (= ought to)	…하면 안 된다 (= ought not to)	…해야 하나요?

E had better / used to

1 had better

	긍정문	부정문
형태	had better+동사원형	had better not+동사원형
충고	…하는 게 좋겠다	…하지 않는 게 좋겠다

2 used to

	과거의 규칙적인 습관	과거의 상태
의미	…하곤 했다	(예전에) …했었다

>> Expression

1 묘사하기

인물의 특징 묻기
- What is ... like?
- How can you describe ...?
- What kind of person(man/woman) is ...?

인물의 특징 묘사하기
- He(She) is ....
- He(She) does ....

인물의 외모 묻기
- What do(es) ... look like?
- How do(es) ... look?

인물의 외모 묘사하기
- He(She) is ....
- He(She) has ....
- He(She) is wearing ....

2 상황에 대해 묻기 / 격려하기

상황에 대해 묻기
- What's wrong?
- What's the matter?
- Why are you sad(disappointed)?

격려하기
- Cheer up!
- Don't give up!
- Take it easy!
- Don't worry!

Believe you can
and you're halfway there.

Theodore Roosevelt

PART

II

듣기 실전 모의고사

01회 » 듣기 실전 모의고사

01 다음을 듣고, 부산의 오늘 오후 날씨로 가장 적절한 것을 고르시오.

02 대화를 듣고, 여자가 구입할 티셔츠로 가장 적절한 것을 고르시오.

03 대화를 듣고, 남자의 심정으로 가장 적절한 것을 고르시오.

① upset ② sad
③ bored ④ embarrassed
⑤ excited

04 대화를 듣고, 여자가 어제 한 일로 가장 적절한 것을 고르시오.

① 쇼핑몰 가기 ② 새 옷 사기
③ 생일 파티 하기 ④ 선물 구입하기
⑤ 할머니 댁 방문하기

05 대화를 듣고, 두 사람이 대화하는 장소로 가장 적절한 곳을 고르시오.

① 병원 ② 약국 ③ 학교
④ 식당 ⑤ 경찰서

06 대화를 듣고, 여자의 마지막 말의 의도로 가장 적절한 것을 고르시오.

① 감사 ② 충고 ③ 허가
④ 비난 ⑤ 동의

07 대화를 듣고, 여자가 한국에 와서 한 일이 아닌 것을 고르시오.

① 쇼핑 하기 ② 미술관 가기
③ 경복궁 구경하기 ④ 청계천 주변 걷기
⑤ 야구 경기 관람하기

08 대화를 듣고, 남자가 대화 직후에 할 일로 가장 적절한 것을 고르시오.

① 자전거 타기 ② 사회 숙제하기
③ 버스 타기 ④ 친구 기다리기
⑤ 엄마 차 타기

09 대화를 듣고, 여자가 Jina Lee에 대해 언급하지 않은 것을 고르시오.

① 나이 ② 직업
③ 최종 학력 ④ 출신 고등학교
⑤ 고용한 직원 수

10 다음을 듣고, 남자가 하는 말의 내용으로 가장 적절한 것을 고르시오.

① bank teller
② credit card
③ cell phone
④ fax machine
⑤ automated teller machine

Answer p. 16

11 다음을 듣고, 여자가 하는 말의 내용과 일치하지 않는 것을 고르시오.

① 여자는 아침에 일어나면 미세먼지 수치를 확인한다.
② 미세먼지는 점점 더 심각해지고 있다.
③ 미세먼지를 해결하기 위해 함께 노력해야 한다.
④ 대중교통 이용을 줄여야 한다.
⑤ 미세먼지에 관해 다른 나라를 탓하지 않아야 한다.

12 대화를 듣고, 남자가 전화를 건 목적으로 가장 적절한 것을 고르시오.

① 가구를 주문하기 위해서
② 상품 주문을 취소하기 위해서
③ 배송 날짜를 변경하기 위해서
④ 기차표를 예매하기 위해서
⑤ 약속 시간을 잡기 위해서

13 대화를 듣고, 남자가 지불해야 할 금액으로 가장 적절한 것을 고르시오.

① 46,000원 ② 48,000원 ③ 50,000원
④ 52,000원 ⑤ 54,000원

14 대화를 듣고, 두 사람의 관계로 가장 적절한 것을 고르시오.

① 의사 – 환자 ② 교사 – 학생
③ 경찰관 – 운전자 ④ 아빠 – 딸
⑤ 버스 운전기사 – 승객

15 대화를 듣고, 남자가 여자에게 부탁한 일로 가장 적절한 것을 고르시오.

① 집 청소 도와주기
② 수학 숙제 도와주기
③ 시험 범위 알려 주기
④ 시험 날짜 알려 주기
⑤ 수학 문제 알려 주기

16 대화를 듣고, 여자가 영화를 보러 갈 수 없는 이유로 가장 적절한 것을 고르시오.

① 엄마가 편찮으셔서
② 다른 약속이 있어서
③ 그 영화를 이미 봐서
④ 남동생을 돌봐야 해서
⑤ 늦게까지 일을 해야 해서

17 다음 그림의 상황에 가장 적절한 대화를 고르시오.

① ② ③ ④ ⑤

18 다음을 듣고, 여자가 슈퍼마켓 이용에 대해 언급하지 않은 것을 고르시오.

① 영업일 ② 영업시간
③ 층별 상품 ④ 회원 혜택
⑤ 무료 주차 시간

[19-20] 대화를 듣고, 남자의 마지막 말에 이어질 여자의 말로 가장 적절한 것을 고르시오.

19 Woman: ______________________

① It was hot and sunny.
② I stayed there for three days.
③ I learned to ride a horse, too.
④ The food there tasted great.
⑤ I'm really looking forward to it.

20 Woman: ______________________

① You are right.
② I usually listen to music.
③ I like hip hop music, too.
④ Why don't you buy the album?
⑤ Let's go to the concert someday.

Dictation Test >> 01회

01 다음을 듣고, 부산의 오늘 오후 날씨로 가장 적절한 것을 고르시오.

M Good morning. It's time for today's ________ ________. In Seoul, it will be sunny all day long, so you will be able to enjoy ________ activities. In Daejeon, it will be cloudy and there will be showers in the afternoon. In Busan, it will rain in the morning, but the rain will ________ and the sun will ________ in the afternoon.

02 대화를 듣고, 여자가 구입할 티셔츠로 가장 적절한 것을 고르시오.

M How may I help you?
W I'm ________ ________ a white T-shirt.
M What about this one over here? It ________ very well.
W Umm.... I don't like the square neck.
M Then how about this one? It has a round neck.
W I don't want any ________ on it. I need a simple one.
M Maybe this is the one you're looking for. Right?
W Perfect! I'll take it.

03 대화를 듣고, 남자의 심정으로 가장 적절한 것을 고르시오.

① upset ② sad
③ bored ④ embarrassed
⑤ excited

W Dongmin, what's ________? You look ________.
M I've been looking for my backpack, but I can't find it.
W Where did you put it?
M It was right here. But now it's gone.
W Really? Are you ________ me?
M Why? I'm very ________.
W Well. You're carrying it right now. ________ your back.
M Oops! I didn't know that.

04 대화를 듣고, 여자가 어제 한 일로 가장 적절한 것을 고르시오.

① 쇼핑몰 가기 ② 새 옷 사기
③ 생일 파티 하기 ④ 선물 구입하기
⑤ 할머니 댁 방문하기

M Sujin, you're ________ a nice muffler.
W Thanks.
M Where did you get it? Did you buy it at the mall?
W No, not really. I went to my grandmother's house yesterday, and she gave it to me as a ________ ________.
M That's a really ________ present. Happy birthday, by the way.
W Thanks. Can you come to my birthday party tomorrow?
M Of course I can.

>> WORDS **all day long** 하루 종일 **shower** 소나기 **square** 정사각형 모양의 **muffler** 목도리, 머플러

Answer p. 16

05 대화를 듣고, 두 사람이 대화하는 장소로 가장 적절한 곳을 고르시오.

① 병원 ② 약국 ③ 학교
④ 식당 ⑤ 경찰서

W What's the matter?
M I have a ________ ________ and I'm coughing a lot.
W Do you have a ________, too?
M No, I guess not.
W Then, take these pills three times a day. Be sure to take them after meals.
M I see.
W If you don't ________ ________ tomorrow, you should go see a doctor.
M Okay, I will.

06 대화를 듣고, 여자의 마지막 말의 의도로 가장 적절한 것을 고르시오.

① 감사 ② 충고 ③ 허가
④ 비난 ⑤ 동의

W You look angry, Juho. What happened?
M I went to the supermarket with my pet dog, but they didn't ________ me ________.
W Why? Because of your dog?
M Yes. They said that no animals were allowed inside the supermarket.
W Umm.... They might be ________ about animals eating the food there.
M But I was ________ my dog in my arms.
W Come on. Put yourself in their ________, and you will understand.

07 대화를 듣고, 여자가 한국에 와서 한 일이 <u>아닌</u> 것을 고르시오.

① 쇼핑 하기 ② 미술관 가기
③ 경복궁 구경하기 ④ 청계천 주변 걷기
⑤ 야구 경기 관람하기

M Kate, are you having fun here in Korea?
W Yeah, I'm having a wonderful time here.
M You arrived two days ago. What did you do?
W Well. On the first day I ________ for clothes and then I went to an art gallery in Insadong.
M I see. What about yesterday?
W I first went to Gyeongbokgung in the morning and ________ around Cheonggyecheon in the evening.
M Sounds fun. What's your plan for today?
W I'm going to watch a ________ ________ at the ballpark.
M I hope you will have a lot of fun there.

WORDS **cough** 기침하다 **guess** …으로 추측된다, …일 것 같다 **take** 복용하다 **pill** 알약 **meal** 식사 **allow** 허락하다 **art gallery** 미술관 **ballpark** 야구장

08 대화를 듣고, 남자가 대화 직후에 할 일로 가장 적절한 것을 고르시오.

① 자전거 타기 ② 사회 숙제하기
③ 버스 타기 ④ 친구 기다리기
⑤ 엄마 차 타기

M Mom, I'm ________.
W Where are you going?
M I'm going to meet my friends at the library. We have to finish the social studies ________ together.
W Are you going to ride your bike? It's raining ________ outside.
M Really? I didn't know that. Then I guess I'll take the bus.
W I'd better give you a ________. Wait just a few minutes.
M All right. Thanks, Mom.

09 대화를 듣고, 여자가 Jina Lee에 대해 언급하지 않은 것을 고르시오.

① 나이 ② 직업
③ 최종 학력 ④ 출신 고등학교
⑤ 고용한 직원 수

W Did you read the article about Jina Lee?
M No, I've ________ ________ about her. Who is she?
W She is a ________ business person. She's only 30 years old, but she is already the CEO of a huge fashion company.
M That's amazing. I bet she majored in business administration.
W That's not true. She graduated from high school, and then she started a small business all ________ ________. Now she has more than 10,000 employees.
M Wow! I want to be a great CEO like her.

10 다음을 듣고, 남자가 하는 말의 내용으로 가장 적절한 것을 고르시오.

① bank teller
② credit card
③ cell phone
④ fax machine
⑤ automated teller machine

M This is ________ when you can't visit a bank. You can take out money any time you want with a bank book or a bank card. It doesn't have to ________ ________ your bank. You can also ________ the money in your account to another account using it. It is like a small bank that you can visit anytime, anywhere.

>> WORDS social studies (학교 교과로서의) 사회 article 기사 business administration 경영학 graduate 졸업하다 employee 직원 bank book (은행) 통장 account 계좌

Answer p. 16

11 다음을 듣고, 여자가 하는 말의 내용과 일치하지 않는 것을 고르시오.

① 여자는 아침에 일어나면 미세먼지 수치를 확인한다.
② 미세먼지는 점점 더 심각해지고 있다.
③ 미세먼지를 해결하기 위해 함께 노력해야 한다.
④ 대중교통 이용을 줄여야 한다.
⑤ 미세먼지에 관해 다른 나라를 탓하지 않아야 한다.

W What is the ________ ________ you do in the morning? In my case, I check the weather forecast. To be more exact, I check the level of fine dust. Fine dust is getting ________ and ________. To deal with this problem, everyone should work together. We can start by using public transportation instead of driving. We can also ________ more trees. Let's not blame other countries but do something about it.

12 대화를 듣고, 남자가 전화를 건 목적으로 가장 적절한 것을 고르시오.

① 가구를 주문하기 위해서
② 상품 주문을 취소하기 위해서
③ 배송 날짜를 변경하기 위해서
④ 기차표를 예매하기 위해서
⑤ 약속 시간을 잡기 위해서

W Hello. Find Wood Furniture. How may I help you?
M I'm calling to ________ my ________.
W May I have your name, please?
M This is Mike Sullivan. I ordered a closet last Sunday.
W Yes, I ________ your order. What do you want to change?
M The ________ date. Can I get it this Wednesday instead of Saturday? I will be out of town during the weekend.
W No problem. We will deliver it to you on July 4th, Wednesday.
M Thank you very much.

13 대화를 듣고, 남자가 지불해야 할 금액으로 가장 적절한 것을 고르시오.

① 46,000원 ② 48,000원
③ 50,000원 ④ 52,000원
⑤ 54,000원

W May I help you, sir?
M Yes. I would like to buy five tickets to the aquarium.
W The ticket ________ 10,000 won per person. But we offer a ten percent ________ to those who are over 65 or under seven years old.
M That's good. My mother is 67 and my youngest daughter is only six.
W Then you can get a discount for two people. Will you pay in ________ or by ________ ________?
M By credit card.
W All right. Here are your tickets.

>> WORDS **fine dust** 미세먼지 **deal with** …을 처리하다 **public transportation** 대중교통 **blame** …을 탓하다 **closet** 벽장, 장롱 **aquarium** 수족관

14 대화를 듣고, 두 사람의 관계로 가장 적절한 것을 고르시오.

① 의사 – 환자 ② 교사 – 학생
③ 경찰관 – 운전자 ④ 아빠 – 딸
⑤ 버스 운전기사 – 승객

M Excuse me, ma'am. You were speeding.
W Did I? I was ________ ________ 40 kilometers per hour.
M You are in the school zone. The ________ ________ in this area is under 30 kilometers.
W Is that so? I didn't know that.
M May I see your driver's license?
W Here you are. Please let it go this once for me.
M Okay, but be careful when you drive. Next time you will get a ________.

15 대화를 듣고, 남자가 여자에게 부탁한 일로 가장 적절한 것을 고르시오.

① 집 청소 도와주기
② 수학 숙제 도와주기
③ 시험 범위 알려 주기
④ 시험 날짜 알려 주기
⑤ 수학 문제 알려 주기

[Telephone rings.]
M Hi, Jian. It's Yuchan.
W Hi. What's up?
M I called you to ask ________ ________.
W What kind of help do you need?
M We have a math test tomorrow. But I can't ________ any of the problems in the textbook. Please help me. I know you're good at math.
W Okay. I will come over to your house in half an hour.
M Thanks a lot. You're a ________!

16 대화를 듣고, 여자가 영화를 보러 갈 수 없는 이유로 가장 적절한 것을 고르시오.

① 엄마가 편찮으셔서
② 다른 약속이 있어서
③ 그 영화를 이미 봐서
④ 남동생을 돌봐야 해서
⑤ 늦게까지 일을 해야 해서

M Are you ________ tonight? Let's go watch a movie. The new Spiderman movie is ________ now.
W I really want to see it, but I can't go out tonight.
M Why is that?
W My little brother is sick. I have to ________ ________ him.
M What about your mom?
W She has to work late, so she asked me to take care of him.
M I see. We can watch the movie some other day.

>> **WORDS** **area** 지역, 구역 **driver's license** 운전면허증 **textbook** 교과서 **take care of** …을 돌보다

Answer p. 16

17 다음 그림의 상황에 가장 적절한 대화를 고르시오.

① ② ③ ④ ⑤

① M How much do they cost all together?
W They're 20,000 won.
② M Are you going to ________ ________ now?
W Yes, here is my room key.
③ M How many books do you read a month?
W I usually read two to three books.
④ M What are you reading?
W I'm reading a ________ novel.
⑤ M I want to check out this book.
W Okay. Please give me your ________ card.

18 다음을 듣고, 여자가 슈퍼마켓 이용에 대해 언급하지 않은 것을 고르시오.

① 영업일　② 영업시간
③ 층별 상품　④ 회원 혜택
⑤ 무료 주차 시간

W Welcome to Green Supermarket. We're ________ from 9 a.m. to 10 p.m. every day. On the first floor, you can find ________ ________ of fresh and processed foods. On the second floor, there are stationery and home decoration items. We have a big ________ ________ on the basement floor. You can park your car there for two hours for free. Enjoy your shopping at Green Supermarket.

[19-20] 대화를 듣고, 남자의 마지막 말에 이어질 여자의 말로 가장 적절한 것을 고르시오.

19 ① It was hot and sunny.
② I stayed there for three days.
③ I learned to ride a horse, too.
④ The food there tasted great.
⑤ I'm really looking forward to it.

M How was your trip to Jeju Island?
W It was fantastic. The weather was great, and everyone in my family had a lot of fun.
M What did you do there?
W I went ________ to Hallasan and ________ on the beautiful beaches.
M Sounds great. Wasn't it cold?
W Not at all. It's much ________ there.
M What ________ did you do?

20 ① You are right.
② I usually listen to music.
③ I like hip hop music, too.
④ Why don't you buy the album?
⑤ Let's go to the concert someday.

W What are you looking at, Minho?
M Look! My ________ hip hop group just released a new album.
W Do you like hip hop music? I didn't know that.
M Yeah. It's my favorite music genre. Don't you like it?
W Not really. I don't like ________ music.
M You ________ like ________ music then.

>> WORDS **processed food** 가공식품 **stationery** 문구류 **decoration** 장식 **basement** 지하층 **release** 공개(발표)하다

02회 » 듣기 실전 모의고사

01 다음을 듣고, 도쿄의 날씨로 가장 적절한 것을 고르시오.

02 대화를 듣고, 남자가 구입할 케이크로 가장 적절한 것을 고르시오.

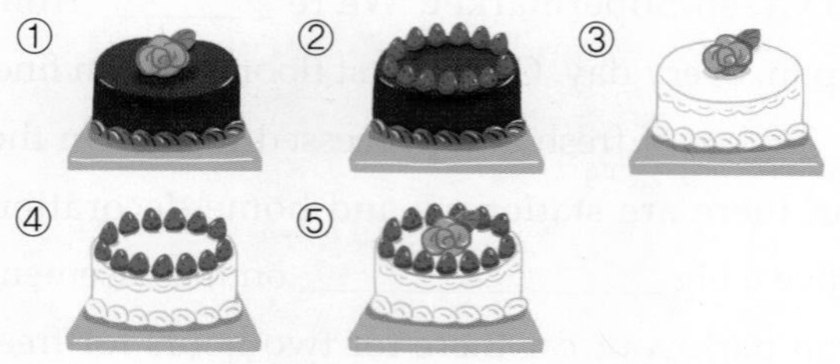

03 대화를 듣고, 남자의 심정 변화로 가장 적절한 것을 고르시오.

① upset → sad
② sad → excited
③ worried → upset
④ excited → disappointed
⑤ disappointed → pleasant

04 대화를 듣고, 여자가 지난 주말에 한 일로 가장 적절한 것을 고르시오.

① 캠핑 가기　② 병원 진료받기
③ 친구 병문안 가기　④ 다리 수술하기
⑤ 아버지 간호하기

05 대화를 듣고, 두 사람이 대화하는 장소로 가장 적절한 곳을 고르시오.

① 학교　② 병원　③ 식당
④ 우체국　⑤ 경찰서

06 대화를 듣고, 남자의 마지막 말의 의도로 가장 적절한 것을 고르시오.

① 동의　② 반대　③ 격려
④ 추천　⑤ 부탁

07 대화를 듣고, 여자가 영어 실력 향상을 위해서 하는 일이 아닌 것을 고르시오.

① 영어 책 읽기
② 영어 영화 보기
③ 영어 라디오 방송 청취
④ 영어로 생각하기
⑤ 영어 토론 동아리 참여

08 대화를 듣고, 남자가 대화 직후에 할 일로 가장 적절한 것을 고르시오.

① 피자 주문하기　② 블로그 만들기
③ 피자 만들기　④ 블로그 방문하기
⑤ 요리 수업 등록하기

09 다음을 듣고, 여자가 안내하는 내용과 일치하지 않는 것을 고르시오.

① 내일 국립 박물관에 갈 것이다.
② 지하철역으로 오전 8시까지 와야 한다.
③ 박물관 입장료를 지참해야 한다.
④ 점심 도시락을 지참해야 한다.
⑤ 교복을 입어야 한다.

10 다음을 듣고, 남자가 설명하는 운동 종목으로 가장 적절한 것을 고르시오.

① basketball　② baseball
③ hockey　④ volleyball
⑤ soccer

Answer p. 21

11 다음을 듣고, 여자가 하는 말의 내용과 일치하지 않는 것을 고르시오.

① 학교 축제는 매년 열린다.
② 축제는 7월 20일에 열릴 것이다.
③ 학생들은 4시까지 강당에 와야 한다.
④ 학교 밴드와 댄스 그룹의 공연이 있을 것이다.
⑤ 간식과 음료가 무료로 제공될 것이다.

12 대화를 듣고, 남자가 한국에 온 목적으로 가장 적절한 것을 고르시오.

① 한국어 강좌를 듣기 위해서
② 한국 문화를 배우기 위해서
③ 한국에 관한 글을 쓰기 위해서
④ 삼촌의 결혼식에 참석하기 위해서
⑤ 처음으로 삼촌을 만나기 위해서

13 대화를 듣고, 두 사람이 만날 시각을 고르시오.

① 7:30 ② 7:45 ③ 7:50
④ 8:00 ⑤ 8:15

14 대화를 듣고, 두 사람의 관계로 가장 적절한 것을 고르시오.

① 담임 교사 - 학생 ② 엄마 - 아들
③ 보건 교사 - 학생 ④ 식당 종업원 - 손님
⑤ 의사 - 환자

15 대화를 듣고, 남자가 여자에게 부탁한 일로 가장 적절한 것을 고르시오.

① 숙제 도와주기
② 침실로 데려다주기
③ 학교에 데려다주기
④ 샌드위치 만들어 주기
⑤ 한 시간 뒤에 깨워 주기

16 대화를 듣고, 여자가 화가 난 이유로 가장 적절한 것을 고르시오.

① 영어 시험을 망쳐서
② 영어 숙제를 못해서
③ 영어 교과서를 어디 뒀는지 몰라서
④ 친구가 영어 교과서에 낙서를 해서
⑤ 친구가 영어 교과서를 잃어버려서

17 다음 그림의 상황에 가장 적절한 대화를 고르시오.

① ② ③ ④ ⑤

18 다음을 듣고, 남자가 안내 방송에서 언급하지 않은 것을 고르시오.

① 비행시간 ② 출발지 ③ 목적지
④ 도착 시간 ⑤ 목적지 날씨

[19-20] 대화를 듣고, 여자의 마지막 말에 이어질 남자의 말로 가장 적절한 것을 고르시오.

19 Man: ______________________________

① I'll pay for yours.
② I can't eat anymore.
③ You can say that again.
④ You should say "let's go Dutch."
⑤ The dessert was better than the main dish.

20 Man: ______________________________

① Soccer is my favorite sport.
② I bet the German team will win.
③ Let's watch the match together.
④ I've never thought about the match.
⑤ They practiced really hard for this match.

Dictation Test » 02회

01 다음을 듣고, 도쿄의 날씨로 가장 적절한 것을 고르시오.

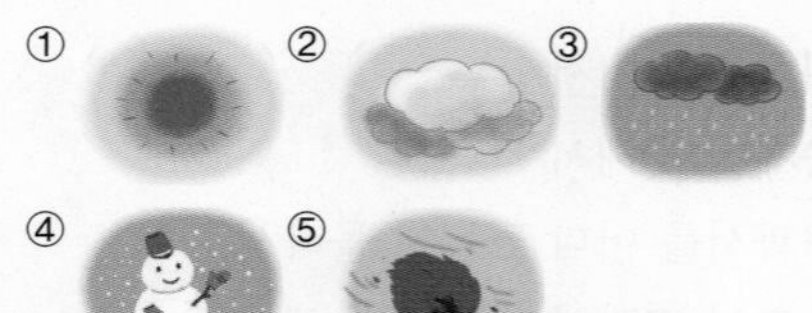

W Hello, everyone. Welcome to the World Weather Report. In New York, it's ________ and the temperature is around 18 degrees Celsius. A pleasant day is expected in London as well. In Tokyo, it's raining ________ and the rain will continue ________ ________. In Beijing, it will be cold and windy. Don't forget to wear a jacket when you go out.

02 대화를 듣고, 남자가 구입할 케이크로 가장 적절한 것을 고르시오.

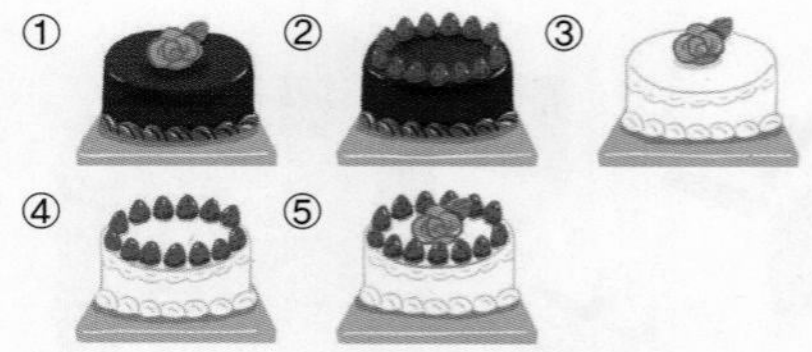

W What can I do for you, sir?
M I'm looking for a cake for my daughter.
W Okay. What about this one? It's ________ among girls.
M She doesn't like chocolate. I need a whipped-cream cake.
W Then, I ________ this one with fruit toppings.
M Umm... I ________ that one with fruit toppings and flower decorations in the middle.
W It's a little ________. Is it okay?
M No problem. I'll take it.

03 대화를 듣고, 남자의 심정 변화로 가장 적절한 것을 고르시오.

① upset → sad
② sad → excited
③ worried → upset
④ excited → disappointed
⑤ disappointed → pleasant

M I have good news for you!
W What is it?
M We have ________ ________ tomorrow!
W Is that so? That's ________ to me. Why is that?
M Tomorrow is May 1st. Everyone has a day off that day.
W That's only for workers. We are students, not workers. So we have school that day. You didn't know that.
M What? That's not ________!

04 대화를 듣고, 여자가 지난 주말에 한 일로 가장 적절한 것을 고르시오.

① 캠핑 가기 ② 병원 진료받기
③ 친구 병문안 가기 ④ 다리 수술하기
⑤ 아버지 간호하기

M Jisu, I heard you were going camping with your family.
W Yeah, that was my plan. But I couldn't go.
M Why? Were you ________ or something?
W Actually, my father was. He fell down the stairs and ________ his ________.
M What a pity! Is he okay now?
W Yes, my mom and I took ________ ________ care of him at the hospital during the weekend. Now, he's at home.
M I hope he gets well soon.
W Thank you.

» WORDS **pleasant** 쾌적한 **expect** 예상[기대]하다 **as well** 또한 **continue** 계속되다 **don't forget to** 반드시 …하다 **whipped-cream** 생크림의 **off** 휴가인 **fall down** 넘어지다 **get well** 건강을 회복하다

Answer p. 21

05 대화를 듣고, 두 사람이 대화하는 장소로 가장 적절한 곳을 고르시오.

① 학교 ② 병원 ③ 식당
④ 우체국 ⑤ 경찰서

W How may I help you?
M I need to mail this ________ to Mokpo, please.
W Okay, let's see how much it weighs.... It's about 2 kilograms. You can send it by ________ mail or ________ ________.
M Regular mail, please. How much will that be?
W Five thousand won. Do you need anything else?
M Oh, yeah! I almost forgot. I need a book of ________, too.
W Okay, your total comes to 8,000 won.

06 대화를 듣고, 남자의 마지막 말의 의도로 가장 적절한 것을 고르시오.

① 동의 ② 반대 ③ 격려
④ 추천 ⑤ 부탁

M Oh, it's noon already. Let's have ________.
W Okay. What do you want to eat?
M I'd like to have Chinese food today.
W Let's go to the new restaurant down the street. I ate there with my family last weekend.
M Really? ________ did ________ like it?
W The *jjajangmyeon* was very delicious, but the *jjamppong* was a little bit ________.
M Umm.... Then, we'd better not go there.

07 대화를 듣고, 여자가 영어 실력 향상을 위해서 하는 일이 <u>아닌</u> 것을 고르시오.

① 영어 책 읽기
② 영어 영화 보기
③ 영어 라디오 방송 청취
④ 영어로 생각하기
⑤ 영어 토론 동아리 참여

M Yuna, that was an amazing ________. I didn't know that you were such a good English speaker.
W Thanks. I'm still trying to ________ my English speaking.
M How do you practice?
W Well, I read a lot of English books, and I listen to an English radio program every morning.
M Wow. That's a lot of effort.
W I also joined an English debate club. We have a regular meeting ________ a ________. I try to think in English as ________.
M I don't think I could do all that.

>> WORDS **mail** (우편으로) 보내다, 부치다 **weigh** 무게가 …이다 **effort** 노력 **debate** 토론

Dictation Test >> 02회

08 대화를 듣고, 남자가 대화 직후에 할 일로 가장 적절한 것을 고르시오.

① 피자 주문하기 ② 블로그 만들기
③ 피자 만들기 ④ 블로그 방문하기
⑤ 요리 수업 등록하기

M Thanks for inviting me to the party.
W I'm glad you could come. ________ ________ to pizza.
M Umm.... This is so delicious. Did you make it yourself?
W Yeah. This is the first time I made pizza.
M Really? How did you make it?
W I just followed the ________ on the blog. There's a useful cooking blog I visit very often.
M Tell me the ________. I'll visit there right now.
W Okay. Check this out.

09 다음을 듣고, 여자가 안내하는 내용과 일치하지 않는 것을 고르시오.

① 내일 국립 박물관에 갈 것이다.
② 지하철역으로 오전 8시까지 와야 한다.
③ 박물관 입장료를 지참해야 한다.
④ 점심 도시락을 지참해야 한다.
⑤ 교복을 입어야 한다.

W Hello, this is your homeroom teacher. Tomorrow, we're going to visit the National Museum. We will go there ________ ________, so please come to the subway station by 8 o'clock in the morning. You can enter the museum for ________, but you must ________ your transportation fee and lunch with you. Everyone should wear the school ________.

10 다음을 듣고, 남자가 설명하는 운동 종목으로 가장 적절한 것을 고르시오.

① basketball ② baseball
③ hockey ④ volleyball
⑤ soccer

M This is a sport that can be played ________ or outdoors. Each team has five players. They have to ________ the ball ________ the other team's basket to score points. The team with the most points wins. A player with the ball can't take more than 3 steps without ________ it.

11 다음을 듣고, 여자가 하는 말의 내용과 일치하지 않는 것을 고르시오.

① 학교 축제는 매년 열린다.
② 축제는 7월 20일에 열릴 것이다.
③ 학생들은 4시까지 강당에 와야 한다.
④ 학교 밴드와 댄스 그룹의 공연이 있을 것이다.
⑤ 간식과 음료가 무료로 제공될 것이다.

W Hello, everyone. I'm the school president, Kim Suyeon. I'm happy to make this announcement. The annual school festival is going to ________ ________ next week. It will begin at 4 p.m. on July 20th. Please come to our auditorium by 3:50. There will be ________ performances by the school band and the dance group. Also, there will be free snacks and beverages. Don't ________ this exciting event!

>> **WORDS** **homeroom teacher** 담임 선생님 **station** 역, 정거장 **transportation** 교통 **fee** 요금 **score** 득점하다 **point** 점수 **school president** 학생회장 **annual** 연례의, 매년의 **auditorium** 강당 **performance** 공연

Answer p. 21

12 대화를 듣고, 남자가 한국에 온 목적으로 가장 적절한 것을 고르시오.

① 한국어 강좌를 듣기 위해서
② 한국 문화를 배우기 위해서
③ 한국에 관한 글을 쓰기 위해서
④ 삼촌의 결혼식에 참석하기 위해서
⑤ 처음으로 삼촌을 만나기 위해서

W Hi, Mark. It's good to see you here in Korea.
M Hi, Mira. I'm glad to see you again, too.
W ________ ________ you here? Are you going to take the Korean language classes like last year?
M Not really. My uncle is going to get married this weekend. I'm here to ________ his wedding.
W Wow, that's good news.
M Yeah. By the way, my Korean improved a lot ________ ________ the Korean language classes I took last year.
W Really? Why don't you say something in Korean?
M All right. Give me a topic, then I'll talk about it.

13 대화를 듣고, 두 사람이 만날 시각을 고르시오.

① 7:30 ② 7:45 ③ 7:50
④ 8:00 ⑤ 8:15

[Cell phone rings.]
W Hi, Tony. This is Jenny.
M Hi, Jenny.
W You know we have to ________ the role play for the English class tomorrow.
M I know, but I have no time at all today. Why don't we practice before class tomorrow?
W That's a good idea. What time shall we meet?
M Let's meet at the school ________ at 8 o'clock.
W But tomorrow is Monday. The first class ________ at 8:30. I'm afraid we would be late for class.
M Then, how about a ________ to eight?
W That would be nice. See you tomorrow.

14 대화를 듣고, 두 사람의 관계로 가장 적절한 것을 고르시오.

① 담임 교사 – 학생
② 엄마 – 아들
③ 보건 교사 – 학생
④ 식당 종업원 – 손님
⑤ 의사 – 환자

W What's wrong with you, Minsu?
M I have a ________ and I feel dizzy.
W What did you eat for breakfast?
M I ________ breakfast. I guess the milk I drank last night was ________.
W Oh, my! Did you visit the school nurse?
M Yes, I took the ________ she gave to me already, but I don't feel ________.
W Okay, I think you should go home now. Let me call your mom.

>> **WORDS** **get married** 결혼하다 **improve** 개선되다 **topic** 주제 **role play** 역할극 **dizzy** 어지러운 **school nurse** 보건 교사

Dictation Test >> 02회

15 대화를 듣고, 남자가 여자에게 부탁한 일로 가장 적절한 것을 고르시오.

① 숙제 도와주기
② 침실로 데려다주기
③ 학교에 데려다주기
④ 샌드위치 만들어 주기
⑤ 한 시간 뒤에 깨워 주기

M Mom, I'm home.
W How was school, Jinsu?
M I had a long day. I'm so ________ and ________.
W Do you ________ me to make you a sandwich or something?
M Thanks, Mom. But I think I'd ________ get some sleep first. I can't move at all.
W Okay. Then go get some sleep.
M Can you ________ me up in an hour?
W Of course I can. I will get your sandwich ready by then.

16 대화를 듣고, 여자가 화가 난 이유로 가장 적절한 것을 고르시오.

① 영어 시험을 망쳐서
② 영어 숙제를 못해서
③ 영어 교과서를 어디 뒀는지 몰라서
④ 친구가 영어 교과서에 낙서를 해서
⑤ 친구가 영어 교과서를 잃어버려서

M Sora, you look upset. What's ________?
W One of my friends borrowed my English textbook last week, but he didn't give it back to me until now.
M We have an English test next week. You should ask him to ________ it.
W I already did. But he told me that he had ________ it.
M Oh, no. You need the book for the test!
W That's ________ ________. I'm so mad.
M Come on, let's see what we can do.

17 다음 그림의 상황에 가장 적절한 대화를 고르시오.

① ② ③ ④ ⑤

① **W** I'm sorry. No food or drink is ________ here.
M Oh, I didn't know that.
② **W** When is the museum closed?
M The museum is ________ all year round.
③ **W** How may I help you?
M I'd like to buy tickets to the special exhibition.
④ **W** Welcome to the National Art Museum.
M Thank you. I'm looking ________ to ________ the artworks here.
⑤ **W** What are you drinking?
M I'm drinking soda.

>> **WORDS** **upset** 화가 난 **borrow** 빌리다 **give back** …을 돌려주다 **mad** 몹시 화가 난 **museum** 박물관, 미술관 **all year round** 일 년 내내 **exhibition** 전시회, 전시 **artwork** 예술품, 미술품

18 다음을 듣고, 남자가 안내 방송에서 언급 하지 않은 것을 고르시오.

① 비행시간 ② 출발지 ③ 목적지
④ 도착 시간 ⑤ 목적지 날씨

M Ladies and gentlemen, good afternoon. Welcome aboard Peace Airlines. This is your captain speaking. Our ________ ________ today will be three and a half hours and we will ________ in Bangkok at 4 p.m. The weather is good. The ________ in Bangkok is now 28 degrees Celsius. We wish you a pleasant flight. Thank you.

[19-20] 대화를 듣고, 여자의 마지막 말에 이어질 남자의 말로 가장 적절한 것을 고르시오.

19 ① I'll pay for yours.
② I can't eat anymore.
③ You can say that again.
④ You should say "let's go Dutch."
⑤ The dessert was better than the main dish.

W Are you finished? I'm done.
M Me, too. The food here is really great.
W I agree. By the way, let's Dutch pay today.
M Dutch pay? What do you ________?
W I mean let's ________ individually.
M Ah ha. Dutch pay is not the ________ ________.
W Then, how should I say it?

20 ① Soccer is my favorite sport.
② I bet the German team will win.
③ Let's watch the match together.
④ I've never thought about the match.
⑤ They practiced really hard for this match.

W What are you thinking about so hard?
M Oh, I'm thinking about the soccer match tomorrow.
W The Korean national soccer team is ________ ________ Germany, right?
M Yeah, I made a bet on the match with my father.
W Who do you think will win?
M I'm ________ the Korean team will win the match.
W Really? But the German team is one of the top-ranked teams. What ________ you ________ our team will win?

>> WORDS captain 기장 finish 끝내다, 마치다 individually 개별적으로 match 시합 national 국가의 top-ranked 최상위의

03회 » 듣기 실전 모의고사

01 다음을 듣고, 금요일의 날씨로 가장 적절한 것을 고르시오.

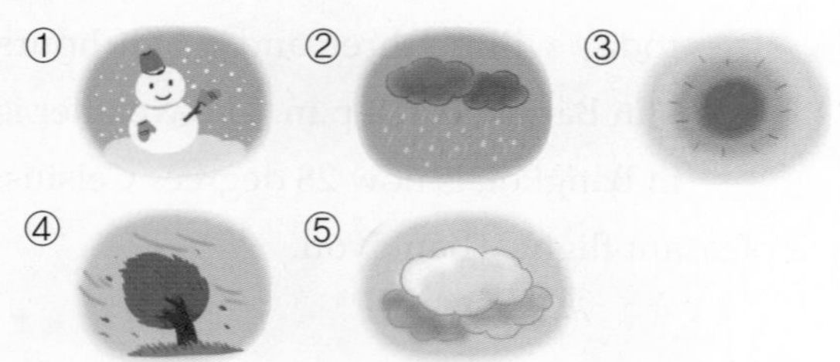

02 대화를 듣고, 남자가 찾고 있는 가방으로 가장 적절한 것을 고르시오.

03 대화를 듣고, 남자의 심정으로 가장 적절한 것을 고르시오.

① proud ② angry
③ envious ④ bored
⑤ embarrassed

04 대화를 듣고, 남자가 어제 한 일로 가장 적절한 것을 고르시오.

① 집들이 하기
② 나무 자르기
③ 파티에 참석하기
④ 병원에서 다리 치료받기
⑤ 아버지를 병원에 모셔다드리기

05 대화를 듣고, 두 사람이 대화하는 장소로 가장 적절한 곳을 고르시오.

① 경찰서 ② 공항 ③ 병원
④ 우체국 ⑤ 식당

06 대화를 듣고, 여자의 마지막 말의 의도로 가장 적절한 것을 고르시오.

① 거절 ② 칭찬 ③ 부탁
④ 추천 ⑤ 동의

07 대화를 듣고, 남자가 등록할 방과 후 수업으로 가장 적절한 것을 고르시오.

① 수학, 영어 ② 과학, 농구
③ 과학, 축구 ④ 축구, 영어
⑤ 수학, 농구

08 대화를 듣고, 남자가 대화 직후에 할 일로 가장 적절한 것을 고르시오.

① 집에 돌아가기
② 학생증 발급받기
③ 문화 센터 방문하기
④ 요가 수업 등록하기
⑤ 할인 방법 알아보기

09 대화를 듣고, 여자가 벼룩시장에 대해 언급하지 않은 것을 고르시오.

① 참가 자격 ② 개최 목적
③ 개최 장소 ④ 개최 시간
⑤ 개최 날짜

10 다음을 듣고, 여자가 하는 말의 내용으로 가장 적절한 것을 고르시오.

① 도시의 소음 문제
② 재활용을 하는 방법
③ 다큐멘터리의 유익함
④ 쓰레기 문제의 해결 방법
⑤ 음식물 쓰레기를 줄이는 방법

Answer p. 26

11 다음을 듣고, 아기 코알라에 대한 내용과 일치하지 않는 것을 고르시오.

① 태어나면 어미의 주머니 속에 들어간다.
② 생후 6개월 동안 어미의 주머니 속에서 자란다.
③ 튼튼하게 자라면 어미의 등으로 간다.
④ 어미의 등에서 6개월을 보낸다.
⑤ 어미의 등에서 자랄 때에는 주머니 속으로 가지 않는다.

12 대화를 듣고, 남자가 전화를 건 목적으로 가장 적절한 것을 고르시오.

① 주문을 취소하기 위해서
② 주문 내역을 확인하기 위해서
③ 주문 내용을 변경하기 위해서
④ 책을 집으로 배송시키기 위해서
⑤ 책의 재고가 있는지 알아보기 위해서

13 대화를 듣고, 여자가 지불해야 할 금액으로 가장 적절한 것을 고르시오.

① 10,000원 ② 20,000원 ③ 30,000원
④ 40,000원 ⑤ 50,000원

14 대화를 듣고, 두 사람의 관계로 가장 적절한 것을 고르시오.

① 의사 – 환자 ② 가게 점원 – 손님
③ 식당 종업원 – 손님 ④ 교사 – 학생
⑤ 수리기사 – 손님

15 대화를 듣고, 여자가 남자에게 부탁한 일로 가장 적절한 것을 고르시오.

① 숙제 끝내기 ② 방 청소하기
③ 세탁기 돌리기 ④ 식료품 사 오기
⑤ 세탁물 찾아오기

16 대화를 듣고, 여자가 밤을 새운 이유로 가장 적절한 것을 고르시오.

① 낮잠을 자서
② 숙제를 해야 해서
③ 커피를 많이 마셔서
④ 해야 할 일이 많아서
⑤ 시험공부를 해야 해서

17 다음 그림의 상황에 가장 적절한 대화를 고르시오.

① ② ③ ④ ⑤

18 다음을 듣고, 남자가 시험 시 유의 사항에 대해 언급하지 않은 것을 고르시오.

① 휴대전화의 전원을 꺼야 한다.
② 듣기에 앞서 문제를 읽어야 한다.
③ 소음을 내서는 안 된다.
④ 시험지에 낙서를 해서는 안 된다.
⑤ 답을 연필로 표시해야 한다.

[19-20] 대화를 듣고, 여자의 마지막 말에 이어질 남자의 말로 가장 적절한 것을 고르시오.

19 Man: ______________________

① I don't like it.
② I'm sure it will be hard.
③ I'm sorry you can't come.
④ I planted some flowers, too.
⑤ Really? Thanks for inviting me.

20 Man: ______________________

① Tomorrow is May 8th.
② Let's go to the bakery.
③ I want a chocolate cake.
④ You should make a card.
⑤ I don't think it's a good idea.

Dictation Test >> 03회

01 다음을 듣고, 금요일의 날씨로 가장 적절한 것을 고르시오.

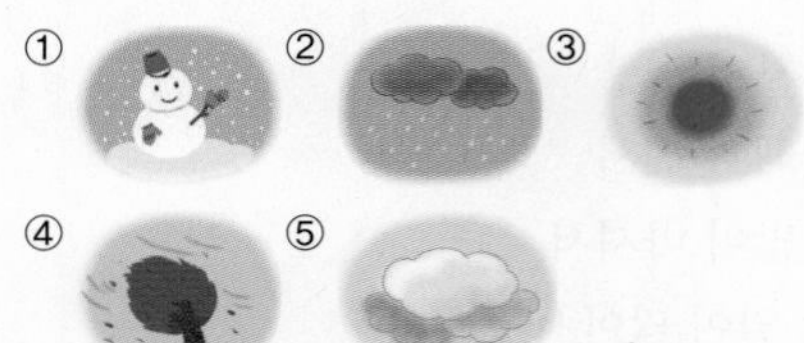

M Good morning, everyone. It's Monday morning and here's the weather report for this week. Now, it's very sunny and cool. In the afternoon, there is a ________ of some rain. Tomorrow, we will see ________ ________ again and the pleasant weather will continue until Friday. The ________ will start again on Saturday morning.

02 대화를 듣고, 남자가 찾고 있는 가방으로 가장 적절한 것을 고르시오.

W Seoul Station's Lost and Found. May I help you?

M I left my bag on the ________ and I'm looking for it.

W What kind of bag is it?

M It's a yellow ________ bag. It is as big as a ________.

W I see. Is there anything else you want to tell us about it?

M Well. It's all yellow and has no patterns on it. But there is a puppy key chain ________ on it.

W Okay. If we find the bag, we will contact you.

03 대화를 듣고, 남자의 심정으로 가장 적절한 것을 고르시오.

① proud ② angry
③ envious ④ bored
⑤ embarrassed

W Wow! Look at that boy! He's really ________ ________ soccer. No wonder his nickname is Messi!

M Is that so? I didn't know that.

W The first half didn't end yet, but he has scored three goals until now.

M That's a lot. I just arrived, so I ________ all of them.

W His parents must be very ________ of him.

M Actually, I am his father.

W Really? You have such a great ________.

M Yes, I think so too.

04 대화를 듣고, 남자가 어제 한 일로 가장 적절한 것을 고르시오.

① 집들이 하기
② 나무 자르기
③ 파티에 참석하기
④ 병원에서 다리 치료받기
⑤ 아버지를 병원에 모셔다드리기

M Did you have a good time at Janet's party yesterday?

W Yes, we had fun. How come you didn't come to the party?

M I was going to go, but something just ________ ________.

W Was it something bad?

M Yeah. My father ________ his leg while cutting a tree.

W Oh, no! Is he all right?

M Yes. Fortunately, it was not that ________. I took him to the hospital right away, and he's getting better now.

>> WORDS lost and found 분실물 취급소 pattern 무늬, 패턴 key chain 열쇠고리 contact 연락하다 nickname 별명 score 득점을 올리다 fortunately 다행스럽게도

Answer p. 26

05 대화를 듣고, 두 사람이 대화하는 장소로 가장 적절한 곳을 고르시오.

① 경찰서 ② 공항 ③ 병원
④ 우체국 ⑤ 식당

W Can I see your ________ and ________?
M Sure. Here they are.
W Okay. How many suitcases will you be checking in?
M Just one suitcase.
W Would you like a window ________ aisle seat?
M A window seat, please.
W This is your ________ ________ and the departure gate.
M What time will we be boarding?
W We will ________ boarding at six. Enjoy your flight.

06 대화를 듣고, 여자의 마지막 말의 의도로 가장 적절한 것을 고르시오.

① 거절 ② 칭찬 ③ 부탁
④ 추천 ⑤ 동의

M Can you do me a favor?
W What is it?
M I have to finish ________ this picture today. Can you do it for me?
W It's your art ________. Why are you asking me to do it?
M I have to go out in 30 minutes. I'm going to play soccer with my friends.
W Then you can do it ________ you play soccer.
M But you're my sister. Please do it for me just this once.
W Kevin, I'm your big sister, and I love you. Still, you should do your ________ work.

07 대화를 듣고, 남자가 등록할 방과 후 수업으로 가장 적절한 것을 고르시오.

① 수학, 영어 ② 과학, 농구
③ 과학, 축구 ④ 축구, 영어
⑤ 수학, 농구

M Look here! The timetable for the after-school classes just came out. I'd like to take one, but I can't decide what to take.
W What are you interested in?
M I'm interested in ________, but I think I should take the science class, too.
W Then you can take ________ of them.
M But most sports classes are on Monday which is the ________ day as the science class.
W Look! There is a ________ class on Friday. So, you can take it with the science class.
M You're right. Now, it's ________.

>> WORDS suitcase 여행 가방 check in (비행기 등을 탈 때) …을 부치다 aisle 통로 board 탑승하다 timetable 시간표

Dictation Test >> 03회

08 대화를 듣고, 남자가 대화 직후에 할 일로 가장 적절한 것을 고르시오.

① 집에 돌아가기
② 학생증 발급받기
③ 문화 센터 방문하기
④ 요가 수업 등록하기
⑤ 할인 방법 알아보기

W Minsu, where are you going?

M I'm going to the community center. I'm thinking about taking a yoga class.

W Oh, I ________ the class last ________.

M ________ did you like it?

W It was great. By the way, you know we can get a ________ ________, don't you?

M No, I didn't know that. How can I get the discount?

W You only have to show your student ID.

M Oh, I think I have to go back home to ________ it.

09 대화를 듣고, 여자가 벼룩시장에 대해 언급하지 않은 것을 고르시오.

① 참가 자격 ② 개최 목적
③ 개최 장소 ④ 개최 시간
⑤ 개최 날짜

W Adam, did you hear about the school ________ market?

M No, I didn't. Can you tell me about it?

W The school is holding a flea market for students.

M Sounds interesting. Can I join it?

W Sure. ________ can join. If you want to sell something, just apply for it on the school website.

M When and where will it be held?

W It's going to be held at the ________ at 2 p.m. on May 2nd.

M It's this Saturday. I think I should join it as a ________.

10 다음을 듣고, 여자가 하는 말의 내용으로 가장 적절한 것을 고르시오.

① 도시의 소음 문제
② 재활용을 하는 방법
③ 다큐멘터리의 유익함
④ 쓰레기 문제의 해결 방법
⑤ 음식물 쓰레기를 줄이는 방법

W Yesterday, I saw a documentary about the ________ ________ in our country. They say we don't have enough space to bury the trash now. What can we do to ________ the problem? The most important thing is not to make waste. We have to recycle and reuse things. We should also try not to ________ food too. The little things we do can make a big ________.

>> WORDS **discount** 할인 **documentary** 다큐멘터리 **space** 공간 **bury** 묻다, 매장하다

Answer p. 26

11 다음을 듣고, 아기 코알라에 대한 내용과 일치하지 않는 것을 고르시오.

① 태어나면 어미의 주머니 속에 들어간다.
② 생후 6개월 동안 어미의 주머니 속에서 자란다.
③ 튼튼하게 자라면 어미의 등으로 간다.
④ 어미의 등에서 6개월을 보낸다.
⑤ 어미의 등에서 자랄 때에는 주머니 속으로 가지 않는다.

W Everyone knows baby koalas live in their mothers' pouches. But do you know ________ ________ they stay there? When a koala is born, it ________ ________ to its mother's pouch and grows there for about six months. When it grows ________ enough, the baby moves to its mother's back and stays there another six months. They still use their mothers' pouches to ________.

12 대화를 듣고, 남자가 전화를 건 목적으로 가장 적절한 것을 고르시오.

① 주문을 취소하기 위해서
② 주문 내역을 확인하기 위해서
③ 주문 내용을 변경하기 위해서
④ 책을 집으로 배송시키기 위해서
⑤ 책의 재고가 있는지 알아보기 위해서

[Telephone rings.]

W Hello. This is Charlie's Bookstore.

M Hello. My name is Daniel Thomson. I ________ three books at your store yesterday.

W Yes. Is there anything I can help you with?

M Actually, I want to ________ something in my order.

W What would you like to change?

M I want to order *Holes* by Louis Sachar ________ ________ *Matilda* by Roald Dahl.

W That's possible. But *Holes* is not in stock now. It will arrive in three days. Is it okay for you?

M No problem. I'll ________ them ________ this weekend.

13 대화를 듣고, 여자가 지불해야 할 금액으로 가장 적절한 것을 고르시오.

① 10,000원 ② 20,000원
③ 30,000원 ④ 40,000원
⑤ 50,000원

M Do you need help?

W Yes, I'm looking for a shirt for my dad.

M What about this one? It's very ________.

W I like it. But it looks ________.

M Don't worry. It's on sale now. Its regular price is 40,000 won, but it's 50 percent ________ now.

W Really? That's great! Then can you ________ a necktie, too? I think I can buy a shirt and a tie.

M Sure. What about this one? It's only 10,000 won now.

W Perfect. I will take them.

>> WORDS **pouch** 주머니 **back** 등 **arrive** 도착하다 **regular price** 정가

14 대화를 듣고, 두 사람의 관계로 가장 적절한 것을 고르시오.

① 의사 – 환자
② 가게 점원 – 손님
③ 식당 종업원 – 손님
④ 교사 – 학생
⑤ 수리기사 – 손님

M What is the matter?
W Look. The printout has spots and is ________.
M Umm... I think it's because of the toner. Let me ________ it ________ a new one.
W Okay.
M Let's print out a ________ of paper for a test. Look. Now it's clean.
W That's right.
M Is there any other problem?
W Oh, one more thing. The paper gets jammed sometimes.
M Let me check the printer. Please ________.

15 대화를 듣고, 여자가 남자에게 부탁한 일로 가장 적절한 것을 고르시오.

① 숙제 끝내기 ② 방 청소하기
③ 세탁기 돌리기 ④ 식료품 사 오기
⑤ 세탁물 찾아오기

W Are you going out, Minho?
M Yes, I am. I'm going to hang out with my friends.
W Did you ________ your homework?
M Yes, Mom. I ________ my room, too.
W Good job. By the way, can you do me a favor?
M Of course I can. What is it?
W On your way home, stop by the cleaner's and pick up the ________, will you?
M Sure. I won't ________.

16 대화를 듣고, 여자가 밤을 새운 이유로 가장 적절한 것을 고르시오.

① 낮잠을 자서
② 숙제를 해야 해서
③ 커피를 많이 마셔서
④ 해야 할 일이 많아서
⑤ 시험공부를 해야 해서

M Juha, you look tired. Didn't you get ________ ________ last night?
W Yeah. I stayed up all night yesterday.
M Why did you do that? Did you ________ for the test?
W Not really.
M Then why did you stay awake?
W I just couldn't go to sleep. I usually drink just one cup of coffee, but I drank two cups yesterday.
M That's it. You couldn't sleep because of the caffeine. Why don't you get some ________?
W I think I should.

>> WORDS printout 인쇄(물) spot 점, 반점 jam 작동하지 못하게 되다 stay up 밤을 새다 caffeine 카페인

Answer p. 26

17 다음 그림의 상황에 가장 적절한 대화를 고르시오.

① ② ③ ④ ⑤

① W I'm sorry. You can't ________ here.
M Sorry. I didn't see the sign.
② W Where is the nearest post office?
M Cross the road here. Then you will see it on your right.
③ W Watch out! There's a ________ ________.
M Oops! I didn't see it. Thanks.
④ W What are you doing?
M I'm just waiting for my friends.
⑤ W The traffic is too ________ today.
M You're right. We're going to be late.

18 다음을 듣고, 남자가 시험 시 유의 사항에 대해 언급하지 않은 것을 고르시오.

① 휴대전화의 전원을 꺼야 한다.
② 듣기에 앞서 문제를 읽어야 한다.
③ 소음을 내서는 안 된다.
④ 시험지에 낙서를 해서는 안 된다.
⑤ 답을 연필로 표시해야 한다.

M Before we start the English listening test, I will give you some instructions. First, make sure to ________ ________ your cell phones before the test. Second, try to read the questions before you listen to the conversations. Next, don't make ________ ________ during the test. Finally, don't forget to ________ your answers with a pencil. Good luck to you.

[19-20] 대화를 듣고, 여자의 마지막 말에 이어질 남자의 말로 가장 적절한 것을 고르시오.

19 ① I don't like it.
② I'm sure it will be hard.
③ I'm sorry you can't come.
④ I planted some flowers, too.
⑤ Really? Thanks for inviting me.

M What did you do last weekend?
W I went to my grandmother's farm and helped her with ________ ________.
M What kind of work did you do?
W Well, I dug out ________ and picked up peppers. I sweated a lot, but it was fun.
M My grandmother lives in a city. I ________ I ________ a farm to visit.
W You can come with me if you want.

20 ① Tomorrow is May 8th.
② Let's go to the bakery.
③ I want a chocolate cake.
④ You should make a card.
⑤ I don't think it's a good idea.

M Tomorrow is Mother's Day.
W Oh, I almost ________. What should we do?
M Why don't we ________ a ________ for mom?
W That's a great idea. Do you have any plans for it?
M I think we ________ a cake and a card. I can bake a cake.
W Okay. What do you want me to do?

>> WORDS instruction 설명, 지시 dig 파다 pepper 고추 sweat 땀을 흘리다

04회 » 듣기 실전 모의고사

01 다음을 듣고, 일요일의 날씨로 가장 적절한 것을 고르시오.

02 대화를 듣고, 남자가 디자인한 가방으로 가장 적절한 것을 고르시오.

03 대화를 듣고, 여자의 심정으로 가장 적절한 것을 고르시오.

① calm ② surprised
③ worried ④ regretful
⑤ disappointed

04 대화를 듣고, 여자가 어제 한 일로 가장 적절한 것을 고르시오.

① 하이킹 ② 배드민턴 ③ 시험공부
④ 아르바이트 ⑤ 놀이공원 방문

05 대화를 듣고, 두 사람이 대화하는 장소로 가장 적절한 곳을 고르시오.

① 공원 ② 화원 ③ 수영장
④ 음식점 ⑤ 식료품점

06 대화를 듣고, 남자의 마지막 말의 의도로 가장 적절한 것을 고르시오.

① 격려 ② 질책 ③ 칭찬
④ 권유 ⑤ 금지

07 대화를 듣고, 남자가 용돈으로 산 것에 해당하지 않는 것을 고르시오.

① 간식 ② 책
③ 잡지 ④ 티셔츠
⑤ 친구 생일 선물

08 대화를 듣고, 남자가 대화 직후에 할 일로 가장 적절한 것을 고르시오.

① 돈 빌려주기
② 휴대전화 충전하기
③ 염색약 골라 주기
④ 염색하는 법 설명해 주기
⑤ 노트북 컴퓨터 건네주기

09 대화를 듣고, 여자가 미술 수업 준비물로 언급하지 않은 것을 고르시오.

① 사진 ② 신문 ③ 가위
④ 풀 ⑤ 도화지

10 다음을 듣고, 남자가 하는 말의 내용으로 가장 적절한 것을 고르시오.

① 작은 키의 장점
② 키가 크는 방법
③ 키가 커 보이는 방법
④ 유행하는 패션 아이템
⑤ 키가 큰 사람들의 공통점

Answer p. 31

11 다음을 듣고, 재활용에 대한 내용과 일치하지 않는 것을 고르시오.

① 재활용 업체는 월요일마다 방문한다.
② 재활용 업체는 비닐봉지를 수거하지 않는다.
③ 비닐봉지는 일반 쓰레기봉투에 담아야 한다.
④ 스티로폼은 수거 대상이 아니다.
⑤ 지저분한 플라스틱 병은 씻어서 배출해야 한다.

12 대화를 듣고, 여자가 전등을 끄는 목적으로 가장 적절한 것을 고르시오.

① 전기세를 아끼기 위해서
② 전구를 오래 쓰기 위해서
③ 아이들의 눈을 보호하기 위해서
④ 어두워 보이도록 하기 위해서
⑤ 아이들이 깨지 않게 하기 위해서

13 대화를 듣고, 남자가 발레 강좌를 수강할 날짜를 고르시오.

① 1일 ② 6일 ③ 8일
④ 13일 ⑤ 30일

14 대화를 듣고, 두 사람의 관계로 가장 적절한 것을 고르시오.

① 교사 – 학생 ② 판매원 – 고객
③ 구청 직원 – 민원인 ④ 복지관 직원 – 교사
⑤ 콜센터 직원 – 고객

15 대화를 듣고, 여자가 남자에게 부탁한 일로 가장 적절한 것을 고르시오.

① 남은 고기 버리기
② 삼겹살 더 사 오기
③ 지퍼백 가져다주기
④ 음식물 쓰레기 버리기
⑤ 냉장고에 남은 고기 넣기

16 대화를 듣고, 꽃이 시든 이유로 가장 적절한 것을 고르시오.

① 꽃이 오래돼서
② 햇빛을 못 봐서
③ 공기가 건조해서
④ 물을 갈아 주지 않아서
⑤ 물에 닿아 있지 않아서

17 다음 그림의 상황에 가장 적절한 대화를 고르시오.

① ② ③ ④ ⑤

18 다음을 듣고, 남자가 아버지에 대해 언급하지 않은 것을 고르시오.

① 성격 ② 신장 ③ 체격
④ 생김새 ⑤ 목소리

[19-20] 대화를 듣고, 남자의 마지막 말에 이어질 여자의 말로 가장 적절한 것을 고르시오.

19 **Woman**: ______________________

① That's interesting.
② Yes, right in the middle.
③ I never knew it was a church.
④ No, Gogh's father was a priest.
⑤ It has been built a few months ago.

20 **Woman**: ______________________

① Is coffee your favorite drink?
② Once you taste it, you'll love it.
③ I prefer to sleep in a nice hotel.
④ Mine either. It's a waste of money.
⑤ I can lend it to you whenever you need it.

Dictation Test » 04회

01 다음을 듣고, 일요일의 날씨로 가장 적절한 것을 고르시오.

W Good morning. Here's today's weather forecast. It's a ________ sunny Saturday and I think many people plan to hang out outside. However, the air is not so clear with high levels of ________ ________. Fortunately, it is expected to rain tomorrow and it will ________ up the air by Monday.

02 대화를 듣고, 남자가 디자인한 가방으로 가장 적절한 것을 고르시오.

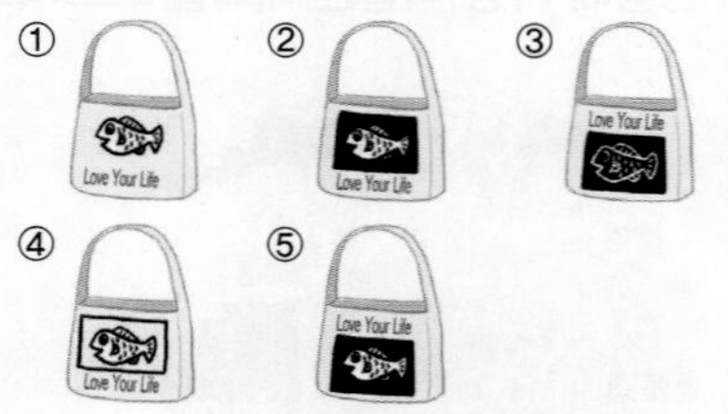

M Hi, Cindy.
W Hey, Mark. I like your bag.
M This is the eco bag that I designed myself.
W Really? I like the way you ________ the white fish in the middle of the black ________.
M Thanks. What do you think about the logo ________ the square?
W Wow, it says, "Love Your Life."
M Right. I hope people start thinking about a ________ life.
W You are amazing.

03 대화를 듣고, 여자의 심정으로 가장 적절한 것을 고르시오.

① calm ② surprised
③ worried ④ regretful
⑤ disappointed

M Sarah, did you do well on the contest yesterday?
W I got ________ place.
M What? I was sure you would ________ first place.
W Well, thanks for comforting me.
M No, I'm not just saying it. I'm ________.
W I was also disappointed but now I feel so refreshed.
M How so?
W I did my best, and there are no ________.
M Good for you.

04 대화를 듣고, 여자가 어제 한 일로 가장 적절한 것을 고르시오.

① 하이킹 ② 배드민턴
③ 시험공부 ④ 아르바이트
⑤ 놀이공원 방문

M Sarah, how about a badminton game after school?
W Sorry, I can't. I can't even ________ well.
M What's wrong? Did you work out hard during the weekend?
W No, I went to the ________ park yesterday and I walked around for almost 12 hours.
M You must ________ had fun, though.
W I rode a roller coaster and a few others. They're fun.
M Let's go there together after the ________.
W Alright.

>> WORDS **hang out** 시간을 보내다 **square** 정사각형 **contest** 대회 **comfort** 위로하다 **disappointed** 실망한 **refreshed** 상쾌한 **regretful** 후회스러운 **work out** 운동하다 **though** 그렇지만

Answer p. 31

05 대화를 듣고, 두 사람이 대화하는 장소로 가장 적절한 곳을 고르시오.

① 공원 ② 화원 ③ 수영장
④ 음식점 ⑤ 식료품점

W Good afternoon. How can I help you?
M I need some flower seeds.
W You can ________ from this shelf.
M Thanks. By the way, the rubber tree I bought here last month almost ________.
W Hmm... how often did you ________ it?
M Every day.
W Maybe that's why. You watered it too ________.
M Alright. Do you have small pots? I want to plant the seeds.
W Follow me. I'll ________ you where they are.

06 대화를 듣고, 남자의 마지막 말의 의도로 가장 적절한 것을 고르시오.

① 격려 ② 질책 ③ 칭찬
④ 권유 ⑤ 금지

W Dad, I want to quit piano lessons.
M Are you serious? You've always said you wanted to ________ in piano in college.
W Yes, but I ________ my mind.
M Can you tell me what happened?
W My piano teacher ________ me whenever I don't practice enough.
M Do you want to have a different teacher? Or you don't want to ________?
W Well, I don't know.
M Try to think about the ________ reason. Then we will talk about it again.

07 대화를 듣고, 남자가 용돈으로 산 것에 해당하지 않는 것을 고르시오.

① 간식 ② 책
③ 잡지 ④ 티셔츠
⑤ 친구 생일 선물

M Mom, can I get some money? I need to buy a T-shirt.
W I gave you the ________ last week, remember?
M I used it up in buying some books.
W You don't ________ me to believe that, do you?
M I really bought a couple of books and magazines.
W And where's the ________ of the money?
M I bought a birthday present for Mina and spent some money on ________ and playing Internet games.
W I think you need to learn to spend money ________.

>> **WORDS** **seed** 씨앗 **shelf** 선반 **rubber tree** 고무나무 **water** 물을 주다 **pot** 화분, 항아리 **plant** 심다 **quit** 그만두다 **college** 대학 **whenever** …할 때마다 **use up** …을 다 쓰다 **believe** 믿다 **a couple of** 두 개의

08 대화를 듣고, 남자가 대화 직후에 할 일로 가장 적절한 것을 고르시오.

① 돈 빌려주기
② 휴대전화 충전하기
③ 염색약 골라 주기
④ 염색하는 법 설명해 주기
⑤ 노트북 컴퓨터 건네주기

W Brian, have you bought the presents for Parents' Day yet?
M I'm still thinking what to buy. Have you?
W I haven't yet, either. But I've been thinking of buying a bottle of hair ________.
M Are you planning to help your parents get their hair dyed?
W Yeah. I heard my Mom ________ about her grey hair.
M That's sad. I think you're a good daughter.
W Thanks. Can I use your cell phone? I want to ________ for a good hair dye.
M It's out of battery now. You can use my laptop ________.
W Thanks so much.

09 대화를 듣고, 여자가 미술 수업 준비물로 언급하지 않은 것을 고르시오.

① 사진　② 신문　③ 가위
④ 풀　⑤ 도화지

W Luke, how's your leg? Are you still in the ________?
M I am. But I'll be able to go to school by next Tuesday.
W I'm so glad to hear that.
M Is there anything I need to ________ for school?
W Yeah. We are taking the art performance test on Tuesday.
M Oh, is it about the collage work ________ one's hero?
W Exactly. So you need to bring a picture of your hero and some newspaper.
M Anything else?
W You need ________ and a glue stick, too.
M Thanks.

10 다음을 듣고, 남자가 하는 말의 내용으로 가장 적절한 것을 고르시오.

① 작은 키의 장점
② 키가 크는 방법
③ 키가 커 보이는 방법
④ 유행하는 패션 아이템
⑤ 키가 큰 사람들의 공통점

M Let me tell you some tips to resolve your concerns. First, choose pants with narrow ________. Wider pants make you look shorter. Second, wear slimmer shoes and ________ bulky ones. The point is to make a long ________ line from your waist to your toes. Third, stay away from shirts with large ________. Keep these in mind if you are ________ about your height.

>> WORDS present 선물 dye 염료; 염색하다 laptop 노트북 컴퓨터 performance test 수행평가 collage 콜라주 hero 영웅 glue stick 풀 narrow 좁은 slim 얇은 bulky 부피가 큰 point 요점 waist 허리 toe 발가락 height 키

Answer p. 31

11 다음을 듣고, 재활용에 대한 내용과 일치하지 않는 것을 고르시오.

① 재활용 업체는 월요일마다 방문한다.
② 재활용 업체는 비닐봉지를 수거하지 않는다.
③ 비닐봉지는 일반 쓰레기봉투에 담아야 한다.
④ 스티로폼은 수거 대상이 아니다.
⑤ 지저분한 플라스틱 병은 씻어서 배출해야 한다.

W Let me tell you about recycling. Recycling companies come and take usable garbage on Mondays. They do not take ________ bags. So please put plastic bags in ________ garbage bags. Also, the companies do not take ________ styrofoam or plastic bottles. So if they got dirty, please clean them before you ________ them ________.

12 대화를 듣고, 여자가 전등을 끄는 목적으로 가장 적절한 것을 고르시오.

① 전기세를 아끼기 위해서
② 전구를 오래 쓰기 위해서
③ 아이들의 눈을 보호하기 위해서
④ 어두워 보이도록 하기 위해서
⑤ 아이들이 깨지 않게 하기 위해서

M Your babies grew taller recently. What's the ________?
W I make them go to bed early.
M When do you get them to sleep?
W My kids go to bed at eight thirty in the evening and fall ________ by nine.
M That early? How is it possible?
W I make them ready for bed and turn ________ all the lights at eight o'clock.
M What good is it to turn off the lights?
W They get the feeling that it's ________ outside and that it's time to go to bed.

13 대화를 듣고, 남자가 발레 강좌를 수강할 날짜를 고르시오.

① 1일 ② 6일 ③ 8일
④ 13일 ⑤ 30일

W Jeffrey, why don't you join the ________ lesson?
M Are you kidding?
W No, I'm serious. There is a boy in my class and he ________ it too.
M I am not of the kind.
W Come on. Try out the free ________ next Wednesday.
M I feel silly but trying wouldn't ________. You mean on June 6th?
W No, on the 13th. It is the 8th today.
M Oh, you're right. What time is it?
W It ________ at 6:30 p.m.

>> WORDS **usable** 사용 가능한 **garbage** 쓰레기 **plastic bag** 비닐봉지 **styrofoam** 스티로폼 **try out** 시험 삼아 해 보다 **silly** 어리석은

14 대화를 듣고, 두 사람의 관계로 가장 적절한 것을 고르시오.

① 교사 – 학생
② 판매원 – 고객
③ 구청 직원 – 민원인
④ 복지관 직원 – 교사
⑤ 콜센터 직원 – 고객

[Telephone rings.]
W Hello. How can I help you?
M Hi. I am a teacher at Daehan Middle School. Can I take my students to the welfare center to do some ________ work?
W Sure. When do you plan to visit?
M Is April 20th okay with you?
W I guess. How many students are you ________?
M We have 15 students in our school volunteer club.
W Okay.
M Is there anything we ________ ________ prepare?
W Nothing ________.

15 대화를 듣고, 여자가 남자에게 부탁한 일로 가장 적절한 것을 고르시오.

① 남은 고기 버리기
② 삼겹살 더 사 오기
③ 지퍼백 가져다주기
④ 음식물 쓰레기 버리기
⑤ 냉장고에 남은 고기 넣기

M Becky, why don't you eat some more?
W I'm so full. We should have ________ less *samgyeopsal*.
M That's true. Let's just throw away the ________.
W No way.
M Do you have any other ________?
W You can make ________ *kimchi-jjigae* with the meat.
M Really?
W Yeah. Let's keep it in the ________. Could you get me a zipper bag?
M Alright.

16 대화를 듣고, 꽃이 시든 이유로 가장 적절한 것을 고르시오.

① 꽃이 오래돼서
② 햇빛을 못 봐서
③ 공기가 건조해서
④ 물을 갈아 주지 않아서
⑤ 물에 닿아 있지 않아서

M Ruth, look at the ________ of flowers in the vase.
W They are so fresh and beautiful.
M Yeah, but look at it more ________.
W Oh, one of the flowers has dried ________.
M You're right.
W What happened to that flower?
M Only that flower hasn't been ________ into the water.
W I can see that.

>> **WORDS** **welfare center** 복지관 **volunteer** 봉사 활동 **throw away** 버리다

Answer p. 31

17 다음 그림의 상황에 가장 적절한 대화를 고르시오.

① ② ③ ④ ⑤

① W Look! The mommy fish finally ________ ________ to a school of baby fish.
M It's amazing.
② W Happy birthday, Brian. Here's your birthday present.
M Thanks. I've always wanted to ________ this toy.
③ W Have you fed the fish yet? They must be hungry.
M I totally forgot.
④ W Where did you buy this toy fish?
M I bought it at the store around the ________.
⑤ W Which T-shirt looks better on me?
M The one with the big fish in the ________ looks better.

18 다음을 듣고, 남자가 아버지에 대해 언급하지 <u>않은</u> 것을 고르시오.

① 성격 ② 신장 ③ 체격
④ 생김새 ⑤ 목소리

M This is a picture of my dad 30 years ago. As you see, I resemble him a lot. He was not as tall as I am and he was much ________ but people say we look so ________. My eyes, nose, and even ears are from him. Besides our ________ are similar. Sometimes my uncles get ________ when I get phone calls for my father.

[19-20] 대화를 듣고, 남자의 마지막 말에 이어질 여자의 말로 가장 적절한 것을 고르시오.

19 ① That's interesting.
② Yes, right in the middle.
③ I never knew it was a church.
④ No, Gogh's father was a priest.
⑤ It has been built a few months ago.

W Look at this picture.
M It's *The Starry Night* by Van Gogh.
W Right. It's my favorite ________.
M It ________ that the tree is alive and the stars are actually ________.
W Yeah. Doesn't the ________ church look so lonely?
M Is there a church in the picture?

20 ① Is coffee your favorite drink?
② Once you taste it, you'll love it.
③ I prefer to sleep in a nice hotel.
④ Mine either. It's a waste of money.
⑤ I can lend it to you whenever you need it.

M What's in the box?
W It is the tent I bought ________.
M The box is too small for a tent.
W Yeah, but there is a ________ tent folded up inside.
M It's amazing. By the way, why did you buy it?
W I've ________ wanted to go camping with my family.
M Really? Well.... Camping is not my cup of ________.

>> WORDS **a school of** 한 무리의 **feed** 먹이를 주다 **totally** 완전히 **lonely** 외로운 **in the middle** 중앙에 **priest** 성직자 **fold** 접다 **prefer** 선호하다 **lend** 빌려주다

05회 » 듣기 실전 모의고사

01 다음을 듣고, 목요일의 날씨로 가장 적절한 것을 고르시오.

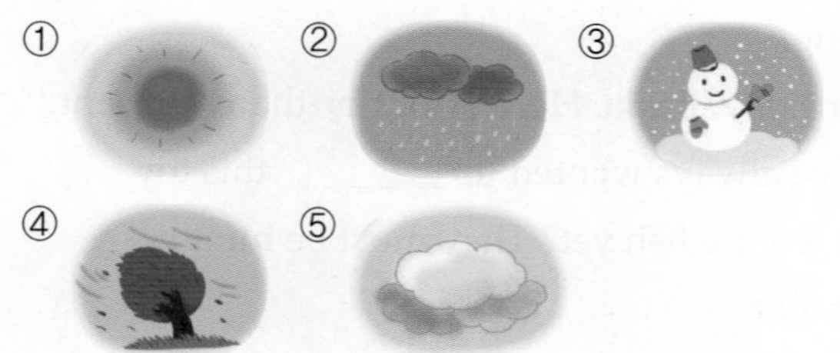

02 대화를 듣고, 여자가 구입한 화분으로 가장 적절한 것을 고르시오.

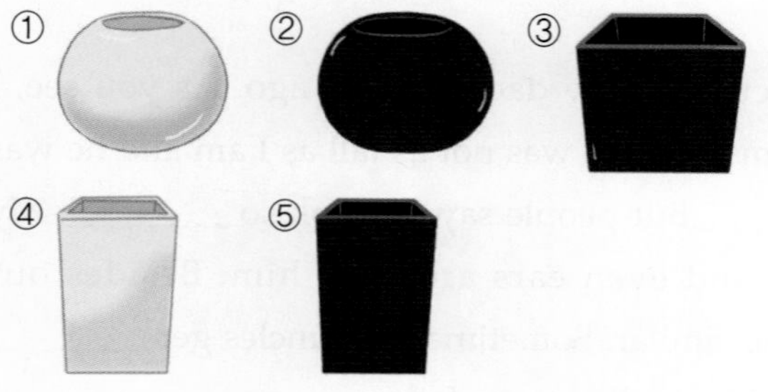

03 대화를 듣고, 남자의 심정으로 가장 적절한 것을 고르시오.

① happy ② relieved
③ bored ④ regretful
⑤ proud

04 대화를 듣고, 여자가 지난주에 한 일로 가장 적절한 것을 고르시오.

① 티셔츠 제작 ② 스마트폰 구입
③ 가족사진 촬영 ④ 가족 티셔츠 주문
⑤ 결혼기념일 선물 구입

05 대화를 듣고, 두 사람이 대화하는 장소로 가장 적절한 곳을 고르시오.

① 호텔 ② 야구장 ③ 수영장
④ 우체국 ⑤ 축구장

06 대화를 듣고, 남자의 마지막 말의 의도로 가장 적절한 것을 고르시오.

① 항의 ② 비난 ③ 의심
④ 칭찬 ⑤ 간청

07 대화를 듣고, 여자가 바자회에서 구입한 항목에 해당하지 않는 것을 고르시오.

① 책 ② 자석 ③ 풍선
④ 머리핀 ⑤ 티스푼

08 대화를 듣고, 여자가 대화 직후에 할 일로 가장 적절한 것을 고르시오.

① 차 태워주기
② 차 수리 맡기기
③ 시계 배터리 교체하기
④ 정확한 시간 알려 주기
⑤ 고장 난 시계 수리하기

09 대화를 듣고, 두 사람이 여행을 떠나기 전에 해야 할 일로 언급하지 않은 것을 고르시오.

① 냉장고에 음식 넣기
② 가스 밸브 잠그기
③ 신문 구독 중지하기
④ 전등 끄기
⑤ 가전제품의 플러그 뽑기

10 다음을 듣고, 여자가 하는 말의 내용으로 가장 적절한 것을 고르시오.

① 학생 상담 일정 안내
② 교내 대회 취소 통보
③ 디즈니 만화 영화 개봉작 홍보
④ 포스터 디자인 대회 참가 안내
⑤ 포스터 디자인 대회 입상자 공고

Answer p. 36

11 대화를 듣고, 남자가 찾는 티셔츠에 대한 내용과 일치하지 않는 것을 고르시오.

① 검정색이다.
② 작년에 구입했다.
③ 호박등이 그려져 있다.
④ 세탁물 바구니에 있다.
⑤ 최근에 입은 적이 없다.

12 대화를 듣고, 남자가 화장실을 청소한 목적으로 가장 적절한 것을 고르시오.

① 용돈을 더 받기 위해서
② 누나에게 자랑하기 위해서
③ 화장실 냄새를 없애기 위해서
④ 아버지를 기쁘게 해드리기 위해서
⑤ 애완동물 목욕 후 정리하기 위해서

13 대화를 듣고, 남자가 구입할 아이스크림의 개수를 고르시오.

① 3개 ② 4개 ③ 5개
④ 6개 ⑤ 7개

14 대화를 듣고, 두 사람의 관계로 가장 적절한 것을 고르시오.

① 판매원 – 고객
② 공장 직원 – 공장주
③ 신발 수리공 – 고객
④ 콜센터 직원 – 고객
⑤ 구두 디자이너 – 판매원

15 대화를 듣고, 남자가 여자에게 부탁한 일로 가장 적절한 것을 고르시오.

① 편지 쓰기
② 우편 발송하기
③ 중국어 가르치기
④ 번역본 검토하기
⑤ 번역기 사용법 알려 주기

16 대화를 듣고, 남자가 헌혈을 할 수 없는 이유로 가장 적절한 것을 고르시오.

① 약을 먹고 있어서 ② 바늘을 무서워해서
③ 빈혈을 앓고 있어서 ④ 최근에 헌혈을 해서
⑤ 16세가 되지 않아서

17 다음 그림의 상황에 가장 적절한 대화를 고르시오.

① ② ③ ④ ⑤

18 다음을 듣고, 남자가 글쓰기에 대해 언급하지 않은 것을 고르시오.

① 흥미로운 제목 ② 주제 선정
③ 알맞은 주제문 ④ 적절한 근거
⑤ 유의어 사용

[19-20] 대화를 듣고, 남자의 마지막 말에 이어질 여자의 말로 가장 적절한 것을 고르시오.

19 Woman: ______________________

① I'll put less water next time.
② I added some salt into water.
③ Maybe you're not hungry at all.
④ They are not as tasty as grilled potatoes.
⑤ I spread butter on the pan and then grilled them.

20 Woman: ______________________

① They won't probably think so.
② I'll turn on the air conditioner.
③ I moved to this apartment five years ago.
④ You're suffering from noise between floors.
⑤ Most apartments have the same problem, you know.

Dictation Test >> 05회

01 다음을 듣고, 목요일의 날씨로 가장 적절한 것을 고르시오.

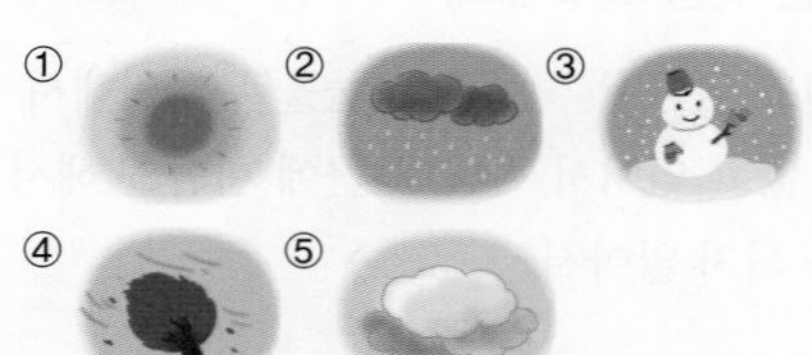

W Here's the weather forecast for this week. The rain will stop by Monday morning and we'll have clear skies ________ the week. However, a ________ ________ is expected on Thursday and you'll have another set of cold ________ days from Friday. So enjoy the nice weather for a couple of days.

02 대화를 듣고, 여자가 구입한 화분으로 가장 적절한 것을 고르시오.

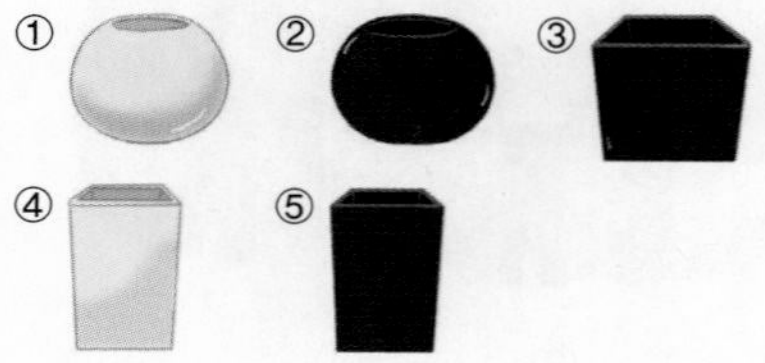

M Can I help you?

W I want to buy a flower pot to plant a ________ ________.

M How about this square-shaped pot?

W I ________ bright colors. This white round-shaped pot looks cute.

M Tomato plants ________ really tall. So you'd better buy a ________ one.

W Then would this white tall rectangular one be okay?

M That'll do.

W Great. I'll take it.

03 대화를 듣고, 남자의 심정으로 가장 적절한 것을 고르시오.

① happy ② relieved
③ bored ④ regretful
⑤ proud

M Good morning, Mia.

W Hi. Did you see the fire engines in front of our ________ ________ last night?

M No, I didn't. What happened?

W There was a fire on the 10th floor.

M Oh, my. Did anybody get ________?

W No, I heard that it was a small fire and it was ________ soon.

M Oh, thank God.

04 대화를 듣고, 여자가 지난주에 한 일로 가장 적절한 것을 고르시오.

① 티셔츠 제작 ② 스마트폰 구입
③ 가족사진 촬영 ④ 가족 티셔츠 주문
⑤ 결혼기념일 선물 구입

M Phoebe, did you change the ________ ________ of your smartphone?

W Yeah, it's the picture of my family.

M When did you take it?

W We took it last week, ________ my parents' anniversary.

M I like the T-shirt all your family members are ________.

W Thanks. I ________ them a month ago.

M Cool. You all look so happy.

>> WORDS a couple of 두 개의 … flower pot 화분 rectangular 직사각형의 fire engine 소방차 anniversary 기념일

Answer p. 36

05 대화를 듣고, 두 사람이 대화하는 장소로 가장 적절한 곳을 고르시오.

① 호텔 ② 야구장 ③ 수영장
④ 우체국 ⑤ 축구장

W Excuse me, sir.
M Yes?
W You cannot enter the ________ without a swimming cap.
M I am wearing a ________ ________ instead.
W I'm sorry but we don't allow baseball caps.
M I see. Where can I borrow one?
W You can borrow one ________ ________ the front desk.
M Thanks.

06 대화를 듣고, 남자의 마지막 말의 의도로 가장 적절한 것을 고르시오.

① 항의 ② 비난 ③ 의심
④ 칭찬 ⑤ 간청

W Ouch!
M Are you alright, Mom?
W I ________ ________ your toy cars again, Philip.
M Oh, I'm sorry. I was just about to clear them up.
W You said the same thing last time. Do you remember what I said?
M That you were going to ________ ________ mine?
W Not quite. I said I was going to ________ them to children in need.
M You can do so next time, really.

07 대화를 듣고, 여자가 바자회에서 구입한 항목에 해당하지 않는 것을 고르시오.

① 책 ② 자석 ③ 풍선
④ 머리핀 ⑤ 티스푼

M How did the ________ go, Linda?
W I had so much fun. My hairpins were ________ ________, you know.
M I'm happy for you. Did you buy some stuff too?
W Yeah. These party balloons, magnets, books and the teaspoon set are what ________ ________ today.
M You did buy a lot of stuff.
W You know what? I bought all of them with just 3,000 won.
M I can't believe it.

>> **WORDS** **swimming cap** 수영 모자 **allow** 허락하다 **front desk** 안내 데스크 **in need** 도움이 필요한 **magnet** 자석 **stuff** 물건

08 대화를 듣고, 여자가 대화 직후에 할 일로 가장 적절한 것을 고르시오.

① 차 태워주기
② 차 수리 맡기기
③ 시계 배터리 교체하기
④ 정확한 시간 알려 주기
⑤ 고장 난 시계 수리하기

W David, why are you still home? Isn't it time for you to take the ________ ________?
M I still have 30 minutes to go. It's 4 o'clock now.
W No, it's 5 o'clock.
M What?
W The clock must be out of ________.
M Oh, no. I must not be late today.
W Hurry up, David.
M Grandma, could you ________ me a ________?
W Alright.

09 대화를 듣고, 두 사람이 여행을 떠나기 전에 해야 할 일로 언급하지 않은 것을 고르시오.

① 냉장고에 음식 넣기
② 가스 밸브 잠그기
③ 신문 구독 중지하기
④ 전등 끄기
⑤ 가전제품의 플러그 뽑기

W Are we all ready to go? We don't want to miss the plane.
M Wait. We have to ________ some things before we depart.
W Like what?
M We should put all the food into the fridge, ________ ________ the gas valves, and so forth.
W You're right. Let me ________ the newspaper subscription for the week.
M Thanks. Are there some other things we need to do?
W Maybe we can pull out the ________ for all of the electronics.
M Great. I guess we are now ready for a trip.

10 다음을 듣고, 여자가 하는 말의 내용으로 가장 적절한 것을 고르시오.

① 학생 상담 일정 안내
② 교내 대회 취소 통보
③ 디즈니 만화 영화 개봉작 홍보
④ 포스터 디자인 대회 참가 안내
⑤ 포스터 디자인 대회 입상자 공고

W Here is an announcement regarding the ________ design contest for the school festival. The ________ of our school festival this year is Disney World. Keep that in mind and try to come up with creative poster ________. If you want to ________ ________ the contest, please visit the teacher's office on the first floor.

>> WORDS miss 놓치다 fridge 냉장고 and so forth … 등등 subscription 구독 pull out 뽑다 electronics 가전제품 announcement 발표 regarding …에 관하여 keep ... in mind …을 명심하다 creative 창의적인

Answer p. 36

11 대화를 듣고, 남자가 찾는 티셔츠에 대한 내용과 일치하지 않는 것을 고르시오.

① 검정색이다.
② 작년에 구입했다.
③ 호박등이 그려져 있다.
④ 세탁물 바구니에 있다.
⑤ 최근에 입은 적이 없다.

M Have you seen my black T-shirt, Mom?
W Which one?
M The one I bought for my Halloween ________ last year.
W I don't quite remember. Can you describe it?
M It is the one with jack-o'-lantern at the back.
W Oh, that one. I don't know where it is. Maybe it's in the ________.
M That's not ________. I haven't worn it recently.

12 대화를 듣고, 남자가 화장실을 청소한 목적으로 가장 적절한 것을 고르시오.

① 용돈을 더 받기 위해서
② 누나에게 자랑하기 위해서
③ 화장실 냄새를 없애기 위해서
④ 아버지를 기쁘게 해드리기 위해서
⑤ 애완동물 목욕 후 정리하기 위해서

M Mia, look what I did.
W Wow, did you finally ________ your room?
M Not only that. I also cleaned up the bathroom.
W Were you planning to ask for a raise in your ________?
M No, I wanted to make Dad happy.
W That's enough to make a cat ________.
M I'm serious. It's Parents' Day soon.

13 대화를 듣고, 남자가 구입할 아이스크림의 개수를 고르시오.

① 3개 ② 4개 ③ 5개
④ 6개 ⑤ 7개

M It's so hot. You'll get a ________ if you stay out there just for five minutes.
W You can say that again. Would you care for some ice cream?
M Why not? Let me go get some ice cream.
W Thanks. Please buy ________ ice cream cones for me.
M That'll make three including mine.
W Oh, Jenny and Jack will be arriving soon. Would you get ________ ________ ________ of them?
M Sure.

>> WORDS describe 묘사하다 jack-o'-lantern 호박등 ask for …을 요구하다 care for …을 좋아하다 including …을 포함하여

14 대화를 듣고, 두 사람의 관계로 가장 적절한 것을 고르시오.

① 판매원 – 고객
② 공장 직원 – 공장주
③ 신발 수리공 – 고객
④ 콜센터 직원 – 고객
⑤ 구두 디자이너 – 판매원

M How can I help you?
W I've ________ these high heels here a week ago and they are very uncomfortable.
M How are they uncomfortable?
W The room for my toes is too tight and ________ ________ hurt.
M In that case, I can ________ the part with a special tool.
W That'll be nice. Do I have to come and grab them later?
M No, you can just wait here. It takes ________ ________ ten minutes.
W Awesome.

15 대화를 듣고, 남자가 여자에게 부탁한 일로 가장 적절한 것을 고르시오.

① 편지 쓰기
② 우편 발송하기
③ 중국어 가르치기
④ 번역본 검토하기
⑤ 번역기 사용법 알려 주기

M Are you still learning Chinese, Ellen?
W I am. It's so interesting.
M Can you help me ________ ________ ________ to my Taiwanese friend?
W Why don't you use a ________ program on the Internet?
M Actually, I did use it and I'm not sure if the translated version is ________.
W So you want me to ________ ________ the translation, right?
M That's right.

16 대화를 듣고, 남자가 헌혈을 할 수 <u>없는</u> 이유로 가장 적절한 것을 고르시오.

① 약을 먹고 있어서
② 바늘을 무서워해서
③ 빈혈을 앓고 있어서
④ 최근에 헌혈을 해서
⑤ 16세가 되지 않아서

M Amy, do you have plans for the weekend?
W I'm planning to ________ my blood. Do you want to join?
M I'd like to, but I can't.
W Aren't you 17 years old yet? I thought your birthday was in February.
M Yeah, my 16th birthday already ________. It's just that I already made a blood donation last month.
W Oh, you need to ________ ________ another month to be able to donate blood.
M That's right.

>> WORDS **high heels** 하이힐 **uncomfortable** 불편한 **toe** 발가락 **tool** 도구 **Taiwanese** 대만 (사람)의 **translate** 번역하다 **blood** 피, 혈액 **donation** 기부 (*v*. donate)

Answer p. 36

17 다음 그림의 상황에 가장 적절한 대화를 고르시오.

① ② ③ ④ ⑤

① W How much is it total?
M Let me pay this time.
② W Would you like to have some more chicken?
M No, thanks. I've already had ________.
③ W I'd like to ________ two boxes of fried chicken.
M Okay. Tell me your address, ma'am.
④ W Where can I throw away the bones?
M Let's put them in this ________ ________.
⑤ W Oops, I don't have any ________. Can I pay by credit card?
M Of course you can.

18 다음을 듣고, 남자가 글쓰기에 대해 언급하지 않은 것을 고르시오.

① 흥미로운 제목 ② 주제 선정
③ 알맞은 주제문 ④ 적절한 근거
⑤ 유의어 사용

M Let me give you some tips for writing. First, you need to give it an interesting ________ that attracts the readers' attention. Next, you should start with a good ________ sentence. Then, write the sentences that ________ the topic sentence. Lastly, use ________ to avoid repeating certain words.

[19-20] 대화를 듣고, 남자의 마지막 말에 이어질 여자의 말로 가장 적절한 것을 고르시오.

19 ① I'll put less water next time.
② I added some salt into water.
③ Maybe you're not hungry at all.
④ They are not as tasty as grilled potatoes.
⑤ I spread butter on the pan and then grilled them.

W Brandon, come and have some corn.
M They are so delicious. Did you ________ them with butter?
W No, I ________ them in water.
M It didn't taste the same when I boiled them last time.
W You shouldn't put too much ________ when boiling.
M I didn't. How are they so tasty?

20 ① They won't probably think so.
② I'll turn on the air conditioner.
③ I moved to this apartment five years ago.
④ You're suffering from noise between floors.
⑤ Most apartments have the same problem, you know.

M Where is this noise from?
W I've ________ ________ the air conditioner.
M It's not the air conditioner. Is your phone vibrating?
W Hmm, no. I guess it's from ________.
M You mean you even can hear your neighbor's phone vibrating?
W I can sometimes hear them ________, you know.
M Maybe you should ________ ________ another apartment.

>> WORDS pay 지불하다 address 주소 bone 뼈 credit card 신용카드 attract 끌어들이다 attention 주목, 관심 repeat 반복하다 taste …한 맛이 나다 boil 삶다, 끓이다 tasty 맛있는 vibrate 진동하다

Memo

중학 영어의 모든 것

VISANG

All that

중학 영어 2-1

Answers

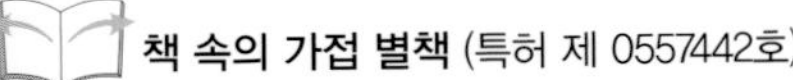

책 속의 가접 별책 (특허 제 0557442호)

'Answers'는 본책에서 쉽게 분리할 수 있도록 제작되었으므로
유통 과정에서 분리될 수 있으나 파본이 아닌 정상제품입니다.

ABOVE IMAGINATION

우리는 남다른 상상과 혁신으로
교육 문화의 새로운 전형을 만들어
모든 이의 행복한 경험과 성장에 기여한다

PART I 실력 다지기

Lesson 01 문장의 형식

Grammar Practice
pp. 12~15

A1 (1)
A2 (1) ⓑ (2) ⓑ (3) ⓒ (4) ⓑ (5) ⓐ (6) ⓑ (7) ⓒ
A3 (1) happy (2) like (3) felt
B1 (1) us English (2) eggs (3) reading books (4) a long letter (5) me the note
B2 (1) to her (2) beautiful (3) merrily (4) for me (5) for us
B3 (1) to us (2) Emily (3) a gift to (4) questions of (5) me a bike
C1 (1) named her dog Pinky (2) keep your room clean (3) his dad to repair the bike (4) kept his brother waiting
C2 (1) King (2) cheerful (3) to stop taking pills (4) crying
D1 (1) laugh (2) to collect (3) set (4) stop
D2 (3)
E1 (1) ○ (2) touch(touching) (3) ○ (4) put(putting)
E2 (1) bake(baking) (2) (to) draw (3) use (4) to read (5) miss

Grammar Test
pp. 16~17

01 ① **02** ③ **03** ① **04** (1) playing soccer (2) singing a song **05** ③ **06** ③ **07** Justin's mother cooked him chicken soup. 또는 Justin's mother cooked chicken soup for him. **08** ④ **09** (1) smoothly → smooth (2) share → to share (3) to take → take **10** ⑤ **11** ③ **12** ⑤ **13** (3) a teddy bear her → her a teddy bear/a teddy bear for her (5) looked happily → looked happy

01 수여동사 make를 써서 〈간접목적어(my mother) + 직접목적어(a card)〉, 또는 〈직접목적어(a card) + for + 간접목적어(my mother)〉의 형태로 쓸 수 있다.

02 ③은 〈수여동사 + 간접목적어 + 직접목적어〉의 어순이고, 나머지는 목적어 뒤에 목적격보어가 쓰인 문장이다.

03 〈let + 목적어 + 동사원형〉 / 〈see + 목적어 + 동사원형(현재분사)〉

04 지각동사 see, watch는 목적격보어로 동사원형이나 현재분사를 취하는데, 진행 중임을 강조하므로 현재분사를 쓴다.

05 감각동사 look 뒤에는 보어로 형용사를 쓴다.

06 〈동사 + 목적어(me) + to go〉의 형태이므로, 목적격보어로 동사원형을 취하는 사역동사 made는 알맞지 않다.

07 수여동사 cook은 뒤에 〈간접목적어 + 직접목적어〉나 〈직접목적어 + for + 간접목적어〉의 형태로 쓸 수 있다.

08 look 뒤에는 보어로 형용사를 써야 하는데 대화 흐름상 happy가 어울리며, buy 뒤에 직접목적어를 먼저 쓰면 간접목적어 앞에 전치사 for를 써야 한다.

09 (1) feel 뒤에는 보어로 형용사를 쓴다. (2) tell은 목적격보어로 to부정사를 쓴다. (3) 사역동사 make는 목적격보어로 동사원형을 쓴다.

10 ① showed ② sent ③ told ④ teaches가 수여동사로 쓰인 문장에서 직접목적어가 먼저 오면 뒤의 간접목적어 앞에 전치사 to를 쓰고, ⑤ made인 경우에는 for를 쓴다.

11 〈보기〉, ③ 주어 + 동사 + 목적어 + 목적격보어 ① 주어 + 동사 + 수식어 ② 주어 + 수여동사 + 간접목적어 + 직접목적어 ④ 주어 + 동사 + 목적어 ⑤ 주어 + 동사 + 주격보어

12 ⑤ make는 사역동사이므로 목적격보어 thinking은 think로 써야 한다.

13 (3) bought 뒤의 목적어는 〈간접목적어 + 직접목적어〉 또는 〈직접목적어 + for + 간접목적어〉로 쓴다. (5) look은 뒤에 보어로 형용사를 쓴다.

Reading
pp. 18~19

1 want our sombreros to look **2** ① **3** ③ **4** ④

[1~2]

세계의 인형들

저는 Sweepy입니다. 저는 독일 출신이고 제 직업은 굴뚝을 청소하는 것입니다. 겨울 동안, 굴뚝 청소부는 사람들이 따뜻하고 안전하도록 돕습니다. 그래서 사람들은 굴뚝 청소부가 그들에게 행운을 가져온다고 생각합니다. 사람들은 굴뚝 청소부가 그들의 결혼식에 오기를 원하기까지 합니다! 여러분이 저를 보시면, 그날은 여러분에게 행운이 있는 날입니다.

제 이름은 Jose이고 이들은 제 마리아치 악단 구성원들입니다. 우리는 민속 음악을 연주하고 항상 우리의 솜브레로, 즉 커다란 모자를 씁니다. 멕시코에서 사람들은 뜨겁고 강한 햇볕에서 시원함을 유지하도록 이 모자를 씁니다. 우리 마리아치 연주자들은 우리의 솜브레로가 화려해 보이길 원합니다. 그래서 우리는 종종 그것들을 여러 다양한 재료들로 장식합니다. 여러분은 우리의 솜브레로 중 어느 것이 가장 마음에 드나요?

1 문장의 동사로 want를 쓰고, 문장 끝의 형용사 fancy 앞에 감각동사 look을 쓴다. look은 want의 목적격보어이므로 to부정사 형태로 써서 〈want+목적어(our sombreros)+목적격보어(to look)〉의 어순으로 문장을 완성한다.

2 ① 독일에서 굴뚝 청소부를 행운의 상징으로 여기기 시작한 때는 언급되지 않았다.

3

> 주목해 주시겠어요? Fantastic Zoo에 오신 것을 환영합니다. 저는 오늘 여러분의 안내원, Helen입니다. 여기 우리의 관광 계획이 있습니다. 우선, 우리는 Bird World에 갈 예정입니다. 지난달에 새로운 공작새가 왔습니다. 공작새의 아름다운 깃털을 즐겨보세요. 그 다음, 우리는 소형 열차를 타고 African Area로 갈 것입니다. 여러분은 코끼리들이 낮잠을 자는 것을 볼 수 있습니다. 우리는 Sunflower Garden에서 점심을 먹을 것입니다. Sunflower Garden으로 가는 길에, 우리는 Green Lake에 들러서 하마들을 볼 것입니다. 점심 식사 후에, 우리는 정문으로 돌아올 것입니다. 질문 있으신가요?

③ African Area에서 코끼리들이 낮잠을 자는 것을 볼 수 있다고 했다.

4

> 여러분은 먼지로 덮인 차를 보면 무슨 생각이 떠오르는가? Scott Wade는 재미있는 생각을 했다. 그는 그것이 예술 작품을 위한 완벽한 화폭이라고 생각했다. 그는 자동차 뒷부분의 먼지 낀 창에 멋진 그림을 그렸다. 그는 더러운 차를 움직이는 미술관으로 바꿨다. 그의 놀라운 작품과 창의성 덕분에, 그는 '먼지의 다빈치'로 알려져 있다. 작품의 아랫부분에, 그는 날짜가 아닌 시간을 썼다. 그것은 그의 작품이 비나 바람에 의해 쉽게 지워질 수 있어서, 날짜를 쓰는 것은 의미가 없기 때문이다.

④ 작품의 아랫부분에 시간을 쓴다.

Expression Test

pp. 20~21

1 ③ **2** kind of movie **3** ④ **4** do you, free time **5** ⑤ **6** ③

1 B가 자신의 관심사를 답하므로 관심사를 묻는 표현인 ③이 빈칸에 알맞다.

2 영화감독이 되겠다는 A의 말에 이어 B가 질문하자 A가 공포 영화를 만들겠다고 답하고 있으므로 B의 질문은 영화의 구체적인 종류를 묻는 표현으로 완성하는 것이 알맞다.

3 관심이 있는지 묻는 말에 B가 관심이 없다고 답했으므로 같은 표현인 I have no interest in it.으로 바꿔 쓸 수 있다.

4 What is your hobby?는 상대방의 취미를 묻는 표현이므로 상대의 여가 활동에 관해 묻는 표현 What do you usually do in your free time?으로 바꿔 쓸 수 있다.

5 B가 랩 음악을 듣는다고 답하고 있으므로 음악의 구체적인 종류를 묻는 표현인 ⑤가 빈칸에 알맞다.

6 (B) 너는 여가 시간에 보통 뭘 하니? – (A) 나는 스케이트 타러 가는 것을 좋아해. – (D) 재미있겠다. 너는 인라인 스케이트를 말하는 거니, 아니면 아이스 스케이트를 말하는 거니? – (C) 나는 보통 인라인 스케이트를 타러 가고, 겨울에는 아이스 링크에서 스케이트를 타.

서술형 평가

p. 22

1 (1) I usually read books. (2) What kind of books do you read? **2** (1) easy (2) a lazy doll (3) sleep (4) to take a rest **3** (1) He wrote a poem to me. (2) I made kites for the children. (3) Can I ask something of you? **4** (1) see my cat play[playing] (2) smell something burn [burning] **5** (1) made me this desk (2) sent it to me (3) bought it for me

1 자신이 자주 하는 행동을 말할 때 부사 usually를 사용해서 말하고 구체적으로 어떤 종류를 물을 때는 〈kind of+명사〉를 사용해 묻는다.

2 (1), (2) 목적격보어로 명사, 형용사를 쓴다. (3) 사역동사(make)의 목적격보어로 동사를 쓰면 원형으로 쓴다. (4) want는 목적격보어로 동사를 쓰는 경우 to부정사로 쓴다.

3 (1) write는 간접목적어 앞에 전치사 to를 쓴다. (2) make는 간접목적어 앞에 전치사 for를 쓴다. (3) ask는 간접목적어 앞에 전치사 of를 쓴다.

4 감각동사(see, hear, feel, smell, watch 등)는 목적격보어로 동사원형 또는 현재분사를 쓴다.

5 수여동사(make, send, buy 등)는 〈동사+간접목적어(…에게)+직접목적어(…을)〉의 어순으로 쓰이며, 직접목적어가 대명사인 경우에는 〈동사+직접목적어+전치사+간접목적어〉의 어순으로 쓰인다.

Final Test

pp. 23~27

01 ① **02** ③ **03** ③ **04** interested in playing chess **05** ③ **06** ④ **07** ④ **08** ① **09** ④ **10** (1) happy (2) introduce **11** ⑤ **12** (1) clean (2) see **13** ③ **14** ⑤ **15** ② **16** ③ **17** (1) for (2) to **18** (1) ⓒ (2) ⓐ (3) ⓒ (4) ⓐ (5) ⓑ (6) ⓑ **19** (1) I told Bill to take care of the dog. (2) I told the boys to be quiet in the classroom. **20** ⑤ **21** tiredly → tired **22** ① **23** ③ **24** (1) bought me a new backpack (2) sent his friend a birthday present **25** ④ **26** ④ **27** ⑤ **28** ② **29** ② **30** ④

01 ①은 동의어 관계이고, 나머지는 모두 반의어 관계이다.

02 ①, ②, ④, ⑤ 직업, 역할 ③ 인형

03 자신이 관심 있는 것을 말할 때에는 I'm interested in .... / I'm into .... 등의 표현으로 나타낼 수 있다.

04 그림은 체스 게임을 하는 모습이고, 관심사를 묻는 A의 말에 대해 B는 체스 게임에 관심 있다는 내용이 알맞다.

05 (C) 너는 무엇에 관심이 있니, Henry? - (A) 나는 이야기를 쓰는 것에 관심이 있어. 너는 어때, Karen? - (D) 나는 운동, 특히 탁구를 좋아해. 나는 탁구 선수가 되고 싶어. - (B) 오, 그거 멋지구나.

06 ④ 그림 그리는 데 관심이 있는지 묻는 A의 질문에 대해 '아니.(Not really.)'라고 답한 후에 그림 그리는 것에 푹 빠져 있다는 말을 덧붙이는 것은 자연스럽지 않다.

07 상대방에게 '무슨 종류의 …을 …하니?'라는 뜻으로 정보를 묻는 표현은 What kind of ... do you ...?로 나타낸다.

08 놀 때 무엇을 하는 것을 좋아하는지 물었으므로 취미를 말하는 대답이 와야 한다. ①은 과거에 한 일을 말하는 표현이다.

09 ④ There is[are] .... 구문에서 주어는 동사 뒤에 쓰는 말(many flowers)이며, There는 유도부사이다.

10 (1) 목적격보어로 형용사를 쓴다. (2) 사역동사 Let의 목적격보어로 동사원형을 쓴다.

11 ⑤ 직접목적어 ①, ③, ④ 목적격보어 ② 주격보어

12 〈사역동사(have)+목적어+동사원형〉의 형태이다.

13 ③ want는 목적격보어로 to부정사를 취한다.

14 지각동사 see가 동사로 쓰였으므로 〈목적어+동사원형 또는 현재분사〉의 어순이 알맞다.

15 want는 to부정사를 목적격보어로 취한다.

16 목적격보어로 동사원형(water)이 온 것으로 보아 빈칸에는 사역동사 made를 써야 한다

17 〈간접목적어+직접목적어〉의 어순을 바꿔 〈직접목적어+전치사+간접목적어〉로 나타낼 때, buy는 전치사 for를, tell은 to를 사용한다.

18 〈동사+목적어+목적격보어〉: ⓐ, (2), (4) / 〈동사+목적어〉: ⓑ, (5), (6) / 〈동사+주격보어〉: ⓒ, (1), (3)

19 '…에게 …하라고 말하다'는 〈tell+목적어+to부정사〉의 형태로 나타낸다.

20 〈보기〉, ⑤ 〈동사+목적어+목적격보어〉 / ① 동사+수식어 ② 동사+목적어 ③ 동사+주격보어 ④ 동사+간접목적어+직접목적어

21 감각동사 look 뒤에는 보어로 형용사를 쓴다.

22 사역동사 make의 목적격보어로는 동사원형을 쓰고, 지각동사 see의 목적격보어로는 동사원형이나 현재분사를 쓴다.

23 smell은 감각동사로 형용사를 보어로 쓴다.

24 (1) 수여동사(bought)+간접목적어(me)+직접목적어(a new backpack) (2) 수여동사(sent)+간접목적어(his friend)+직접목적어(a birthday present)

25

> Lantern Festival은 중국과 다른 아시아 국가에서 기념하는 기념일이다. 그것은 봄 축제 마지막 날에 열린다. 그것은 새로운 음력의 첫 보름달을 기념한다. 그 축제 동안, 집들은 화려한 등으로 장식되는데, 종종 그 위에 수수께끼를 쓰기도 한다. 누구든 그 수수께끼를 정확하게 푼다면, 수수께끼를 만든 사람은 푼 사람에게 작은 선물을 준다.

④ 수수께끼를 푼 사람에게 선물을 준다는 내용이 알맞다.

26

> 여러분은 화산이 궁금한가? 여러분은 집에서 화산을 만들 수 있다. 빈 플라스틱 병을 하나 구해라. 그 병을 구멍을 제외하고 찰흙으로 덮어라. (C) 그것을 온수로 채워라. (A) 그 액체에 베이킹 소다 두 숟가락을 넣어라. (B) 식초를 화산에 천천히 붓고 분화를 기다려라. 용암이 천천히 여기저기로 흐를 것이다!

병과 찰흙으로 만든 화산을 (C) 온수로 채우고 (A) 온수에 베이킹 소다를 넣고 (B) 화산에 식초를 천천히 넣으며 분화를 관찰하는 순서가 알맞다.

[27~28]

> 안녕, 진수야!
> 내 이메일에 그렇게 빨리 답장해 주다니 고마워. 또, 인천 공항에서 호텔까지 태워 준다고 말해 준 것도 고마워. 나는 드디어 짐을 다 쌌어. 나는 매우 설레. 나는 Airbus A380을 Heathrow 공항에서 타고 인천 국제공항에 오전 10시 30분에 도착할 거야. 6번 도착 출구 앞에서 11시 30분에 만나자. 만약 변경되는 게 있으면 네게 알려 줄게. 나는 한국을 방문하는 것을 고대하고 있어.
> 사랑을 담아, Lucy가

27 Lucy는 인천 공항에 도착하여 진수를 만나기로 했다.

28 ② 사역동사 let은 목적격보어로 동사원형이 온다.

[29~30]

> 나는 7반의 Sarah Parrott이야. 나는 오래된 손거울을 찾고 있어. 나는 그 위에 내 이름의 머리글자, SP를 새겼어. 내 생각에는 2층의 여자 화장실 손 건조기 위에 그것을 두고 온 것 같아. 그것은 매우 오래되어 보이고 여기저기 흠집이 나 있어. 하지만 그것은 할머니께서 내게 주신 것이어서 내게는 매우 소중해. 만약 누군가 그걸 찾는다면, 여기에 댓글을 달거나 내게 문자를 보내 줘. 내 전화번호는 099-0094-9400이야.

29 ② 잃어버린 손거울에는 자신의 이름 머리글자인 SP가 새겨져 있다고 했다.

30 ⓓ 직접목적어를 대명사로 쓰는 경우에는 〈동사+직접목적어+전치사+간접목적어〉의 어순으로 써야 하므로 my grandma gave it to me로 쓰는 것이 알맞다.

Lesson 02 to부정사

Grammar Practice

pp. 32~35

A1 (1) ⓑ (2) ⓒ (3) ⓐ (4) ⓑ (5) ⓐ (6) ⓒ

A2 (1) It, to live (2) exciting to learn (3) To finish your work

B1 (1) questions to answer (2) friends to play with (3) something to drink (4) to tell you about it

B2 (1) to tell (2) to read (3) to do (4) to write, on

C1 (1) to check (2) to win (3) to know (4) to understand

C2 (1) ⓐ (2) ⓒ (3) ⓑ (4) ⓓ

D1 (1) you (2) me (3) children (4) her

D2 (1) for you (2) for Gina (3) of you (4) for me

D3 (1) careless of Sally (2) rude of him (3) impossible for Tommy (4) silly of her

E1 (1) too (2) to take (3) so (4) great enough (5) how (6) to finish (7) where

E2 (1) should (2) enough (3) couldn't (4) so, can (5) to stay

Grammar Test

pp. 36~37

01 ④ **02** ⑤ **03** ⑤ **04** for, of **05** ⑤ **06** ⑤ **07** It was very wise of you to say so. **08** ② **09** old enough to **10** ② **11** ⑤ **12** ⑤ **13** I went to the bakery to buy some bread. **14** ④

01 빈칸에는 주어 역할을 할 수 있는 to부정사가 와야 알맞다.

02 앞에 나온 명사 a chair를 꾸미는 to부정사를 써야 하며, 의미상 a chair는 to sit on에서 전치사 on의 목적어이다.

03 • 〈too+형용사+to부정사〉: 너무 …해서 …할 수 없는
• 〈where+to부정사〉: 어디에 …해야 할지

04 첫 번째 빈칸에는 형용사가 necessary이므로 의미상 주어는 〈for+목적격〉으로 나타낸다. 두 번째 빈칸에는 사람의 성격을 나타내는 형용사인 kind가 쓰였으므로 의미상 주어는 〈of+목적격〉으로 나타낸다.

05 ⑤는 promised의 목적어로 쓰인 명사적 용법이며 나머지는 모두 부사적 용법으로 쓰였다. ① 감정의 원인 ② 판단의 근거 ③ 결과 ④ 목적

06 to부정사의 의미상 주어가 〈of+목적격〉이므로 빈칸에는 사람의 성격이나 성질을 나타내는 형용사를 써야 한다.

07 to부정사의 의미상 주어는 보통 〈for+목적격〉으로 나타내지만 앞에 있는 형용사가 사람에 대한 평가나 사람의 성격을 나타내는 경우에는 〈of+목적격〉을 쓴다.

08 〈의문사+주어+should+동사원형〉은 〈의문사+to부정사〉의 형태로 바꿔 쓸 수 있다.

09 '…할 만큼 충분히 …한(하게)'은 〈형용사(부사)+enough+to부정사〉를 써서 표현할 수 있다.

10 '…할 만큼 충분히 …한(하게)'의 뜻은 〈형용사(부사)+enough+to부정사〉로 나타낸다.

11 〈too+형용사(부사)+to부정사〉는 〈so+형용사(부사)+that+주어+can't …〉로 바꿔 쓸 수 있다. 주어진 문장의 시제가 과거이므로 couldn't로 써야 한다.

12 〈보기〉와 ⑤는 '…하기 위하여'의 뜻으로 목적을 나타내는 to부정사의 부사적 용법이다. ① 형용사를 꾸미는 부사적 용법 ② 명사를 꾸미는 형용사적 용법 ③ 목적어 역할을 하는 명사적 용법 ④ 감정의 원인을 나타내는 부사적 용법

13 '…하기 위하여'의 뜻으로 목적을 나타내는 to부정사를 이용하여 연결한다.

14 〈형용사+enough+to부정사〉는 〈so+형용사+that+주어+can …〉으로 바꿔 쓸 수 있는데, 현재시제이므로 조동사 can을 쓴다.

Reading

pp. 38~39

1 ① **2** too dependent on my smartphone to do **3** ③ **4** ⑤

[1~2]

나의 디지털 탈출 여행 이야기

지난 여름에, 저는 새롭고 색다른 체험을 했습니다. 바로 스마트폰 없이 Barcelona로 떠났던 가족 여행입니다. 우리의 첫날은 힘들었습니다. Reial 광장 근처에 있는 우리의 게스트하우스로 가는 길에 우리는 길을 잃었습니다. 아빠는 지도를 보고, 몇 개의 스페인어 단어로 방향을 묻느라 바빴습니다. 우리의 게스트하우스가 광장 바로 옆에 있었음에도 불구하고, 우리가 거기에 도착하는 데 약 2시간이 걸렸습니다. 다음 날, 우리는 현지의 작은 음식점에서 해산물 볶음밥을 먹었습니다. 음식은 좋았습니다. 저는 정말로 음식의 사진을 찍어서 그것을 제 블로그에 게시하고 싶었습니다. 하지만 제 전화가 없어서, 저는 그냥 그 순간을 즐기기로 했습니다. 남은 며칠 동안 우리는 점점 더 지역민들에게 의지했습니다. 우리는 그곳의 여러 다양한 사람들을 만나고 그들과 이야기할 수 있었습니다. 또 우리 가족은 내내 어디서나 서로 많이 이야기했습니다. 여행을 떠나기 전, 저는 제 스마트폰에 너무 의존해서 저는 그것 없이는 아무것도 하지 못했습니다. 하지만 이제 저는 제가 그것 없이도 순간을 즐길 수 있다는 것을 압니다.

1 ⓐ 뒤에 이어지는 내용에서, 여행 첫날, 광장 바로 옆에 있는 숙소를 찾을 때, 길을 잃고 2시간이나 헤맸다는 내용이 나오므로 nice를 부정적인 의미의 형용사 terrible 정도로 고쳐야 한다.

2 〈so+형용사+that+주어+can't〉 = 〈too+형용사+to부정사〉

3

> 여러분은 몇몇 '한정판' 야구 모자나 옷을 사기 위해 줄을 선 경험이 있는가? 그렇다면 여러분은 아마도 FOMO를 느꼈을 것이다. 그 단어(FOMO)는 '놓치고 싶지 않은 마음'을 의미한다. 만약 상품이 빨리 팔리고 있어서 여러분이 그것을 얻을 수 없을 것이라고 생각한다면, 여러분은 그것을 사러 달려갈 가능성이 크다. 그러므로, 많은 회사들이 FOMO를 영업에서 많이 사용한다. 예를 들어, Apple은 한정된 수의 휴대전화를 출시할 때 사람들이 그것들을 사고 싶게 만들기 위해 이 전략을 사용한다.

어떤 상품이 인기가 많아 빨리 팔릴 것이라고 생각되면 달려가서 사야 할 것 같은 느낌을 FOMO라고 지칭하고 있으므로 ⓒ는 you're likely to rush to buy it으로 고쳐야 한다.

4

> 기이한 기계가 Franklin 연구소 과학 박물관에 도착했다. 그것은 어린 소년처럼 생겼는데, 그러나 아무도 그것에 대해 몰랐다. 큐레이터들은 오래된 부품들을 조립하고 모터에 시동을 걸었다. 그러자, 그 기계는 살아 움직였다. 그것은 그 눈을 뜨고, 놀라운 움직임으로 손으로 펜을 쥐고 시를 썼다. 그 기계는 프랑스어로 이런 말을 썼다. 'Maillardet의 로봇이 씀.' 이 기계는 스위스 시계공인 Henri Maillardet가 만들었다. 18세기에 시계공들은 종종 그들의 기술을 뽐내기 위해 이런 기계를 발명했다.

⑤ 스위스 시계공인 Henri Maillardet가 만들었다고 했다.

Expression Test

pp. 40~41

1 ③ **2** ③ **3** ① **4** How do(can), to **5** ⑤ **6** two blocks, next

1 라디오를 고칠 수 있는지 묻는 질문에 B가 미안하다고 답하고 있으므로, 라디오 고치는 방법을 알려 주겠다는 ③은 알맞지 않다.

2 '가장 가까운 은행이 어디 있나요?'의 뜻으로 길을 묻는 말이다. ③은 거리를 묻는 표현이다.

3 ① 운전할 수 있는지 묻는 말에 대해 자신에게 잘됐다는 답은 어색하다.

4 How do(can) I get to ...?는 길을 묻는 표현으로, get to는 '…에 도착하다'라는 뜻이다.

5 능력 여부를 묻는 표현은 Can you tell me how to ...?, Do you know how to ...? 등으로 나타낼 수 있다.

6 서점은 두 블록 가서 왼쪽으로 돌면 빵집 옆에 있다.

서술형 평가

p. 42

1 (1) do you know where the repair shop is (2) It's across from the park. **2** (1) hot that I can't drink it (2) big that I couldn't eat it alone **3** (1) to have breakfast (2) to take some pictures (3) Grand Theater to watch the musical *Lion King* **4** (1) a pen to write with (2) some dessert to eat(to eat some dessert) **5** (1) to do my homework (2) me to turn off lights

1 길을 물을 때는 Do you know where ... is?로 표현할 수 있다. across from은 '…의 건너편에 있다'라는 뜻이다.

2 〈too+형용사+to부정사〉 = 〈so+형용사+that+주어+can't〉

3 to부정사가 부사적 용법으로 쓰여 '…하기 위하여'라는 뜻의 목적을 나타낼 수 있다.

4 (1) to부정사가 앞에 있는 명사를 꾸며서 '…할, …하는'의 의미로 형용사 역할을 할 수 있다. (2) 형용사적 용법의 to부정사, 또는 명사적 용법의 to부정사로 문장을 완성한다.

5 want, ask는 to부정사를 목적격보어로 취하는 동사이다. 문장을 바꿔 쓸 때 인칭대명사의 인칭 표시에 유의한다.

Final Test

pp. 43~47

01 ① **02** (1) direction (2) chat (3) scene **03** ③ **04** long, take **05** ③ **06** (B) → (A) → (C) **07** ① **08** I am not able to swim. **09** ⑤ **10** anything to eat **11** ④ **12** ③ **13** (1) to buy (2) to shop **14** ④ **15** (1) It was kind of him to visit me when I was ill. (2) Dad taught me how to play chess. **16** ④ **17** what to eat **18** ① **19** for, of **20** ① **21** ③ **22** to borrow **23** to try **24** ③ **25** ④ **26** ④ **27** ⑤ **28** ③ **29** ⑤ **30** ③

01 ①은 반의어 관계이고, 나머지는 모두 유의어 관계이다.

02 (1) direction은 '방향' (2) chat with는 '…와 이야기를 나누다' (3) scene of the accident는 '사건의 현장'의 의미이다.

03 ①, ②, ④, ⑤는 공원으로 가는 길을 묻는 표현이고 ③은 공원으로 가는 교통수단을 묻는 표현이다.

04 B가 도서관에 가는 데 걸리는 시간을 답했으므로 A는 도서관에 가는 데 걸리는 소요 시간을 묻는 것이 알맞다. 소요 시

간을 묻는 표현은 How long does it take to ...?를 쓴다.

05 B의 대답과 A의 마지막 말로 보아, 도와줄 수 있는지 물어보는 ③이 알맞다. Can you ...?는 '…할 수 있니?'라는 의미이다.

06 A: 이 주변에 우체국이 있나요? – (B) 네, 이 근처에 하나 있어요. – (A) 잘됐네요. 거기에 어떻게 가나요? – (C) 두 블록 곧장 가서 오른쪽으로 도세요. 당신 왼편에 있어요.

07 어떤 일을 할 수 있는지 묻는 표현인 Do you know how to ...?와 바꿔 쓸 수 있는 것으로 Can you ...? / Are you good at ...? 등이 있다.

08 A의 제안에 B가 거절의 답을 했으므로 빈칸에는 수영을 할 수 없다는 의미의 말을 써야 한다. 〈be동사+not+able+to부정사〉는 '…할 수 없다'라는 의미이다.

09 〈보기〉와 ⑤는 앞에 있는 명사를 꾸미는 to부정사의 형용사적 용법으로 쓰였다.

10 앞에 배고프다는 말이 있으므로 먹을 것을 찾는 말로 빈칸을 완성한다. anything을 꾸미는 말은 그 뒤에 쓴다.

11 주어 His dream을 보충 설명하는 to부정사가 알맞다.

12 체육관에 간 목적으로 알맞은 것은 '배드민턴을 치기 위해서'이다.

13 두 번째 문장이 앞 문장에 대한 '목적'을 나타내므로 to부정사를 이용하여 바꿔 쓸 수 있다.

14 〈for+목적격〉이 의미상 주어이므로 사람에 대한 판단이나 성격을 나타내는 형용사인 silly는 알맞지 않다.

15 (1) 사람의 성격을 나타내는 형용사 kind가 쓰였으므로 to부정사의 의미상 주어는 〈of+목적격〉으로 나타낸다. (2) 〈의문사+to부정사〉로 나타내므로 playing은 to play로 써야 한다.

16 '너무 …해서 …할 수 없는'의 의미는 〈too+형용사+to부정사〉로 나타낸다.

17 〈what+to부정사〉는 '무엇을 …할지'의 의미이다.

18 ①은 날씨를 나타내는 비인칭 주어이고, 나머지는 모두 가주어이다.

19 형용사가 impossible인 경우에는 〈for+목적격〉으로 to부정사의 의미상 주어를 나타내고, 사람에 대한 평가인 foolish이면 〈of+목적격〉으로 쓴다.

20 '…할 만큼 충분히 …한[하게]'의 뜻은 〈형용사[부사]+enough+to부정사〉로 나타낸다.

21 ③은 명사적 용법이고, 나머지는 모두 부사적 용법으로 쓰였다.

22 목적을 나타내는 to부정사의 부사적 용법으로 써야 한다.

23 encourage는 to부정사를 목적격보어로 취하는 동사이다.

24 ① contact → contacting ② saying → to say ④ enough smart → smart enough ⑤ buying → to buy

25

제 이름은 Antonia이고 저는 이국적인 악기로 연주하는 것을 좋아해요. 저는 3년 전에 제 아일랜드 친구로부터 백파이프 연주하는 법을 배웠어요. 우리 아빠는 저에게 하프 연주하는 것을 가르쳐 주셨어요. 저는 젬베도 잘 연주할 수 있어요. 저는 인터넷으로 영상을 보고 스스로 배웠어요. 저는 제 실력을 뽐내기 위해 Teen Talent Show 오디션에 참가를 신청해요. 여러분 모두가 제 공연을 즐기길 바라요.

④ 인터넷 영상을 보고 스스로 젬베 연주법을 배웠다고 했다.

26

여러분은 공통점이 없는 두 사람이 사랑에 빠질 수 있다고 생각하나요? 지난 주말 제 아들과 저는 Me Before You라는 영화를 봤는데, 우리는 그 이야기가 매우 좋았습니다. 영화에서, 한 여자는 목숨을 끊으려는 남자와 사랑에 빠졌습니다. 만약 여러분이 유머가 가득한 감동적인 이야기를 원한다면, 이 영화는 여러분에게 안성맞춤입니다. 이 명작을 보며 여러분은 웃고, 울고 그리고 미소 지을 것입니다.

영화를 감상한 소감을 말하므로 ④ a movie review(영화 감상평)가 알맞다.

[27~28]

Anna에게

사랑의 도시, 비엔나에 오신 것을 환영합니다!

제 아파트는 작지만 당신이 이틀을 머물기에는 충분히 아늑할 겁니다. 냉장고 안에 있는 음식은 모두 당신을 위한 것입니다. 달걀, 우유, 잼과 버터가 있습니다. 파스타와 빵은 주방에 있는 선반 위에 있습니다. 만약 당신에게 필요한 게 있으면, Goldberg 가의 꽃집 옆에 편의점이 있습니다. 내 집처럼 편하게 지내세요. 질문이 있으면 제게 이메일을 보내세요. 즐겁게 머물기를!

사랑을 담아, Stella가

27 ⑤ 사과는 언급되지 않았다.

28 '…할 만큼 충분히 …한'을 뜻하는 〈형용사+enough+to부정사〉 구문이 쓰이고, to부정사의 의미상 주어가 문장의 주어와 다를 때, 〈for+목적격〉의 형태로 to부정사 앞에 온다.

[29~30]

<u>생일 초의 전통은 어디에서 기원했는가?</u> 한 가지 가능한 이론은 이 전통이 고대 그리스에서 시작됐다는 것이다. 그리스인들은 달의 여신인 Artemis를 기리기 위해 둥근 케이크를 만들곤 했다. 그들은 달의 불빛을 나타내기 위해 케이크 위에 초를 켰고, 그들은 초에서 나오는 연기가 사람들의 기도를 하늘에 있는 신들에게 전달한다고 믿었다. 몇몇 학자들은 그 전통이 사실은 독일에서 시작됐다고 믿는다. 독일인들은 초를 '생명의 빛'을 나타내기 위해 케이크 위에 꽂았다.

29 글의 내용으로 보아 생일 초 전통의 기원에 관한 질문이 알맞다.

30 ⓐ와 ③은 '…하기 위하여'라는 뜻의 목적을 나타내는 to부정사의 부사적 용법으로 쓰였다.

Lesson 03 동명사

Grammar Practice pp. 52~55

A1 (1) making (2) doing (3) answering (4) taking

A2 (1) ⓐ (2) ⓒ (3) ⓑ (4) ⓑ (5) ⓐ (6) ⓑ (7) ⓐ (8) ⓒ (9) ⓒ (10) ⓒ

B1 (1) trying (2) hearing (3) using (4) taking (5) finding

B2 (1) go fishing (2) looking forward to hearing (3) is busy preparing

B3 (1) Thank you for inviting (2) is good at making (3) feel like traveling

C1 (1) to go (2) watching (3) to switch (4) to keep (5) to visit (6) closing (7) to lose (8) coming (9) making (10) to see

C2 (1) to open → opening (2) to fold → folding (3) studying → to study (4) to watch → watching (5) to visit → visiting

D1 (1) ⓐ (2) ⓐ (3) ⓑ (4) ⓑ (5) ⓐ (6) ⓑ (7) ⓐ (8) ⓑ (9) ⓐ (10) ⓐ

D2 (1) Potter 씨는 재미있는 만화 캐릭터를 그리고 있다. (2) 음악을 듣는 것은 나를 더 기분 좋게 해준다. (3) 춤추고 있는 소녀를 보러 가자. (4) 저 달리고 있는 소녀가 내 여동생이다. (5) 너는 침낭이 필요할 거야. (6) 나는 새 세탁기를 사고 싶어. (7) 밤에 강에서 수영하는 것은 위험하다.

Grammar Test pp. 56~57

01 skating 02 going 03 ④ 04 ④ 05 ④ 06 ⑤ 07 I practice playing the drums almost every day. 08 ③ 09 gives up eating 10 ② 11 to call Mina 12 ③ 13 (1) Tyler는 Tom의 집에 방문하기로 한 것을 기억해서 급히 거기에 갔다. (2) Bobby는 이어폰 샀던 것을 잊고, 다시 하나를 샀다.

01 전치사 다음에 동사가 목적어로 올 때는 동명사의 형태로 쓴다.

02 과거의 일을 나타낼 때는 remember 다음에 동명사가 온다.

03 나머지는 모두 동명사인 반면에 ④의 watching은 진행의 의미를 나타내는 현재분사이다.

04 동사를 목적어로 쓸 때 finish 다음에는 동명사로, decide 다음에는 to부정사로 쓴다.

05 Why don't you ...?는 '…하는 게 어때?'라는 뜻으로 How about -ing?와 바꿔 쓸 수 있다. on -ing는 '…하자마자'의 뜻으로 as soon as와 의미가 같다.

06 start, begin, like, love는 동명사와 to부정사를 모두 목적어로 취하지만, avoid는 동명사만 목적어로 취한다.

07 practice는 동명사를 목적어로 취하는 동사이다.

08 '…하고 싶다'는 의미는 feel like -ing 형태로 나타낸다.

09 그림은 살을 빼기 위해 햄버거를 먹는 것을 거부하는 학생의 모습이므로, 햄버거 먹기를 포기했다는 내용이 와야 한다. give up(포기하다) 뒤에는 동명사를 쓰므로 빈칸에는 gives up eating이 알맞다.

10 ② write a letter가 앞의 girl을 꾸미도록 write를 현재분사 writing으로 고쳐야 한다.

11 민호는 미나에게 전화해야 하는 것을 잊은 상황이므로 미래의 일을 나타내도록 forgot 뒤에 to부정사를 써서 문장을 완성한다.

12 ③ '…하자마자'는 on -ing로 나타낸다. (To hearing → On hearing)

13 (1) remember + to부정사: …할 것을 기억하다(미래)
(2) forget + 동명사: …했던 것을 잊다(과거)

Reading pp. 58~59

1 ⑤ 2 ③ 3 ④ 4 ②

[1~2]

우승 몇 초 전

카트 경주용 경기장에서 많은 사람들이 열렬히 응원을 하고 있습니다. Max는 다섯 바퀴를 더 가야 합니다. 그는 자신과 떨어져 앞에 있는, 경주의 선두 주자인 Simon의 차를 보고, 가속 페달을 더 강하게 밟습니다. 우승자는 세계적으로 유명한 레이싱 선수인 L. J. Richards를 만나게 되기 때문에 Max는 정말로 경주에서 우승하고 싶습니다. Max는 심판이 하얀 깃발을 흔드는 것을 봅니다. 그것은 마지막 바퀴라는 의미입니다. Max는 Simon 바로 뒤에 있습니다. 결승선이 점점 가까워집니다. "나는 할 수 있어!" Max는 크게 말합니다. 그는 자신의 심장이 강하게 뛰는 것을 느낄 수 있습니다. 카트들이 결승선으로 돌진합니다. 누가 우승자일까요?

Max는 자신이 2등을 한 것을 알기 때문에 그의 눈은 눈물이 가득합니다. "울 필요 없다, 얘야." 어느 남자의 목소리가 말합니다. 그의 앞에 서 있는 남자는 L. J. Richards입니다. "감사합니다, 하지만 저는 우승자가 아니에요."라고 Max가 말합니다. "네가 경주에서 우승하지는 못했더라도 너는 최선을 다했어. 그게 중요한 거지!"라고 L. J. Richards가 말합니다.

1 ⓔ 문장의 동사는 L. J. Richards 앞에 있는 is이고, 밑줄 친 부분은 The man을 꾸미는 역할을 하도록 현재분사 standing으로 고쳐야 한다.

2 ③ L. J. Richards가 Max를 위로하며 경주에서 우승하지는 못했지만 최선을 다한 것이 중요하다고 말하고 있으므로, 빈칸에는 ③이 알맞다.

3

Alex Scott은 보통의 아이였다. 불행히도, 1997년에 Alex는 소아암 진단을 받았다. Alex가 네 살일 때, 그녀는 자신의 집 앞에 레모네이드 판매대를 만드는 계획을 생각해냈다. 그녀는 자신이 번 모든 돈을 소아암 연구에 기부했다. 소문이 퍼졌고 그녀는 2천 달러를 모금했다. 매년 레모네이드를 팔아서 그녀는 100만 달러 이상을 모금했고 소아암에 대한 인식을 일깨웠다. Alex가 죽은 뒤, 그녀의 부모님은 소아암 연구를 위한 Alex 레모네이드 판매대 재단을 설립했다.

④ Alex는 레모네이드를 팔면서 소아암에 대한 인식을 높였다고 했다.

4

Bessie Coleman이 어렸을 때, 비행기를 타고 하늘을 나는 것은 아직 꿈에 불과했다. 하지만 Bessie가 젊은 여성이 되었을 때, 그녀의 오빠들은 제1차 세계 대전 중에 봤던 조종사들에 관한 재밌는 이야기를 그녀에게 해 주었다. Bessie는 모험적인 정신을 가졌다. 그녀는 조종사가 되기로 결심했다. 그러나 그 당시에는 어떤 비행 학교도 여성이나 유색 인종을 받아주지 않았다. 자신의 꿈을 포기하는 것 대신, Bessie는 돈을 벌어서 스스로 프랑스어를 배웠다. 마침내, 그녀는 프랑스의 비행 학교에 입학을 허가받았고 최초의 아프리카계 미국인 여성 조종사가 되었다.

Bessie는 조종사가 되는 것이 꿈이었다.

>> Expression Test

pp. 60~61

1 ④ **2** (C) → (A) → (B) **3** ② **4** forget to **5** ④ **6** ③

1 나머지는 '그게 무슨 뜻이니?'라고 설명을 요청하는 표현이고 ④는 상대방의 의견을 묻는 표현이다.

2 A: Eric, 너 좀 나아졌니? – (C) 네, 엄마. – (A) 다행이구나. 하지만 약을 먹어야 하는 것을 기억하렴. – (B) 네, 그럴게요.

3 상기시켜 줄 때 사용하는 Don't forget to ....는 Remember to .... 또는 Make sure to ....로 바꿔 쓸 수 있다.

4 Make sure (that) ....는 '반드시 …하도록 해.'라는 의미로 상기시켜 주는 표현이며 Don't forget to ...., Be sure to ...., Make sure to .... 등과 바꿔 쓸 수 있다.

5 빈칸 뒤에서 A가, 앞에서 자신이 한 말의 의미를 설명하므로, B의 빈칸에는 A가 말한 표현에 대한 설명을 요청하는 말이 알맞다.

6 ⓒ finally는 '마지막으로'라는 의미로, 열거하는 말에서 가장 마지막 순서를 이야기할 때 사용하는 것이 알맞다.

>> 서술형 평가

p. 62

1 (1) What do you mean (by that)? / What does that mean? (2) don't forget to bring an umbrella **2** (1) I tried playing the guitar (2) enjoys swimming in the sea **3** (1) Riding(To ride) (2) cooking (3) waiting **4** (1) worth watching (2) feel like quitting (3) look forward to seeing **5** (1) to do (2) to exercise (3) eating (4) to skip

1 설명을 요청할 때는 What do you mean?을 사용하고, 상기시킬 때는 Don't forget to .... 표현을 쓴다.

2 (1) try -ing: 시험 삼아 …해 보다 (2) enjoy는 동명사를 목적어로 취한다.

3 (1) 문장의 주어 자리이므로 동명사나 to부정사를 써야 한다. ride a skateboard: 스케이트보드를 타다 (2) 전치사 at의 목적어로 동명사를 쓴다. cook fish: 생선 요리를 하다 (3) mind는 동명사 목적어를 취한다. wait for a while: 잠시 기다리다

4 (1) be worth -ing: …할 가치가 있다 (2) feel like -ing: …하고 싶다 (3) look forward to -ing: …하기를 고대하다

5 (1), (2) decide와 plan은 to부정사를 목적어로 취한다. (3) stop+동명사: …하기를 멈추다 (4) try+to부정사: …하려고 애쓰다

>> Final Test

pp. 63~67

01 ④ **02** ② **03** stand **04** ② **05** (B) → (A) → (C) → (D) **06** ① **07** you mean (by that) **08** ⑤ **09** ③ **10** ② **11** ④ **12** Drawing **13** ④ **14** ⑤ **15** learning(to learn) **16** ⑤ **17** ③ **18** to send → sending **19** ⑤ **20** (1) joining (2) finding **21** ⑤ **22** (1) 너는 소금과 후추 사는 것을 잊어서는 안 된다. (2) 너는 소금과 후추 샀던 것을 잊었다. **23** ④ **24** I'll go to shopping with my mother. → I'll go shopping with my mother. **25** ④ **26** ③ **27** ② **28** ③ **29** ④ **30** ⑤

01 ④는 유의어 관계이고, 나머지는 모두 반의어 관계이다.

02 '손이나 손가락을 누군가 또는 어떤 물건 위에 놓다'는 '만지다, 접촉하다'를 뜻하는 touch를 의미한다.

03 '일어서다, 참다, 가판대'의 뜻을 모두 나타내는 단어는 stand이다.

04 Don't forget to ....는 '…할 것을 잊지 마.'라는 의미로 기

억을 상기시켜 주는 표현이며 Be sure to .... / Make sure to .... 등과 바꿔 쓸 수 있다.

05 A: Lucas, 네가 내 개를 돌봐줄 수 있니? – (B) 물론이지. 내가 알아야 할 게 있니? – (A) 응. 개를 혼자 있게 하면 안 돼. – (C) 알았어. 또 다른 건? – (D) 음, 먹이를 충분히 주는 것을 잊지 마.

06 ① Don't forget to ....를 써서 상기시키는 말에 대해 답하는 말로는 Okay, I won't.가 자연스럽다.

07 '그게 무슨 뜻이니?'라고 의미를 물을 때 What do you mean (by that)?을 쓴다.

08 내일 비가 올 테니 우산을 챙기는 것을 잊지 말라고 상기시켜 주는 표현이 빈칸에 알맞다. ⑤는 '우산을 가져갈 필요가 없다'의 의미로 알맞지 않다.

09 절차나 방법을 설명할 때, First(첫째로) 다음에 나올 말은 Second 또는 Then으로 시작하는 것이 알맞다. ③ Third는 어색하다.

10 ② forget 뒤에 동명사가 오면 '…한 것을 잊다'라는 뜻으로 과거의 일을 나타내고, to부정사가 오면 '…할 것을 잊다'라는 뜻으로 미래의 일을 나타낸다.

11 주어 역할을 하는 것은 to부정사나 동명사 모두 가능하지만, 전치사의 목적어 역할을 할 수 있는 것은 동명사이다.

12 to부정사와 동명사는 모두 주어 역할을 하며, 의미상 차이는 없다.

13 stop은 동명사를 목적어로 취하는 동사이다.

14 '…하느라 바쁘다'라는 의미의 be busy -ing가 쓰인 문장이다. 빈칸에는 동명사 helping이 알맞다.

15 동사 start 다음에는 동명사와 to부정사가 모두 목적어로 올 수 있다.

16 ① meet → meeting ② Take → Taking(To take)
③ washing → to wash ④ to cry → crying

17 love, start, begin, like는 동명사와 to부정사를 모두 목적어로 취할 수 있지만, ③ enjoy는 동명사만 목적어로 취한다.

18 last weekend는 과거를 나타내므로 '…했던 것을 기억하다'를 나타내기 위해 목적어로 동명사 sending이 와야 한다.

19 '…하기를 고대하다'는 look forward to -ing로 나타낸다.

20 (1) How about -ing?: …하는 게 어때? (2) have difficulty -ing: …하는 데 어려움이 있다

21 plan 다음에는 to부정사가, enjoy 다음에는 동명사가 목적어로 쓰인다.

22 forget 다음에 to부정사가 오면 미래의 일을, 동명사가 오면 과거의 일을 나타낸다.

23 ④는 진행의 의미를 나타내는 현재분사이지만 나머지는 ①, ② 목적어 ③ 보어 ⑤ 주어 역할을 하는 동명사이다.

24 '쇼핑하러 가다'라는 의미이므로 go shopping이 되어야 한다.

25

> 공기 중에 있는 먼지를 보는 것은 쉽지 않다. 그것은 매우 작다. 아무도 먼지를 좋아하지 않는다. 우리는 먼지를 없애기 위해 씻고, 닦아 내고, 걸레질을 한다. 많은 양의 먼지는 요즘 우리를 아프게 만든다. 그러나 여전히 우리는 먼지를 필요로 한다. 공기 중에 있는 먼지는 태양의 강한 빛을 차단하고 우리의 눈을 보호한다. 그것 없이, 우리는 비나 눈을 볼 수 없다.

주어진 문장은 먼지가 필요하다는 내용으로, 먼지의 긍정적인 역할에 관한 내용이 나열되기 전인 ④에 와야 한다.

26

> 유명한 작곡가, Dvorak은 기차 소리를 좋아했다. 기차 소리를 듣는 것은 그가 가장 좋아하는 취미가 되었다. 그는 기차를 너무 많이 좋아해서 심지어 기차역 근처로 이사를 갔다. 그는 소리만 듣고도 기차의 종류를 구별할 수 있었다. 그의 기차를 향한 사랑은 그의 클래식 음악인 '신세계 교향곡'에 영향을 미쳤다.

Dvorak은 기차 소리를 좋아했고 그것은 그의 음악에 영향을 미쳤다.

[27~28]

> 여러분은 인터넷으로 중고 물품을 사 본 적이 있는가? 그렇다면, 여러분은 공유 경제를 경험한 것이다. 공유 경제는 특정 상품, 서비스, 기술을 공유하는 것이 더 효율적이라는 생각을 토대로 한다. 그것은 사용 가능한 상품과 서비스 그리고 시간의 비용을 줄일 수 있기 때문에 효율적이다. 예를 들면, 만약 여러분이 드라이버를 오직 일 년에 한 번 사용해야 한다면, 자신만의 것을 사는 것보다 10달러를 주고 이웃에게 빌리는 것이 더 낫다.

27 ⓑ 접속사 that이 이끄는 절 안에서 주어 역할을 해야 하므로 동명사 형태인 sharing으로 고쳐야 한다.

28 공유 경제란 새로 물건을 사는 것보다 빌리는 게 효율적이라는 것이므로 빈칸에는 ③ '자신만의 것을 사는 것'이 알맞다.

[29~30]

> 16세 소녀인 Jessica Watson은 2009년 10월 18일 요트로 출항했다. 많은 사람들은 그녀가 작은 요트를 타고 세계 일주를 하는 것을 걱정했다. 그러나 그녀는 스스로 도전하는 것을 즐겼다. 무엇도 그녀를 막을 수 없었다. 그녀는 북동쪽으로 향하여 남태평양을 가로질러 대서양을 건너 남아프리카로 향했다. 그 여정 동안, 그녀의 요트는 몇 번이나 전복되었고 그녀는 큰 폭풍을 만났다. 그렇다고 하더라도 그녀는 포기하지 않았다. 7개월 후, 그녀는 호주로 안전하게 돌아왔다.

29 ④ 요트가 뒤집어지고 폭풍이 불어도 세계 일주를 포기하지 않았다고 했다.

30 밑줄 친 challenging과 ⑤는 목적어로 쓰인 동명사이다. ①, ④ 동명사 보어 ② 현재분사 ③ 동명사 주어

Lesson 04 분사, 수동태

>> Grammar Practice

pp. 72~75

A1 (1) playing (2) talking (3) left (4) made (5) parked

A2 (1) repaired (2) following (3) satisfied (4) broken (5) spoken

B1 (1) ⓐ (2) ⓒ (3) ⓐ (4) ⓒ (5) ⓑ (6) ⓑ (7) ⓐ

B2 (1) ⓑ (2) ⓐ (3) ⓑ (4) ⓐ (5) ⓐ (6) ⓑ (7) ⓑ

C1 (1) exciting (2) amazed (3) shocked (4) satisfying (5) confused

C2 (1) confused, confusing (2) excited, exciting

D1 (1) is loved (2) discovered (3) were eaten (4) Were, made (5) Is, taught

D2 (1) wasn't opened by (2) didn't make (3) weren't baked by

E1 (1) will be taught (2) are being corrected

E2 (1) must be cleaned (2) will be built (3) may be hidden

F1 (1) by people (2) by someone (3) by them (4) by somebody

F2 (1) will be satisfied with (2) were surprised at (3) was covered with

>> Grammar Test

pp. 76~77

01 ⑤ **02** ④ **03** ④ **04** playing the violin **05** ⑤ **06** ④ **07** ② **08** ① **09** ② **10** was built, is owned by, is used **11** ② **12** ③ **13** Math questions were solved very easily by her.

01 '(물을) 마시고 있는'이라는 능동, 진행의 의미로 The cats를 꾸미므로 현재분사가 알맞다.

02 '부서진'이라는 수동, 완료의 의미로 cars를 꾸미므로 과거분사가 알맞다.

03 '(셔츠를) 입은'이라는 능동의 의미이므로 현재분사가 알맞다.

04 주어진 문장은 '바이올린을 연주하고 있는 그 소녀는 Dave의 여동생이다.'로 쓸 수 있다. playing the violin이 The girl을 꾸미는 문장으로 완성한다.

05 • be satisfied with: …에 만족하다 • be interested in: …에 관심이 있다

06 ⓐ 주격보어로 쓰인 동명사 ⓑ face를 꾸미는 현재분사 ⓒ 진행시제를 만드는 현재분사 ⓓ stick의 용도를 나타내는 동명사 ⓔ '신나는'의 의미인 현재분사

07 ② 수동태의 의문문은 〈be동사+주어+과거분사+by+목적격?〉의 어순이어야 한다. (direct → directed)

08 ① Felix가 피곤한 것이므로 tired로 써야 한다.

09 ② her name이 불려진 것이므로 called로 써야 한다.

10 내용상 모두 수동태가 되어야 하고 첫 번째 빈칸의 내용은 1967년도에 대한 것이므로 과거형을 써야 한다.

11 과거형 수동태는 〈was(were)+과거분사〉 형태이다.

12 조동사 수동태는 〈조동사+be+과거분사〉 형태이다.

13 밑줄 친 문장의 목적어 math questions를 주어로 하여 수동태 문장을 완성한다.

>> Reading

pp. 78~79

1 Her long hair must be lowered by Rapunzel **2** But **3** ③ **4** ③

[1~2]

가능한가, 불가능한가

애니메이션 영화에서 놀라운 일들이 가능하다. 하지만 그것이 실생활에서 실제로 가능할까?

당신의 머리카락을 내려 줘요, Rapunzel!

애니메이션에서 Rapunzel은 그녀의 탑으로 사람들을 들이기 위해 그녀의 긴 머리카락을 내려 줘야 한다. 하지만 사람의 머리카락이 정말 사람을 지탱할 수 있었을까?

놀랍게도 그렇다! 머리카락 한 올은 100그램을 지탱할 수 있고 평균적으로 머리에는 약 12만 개의 머리카락이 있다. 그 모든 머리카락이면 코끼리 두 마리를 지탱할 수 있다! 그녀의 머리카락으로 Rapunzel은 사람을 지탱할 능력이 있다. 하지만 그녀는 그녀의 머리카락을 강하고 무거운 뭔가의 둘레에 감아야 한다. 그러지 않으면, 그녀는 목이 매우 아플 것이다.

1 조동사가 들어간 문장이므로 〈조동사+be+과거분사〉의 형태로 수동태 문장을 만든다.

2 (A) Rapunzel이 머리카락으로 사람을 든 사실과, 그것이 실제 가능할지 묻는 것, (B) Rapunzel이 머리카락으로 사람을 지탱할 수 있다는 사실과, 그러기 위한 전제 조건은 각각 역접의 관계이므로 빈칸에는 But이 알맞다.

3

Safe Home for Children을 돕는, 아홉 번째 연례 벼룩시장이 6월 2일과 3일, 토요일과 일요일에 Green Park에서 열릴 예정이다. Safe Home for Children은 전쟁에서 버려진 아이들을 돕기 위해 1985년에 설립되었다. 요즘 이 기관은 전쟁 난민촌에 있는 아이들을 돕는다. 판매는 오전 10시에 시작한다. 누구나 벼룩시장에서 물품을 사고 팔

수 있다. 물품을 팔고 싶은 사람들은 자리와 텐트를 대여하기 위해 Rena Danes에게 미리 연락을 해야 한다. 점심시간 동안 무료 간이식당을 이용할 수 있을 것이다.

③ Rena Danes를 어디서 만날 수 있는지 언급되지 않았다.

4

Boxing Day는 크리스마스의 다음 날에 기념되는 기념일이다. 그것은 영국에서 유래하였고 지금은 호주와 캐나다와 같은 많은 국가에서 기념된다. Boxing Day가 언제 시작되었는지는 아무도 확실히 알지 못한다. 몇몇은 몇 세기 전이라고 믿는다. 주인들은 크리스마스 동안 하인들의 수고를 보상하기 위해 상자에 담은 선물을 하인들에게 주곤 했다. 요즘 그것은 이제 휴식과 쇼핑의 날이다. 쇼핑몰들은 Boxing Day 세일에 쇼핑하려고 온 사람들로 가득 찬다.

③ 크리스마스 동안 주인들이 하인들이 수고한 데 대한 보답으로 주인들이 하인들에게 선물을 줬다고 했다.

Expression Test

pp. 80~81

1 ⑤ **2** How(What) **3** ③ **4** ③ **5** ① **6** ②

1 I can't wait.는 '나는 (…하는 것을) 몹시 기대하고 있다.'라는 뜻으로 기대를 나타내는 표현이다.

2 B가 좋은 생각이라고 말하며, 그림 보는 것을 좋아한다고 답했으므로, A의 말은 미술관에 가자고 제안하는 표현이 알맞다. 빈칸 뒤에 about going이 있으므로, 빈칸에는 How나 What이 알맞다.

3 A: 우리 현장 학습이 다음 월요일이지, 그렇지? - (B) 그래. 나는 그것을 고대하고 있어. 그런데 우리 어디로 가니? - (C) 우리는 음악 박물관에 갈 거야. - (A) 멋지구나.

4 ①, ②, ④, ⑤는 저녁 식사 후에 조깅을 하자는 제안의 표현이고, ③은 저녁 식사 후에 조깅을 할지 묻는 표현이다.

5 B가 제안에 대한 거절의 대답을 했으므로 그 이유가 이어져야 한다. ① '피곤해서 저녁을 함께 먹을 수 없다'라는 흐름이 자연스럽다.

6 I'm really looking forward to ....는 기대를 말하는 표현으로 I can't wait to ....와 바꿔 쓸 수 있다.

서술형 평가

p. 82

1 (1) let me help you (2) I'm looking forward to my family trip **2** (1) was taken (2) It was sent **3** (1) were thrown → threw (2) exciting → excited **4** (1) carrying books to(into) the library (2) fixing the broken fence **5** (1) was invited (2) sitting (3) was surprised

1 도움을 제안할 때 Let me help you.라는 표현을 쓰고, 기대를 표현할 때는 I'm looking forward to ....를 써서 나타낸다. to 뒤에는 명사나 동명사를 쓴다.

2 주어가 행동을 당할 때 〈be동사+과거분사(+by+행위자)〉의 형태로 수동태를 쓴다.

3 (1) '파티를 열었다'라는 능동의 의미이므로 threw (2) '신이 난 소년'이라는 의미로 수동의 의미이므로 과거분사 excited

4 빈칸에는 분사를 이용하여 각 문장의 주어를 꾸미는 말을 쓰는 것이 알맞다. 분사를 이용하여 능동, 진행의 의미일 때는 현재분사를, 수동, 완료의 의미일 때는 과거분사를 쓴다.

5 (1) 차 마시는 모임에 초대되었으므로 수동태로 표현한다. (2) 가운데 앉아 있는 사람이므로 The person을 꾸미는 현재분사를 쓴다. (3) 쥐가 차 따르는 것을 보고 놀란 것을 수동태로 표현한다.

Final Test

pp. 83~87

01 ② **02** ③ **03** ① **04** looking forward to **05** can't wait to **06** ③ **07** (B) → (C) → (A) **08** ④ **09** ④ **10** (a) scored (b) was scored **11** ④ **12** ③ **13** ⑤ **14** ④ **15** ④ **16** The teacher sent him out of the classroom. **17** ② **18** with **19** ② **20** ② **21** ④ **22** ④ **23** ③ **24** ④ **25** ③ **26** ② **27** ⑤ **28** ④ **29** ④ **30** ③

01 '종이나 천 같은 것을 감아서 어떤 것을 덮다'는 wrap(포장하다, 싸다)에 해당하는 영영풀이이다.

02 ability(능력): 뭔가를 수행하는 데 필요한 육체적, 정신적 힘 또는 기술(skill)

03 let down(내리다) = lower(내리다, 낮추다)

04 A가 마지막에 I can't wait!라고 말하는 것으로 보아 A는 미나의 생일 파티를 고대하고 있음을 알 수 있으므로 빈칸에는 (I'm) looking forward to가 알맞다.

05 나는 …하는 것을 매우 기대해: I can't wait to ....

06 B가 가격을 묻고 있는 것으로 보아, B는 물건을 사려는 손님이고, A는 점원이다. 빈칸에는 손님을 맞아 '도와 드릴까요?'라고 묻는 말이 자연스럽다.

07 (B) 나는 이번 월요일이 매우 기대돼. - (C) 왜? 네게 특별한 계획이라도 있니? - (A) 응, 나는 탁아소에서 아이들을 위해 봉사활동을 할 계획이야.

08 ④ 긍정적으로 생각하라는 A의 말에 B가 동의하는 말을 한 후 좋은 생각이 아니라는 응답을 하는 것은 어색하다.

09 A가 콘서트에 가자고 하자 다음 주 시험을 위해 공부해야 한다고 했으므로 빈칸에는 거절하는 표현이 알맞다. ④는 제안에 긍정적으로 답하는 표현이다.

10 (a) 'Maradona가 첫 번째 골을 기록했다.' → 능동태
(b) 'Maradona에 의해 첫 번째 골이 기록되었다.' → 수동태

11 • 내가 로봇 만들기에 흥미로운 감정을 느끼게 되는 것(수동)이므로 과거분사가 알맞다. • 로봇 만들기가 흥미로운 감정을 유발하는 것(능동)이므로 현재분사가 알맞다.

12 • '(검은 드레스를) 입고 있는'이라는 의미로 The girl을 꾸미므로 현재분사가 알맞다. • '(이탈리아에서) 구입된'이라는 의미로 the bag을 꾸미므로 과거분사가 알맞다.

13 • 문장 끝에 by my mother가 있고 주어가 복수이므로 빈칸에는 수동태 의문문을 이끄는 Were가 알맞다. • 문장 끝에 by children이 있고 빈칸 앞에 should가 있으므로 빈칸에는 수동태 문장을 구성하는 be eaten이 알맞다.

14 by Edgar Allen Poe로 보아 수동태(be동사+과거분사)이고, 주어가 단수이므로 be동사로 was를 써야 한다.

15 by my brother로 보아 수동태 문장이며, 진행형 수동태는 〈be동사+being+과거분사〉 형태로 나타낸다.

16 수동태 문장의 행위자(The teacher)를 주어로, 수동태 문장의 동사 was sent가 과거이므로, 과거 동사 sent를 써서 능동태 문장을 만든다.

17 ② 수동태 부정문은 〈be동사+not+과거분사+by+목적격〉 형태이다. (didn't broken → weren't broken)

18 • be covered with: …으로 덮여 있다 / • be pleased with: …에 기뻐하다

19 ② 행위자가 불분명하면 〈by+목적격〉을 생략할 수 있다.

20 ①, ③, ④, ⑤는 '잠을 자고 있는'이라는 의미로 뒤의 명사를 꾸미는 현재분사이고, ②는 '잠을 자기 위한'의 의미로 '용도'를 나타내는 동명사이다. / sleeping bag: 침낭

21 ④ '…에 의해 만들어지다'는 수동의 의미이므로 was made by가 되어야 한다.

22 ④ 진행형 수동태: 〈be동사+being+과거분사〉

23 분사가 다른 어구와 함께 명사를 꾸밀 때는 명사의 뒤에 온다.
→ I bought a shirt made in France.

24 ⓐ '이야기를 하고 있다.'라는 의미이므로 talked는 진행의 의미인 talking으로 ⓒ '삶아진'이라는 완료의 의미로 eggs를 꾸미도록 boiled로 ⓓ 광경이 놀라운 감정을 유발하는 것(능동)이므로 amazing으로 쓴다.

25

> 하늘로 수백의 음식들을 출력하는 기계를 발명하는 한 과학자에 관한 애니메이션 영화가 있었다. 핫도그와 치킨들로 가득 찬 하늘을 상상해 보라. 사실, 이것은 가능하다. 3D 프린터는 이제 음식을 출력할 수 있다. 식용 잉크로 3D 프린터는 신선한 햄버거를 출력할 수 있다. 여러분은 그것의 맛이 걱정되는가? 걱정하지 마라. 그것은 맛이 훌륭하다.

뒤에 식용 잉크로 음식을 출력하는 것이 가능하다는 내용이 오므로 빈칸에는 '가능한'의 의미인 possible이 알맞다.

26

> 옛날에, 사람들은 물건을 사거나 팔 때 돈을 사용하지 않았다. 대신에, 그들은 물건을 교환했다. 이후에, 사람들은 특이한 것들을 돈으로 사용하기 시작했다. 예를 들어, Yap이라 불리는 작은 섬의 사람들은 큰 덩어리의 돌을 돈으로 사용했다. 몇몇 아시아 국가에서는 차가 돈으로 쓰였다. 고대 로마 군인들은 소금을 봉급으로 받았다. 우리는 그 사회의 사람들이 그것을 돈으로 사용하기로 약속하면 어떤 것도 돈이 될 수 있다고 말할 수 있다.

돈이 거래의 수단으로 활용되기 시작한 때, 화폐 역할을 했던 다양한 물건들이 빈칸 앞에 나열되어 있다. 문맥상, 사회의 사람들이 동의하면 '어떤 것도 돈이 될 수 있다'는 내용이 빈칸에 알맞다.

[27~28]

> 직업 체험의 날에 우리 반은 방송국에 방문했다. 거기서 나는 앵커들이 뉴스를 전하는 책상에 앉았다. 정면에 걸린 화면이 두 개 있었다. 나는 그 화면에 쓰여 있는 뉴스 대본을 크게 읽었다. 다른 화면에서 나는 TV에 나오는 내 모습을 볼 수 있었다. 나는 진짜 뉴스 앵커처럼 보였다. 그 다음에 우리는 구내식당에 가서 점심을 먹었다. 운 좋게도, 나는 내가 제일 좋아하는 앵커가 커피를 마시는 것을 보았다. 아주 기억에 남는 하루였다.

27 직업 체험의 날에 방송국에 방문해서 앵커 역할을 체험해 보고, 방송국 구내식당에서 앵커도 만난 것에 대해 운이 좋았다는 것으로 보아 글쓴이는 '신이 난' 상태이다.

28 (A) 화면이 걸려 있다는 능동의 의미이므로 현재분사가, (B) 글씨가 적혀 있는 것과 (C) 보이는 것은 수동의 의미이므로 과거분사가 알맞다.

[29~30]

> 인도 시골에는 학교와 학생들을 위한 자원이 충분하지 않다. 대부분의 학생들은 적절한 책상을 가지고 있지 않다. 비영리 단체 Aarambh는 Help Desk라고 불리는 창의적인 해결책을 생각해 냈다. 그것은 상자용 종이로 만들어진다. 그것은 일종의 '업사이클'이다. 그 판지 책상은 책가방으로 멜 수 있지만 특별한 방법으로 접히면, 그것은 책상으로 변한다. 그것은 생산하는 데 비용이 20루피밖에 들지 않는다.

29 ④ Help Desk는 가방으로 활용할 수 있으나, 옷으로 활용할 수 있는지는 알 수 없다.

30 ⓐ 주어 resources가 복수이므로 there are가 알맞다. ⓑ 현재시제의 have의 부정문 don't have ⓒ be made of: …으로 만들어지다 ⓓ '착용될 수 있다'의 의미가 되도록 be worn ⓔ '특별한 방법으로 접힐 때'의 의미가 되는 수동태 is folded

Lesson 05 조동사

Grammar Practice pp. 92~95

A1 (1) bake (2) take (3) could (4) able to (5) were (6) be able to (7) answer
A2 (1) you can't (2) Were, wasn't (3) Can(May)
B1 (1) You may have my seat. (2) Lydia may be hungry. (3) May I have these cookies?
B2 (1) turn (2) may not (3) be studying (4) join (5) not rain (6) lose (7) make (8) be
B3 (1) Stella may not be in the garden. (2) It may sound strange, but it's true. (3) You may not use my computer. (4) Daisy may not stay at home this weekend.
C1 (1) ⓐ (2) ⓑ (3) ⓑ (4) ⓐ (5) ⓑ (6) ⓐ
C2 (1) has to (2) need not (3) doesn't have(need) to
D1 (1) should (2) should not (3) should not
E1 (1) had (2) used (3) be (4) finish (5) better not
E2 (1) used to (2) had better (3) had better not
E3 (1) coaches → coach (2) tells → tell (3) had not better → had better not

Grammar Test pp. 96~97

01 ③ **02** not better → better not **03** ⑤ **04** ⑤
05 (1) have to (2) Are, able (3) ought(have) to **06** ⑤
07 must(should) **08** ③ **09** ⑤ **10** ④ **11** ③ **12** (1) may (might) be sick (2) doesn't have(need) to **13** ③

01 〈보기〉와 ③의 must는 '강한 추측'을 나타내고, 나머지는 모두 '의무'를 나타낸다.
02 had better의 부정문은 〈had better not+동사원형〉이다.
03 ⑤ had better는 '…하는 게 좋겠다'의 의미이고, shouldn't는 금지를 나타낸다.
04 지금은 탈 수 없지만 곧 탈 수 있게 될 것이라는 흐름이므로 미래형이 알맞다. can의 미래형은 will be able to로 표현한다.
05 (1) must가 '…해야 한다'라는 의무의 뜻일 때는 have to로 바꿔 쓸 수 있다. (2) can은 be able to로 바꿔 쓸 수 있고, be able to가 들어간 문장의 의문문은 〈be동사+주어+able to+동사원형 …?〉의 형태가 된다. (3) should는 의무의 뜻으로 ought to로 바꿔 쓸 수 있다.
06 첫 번째 빈칸에는 과거의 일이고 '…해야 했다'의 뜻이 되어야 하므로 had to가 알맞다. 두 번째 빈칸에는 과거의 일이고 '…할 수 있었다'의 뜻이 되어야 하므로 could가 알맞다.
07 〈must(should) not+동사원형〉은 '…하면 안 된다'의 뜻으로 금지를 나타내는 표현이다.
08 '체중이 많이 나간다'라는 말에 대한 충고의 표현이 이어지는 것이 적절하다. should, need to, ought to, had better 등은 충고의 표현으로 쓰인다.
09 B의 말은 화가 난 여자 친구에게 꽃을 사 주고 사과해야 한다는 충고이므로 '…할 필요 없다'의 의미인 need not은 알맞지 않다.
10 '…을 사용해도 되나요?'의 뜻이 되어야 하므로 허가를 구하는 Can I use ...? 또는 May I use ...?를 써야 한다.
11 ③ '…하곤 했다'는 과거의 습관을 나타낼 때는 〈used to+동사원형〉의 형태로 쓴다.
12 (1) '…일지도 모른다'는 추측의 표현은 may 또는 might를 써서 나타낸다. (2) '…할 필요가 없다'는 표현은 don't have(need) to를 써서 나타낸다. 주어가 3인칭 단수이므로 doesn't로 쓴다.
13 must가 '…임에 틀림없다'라는 의미로 강한 추측을 나타낼 때는 have to와 바꿔 쓰지 않는다.

Reading pp. 98~99

1 ① 2 could 3 ④ 4 ④

[1~2]

제 얘기에 채널을 고정하세요.
랩을 하세요.

안녕하세요. 저는 MC Joy입니다. 여러분은 자신만의 랩 가사를 쓰고 싶은가요? 모든 것이 랩을 위한 이야기가 될 수 있기 때문에 여러분은 무엇에 관해서든 랩을 할 수 있어요. 저는 제가 버스에 있을 때, 샤워 중에, 또는 침대에서 아이디어를 얻어요. 저는 제 생각을 적고, 제가 랩 가사를 쓸 때 그것을 사용해요. 랩 가사를 쓰는 데는 규칙이 없어요. 여러분은 오늘 시작할 수 있어요!

기이한 애완동물

"기이한 애완동물"에 오신 걸 환영합니다! 애완동물 키우기는 즐겁습니다. 오늘 저는 제 애완 고슴도치, Polly를 소개하겠습니다. 제가 처음 Polly를 만났을 때, 그 아이는 무척 두려워했습니다. 그 애가 자신의 가시를 세웠기 때문에, 저는 그 애를 들지 못했어요. 저는 그 애의 우리에 제 티셔츠를 뒀고 그 애는 제 체취에 익숙해졌습니다. 마침내 저는 제 손에 그 애를 들 수 있었습니다. 이제 Polly는 제 절친한 친구이고 항상 저를 행복하게 합니다.

1 (A) 빈칸 뒤에 나열된 상황은 랩 가사를 위한 아이디어를 얻는 때이므로 접속사 when이 알맞다. (B) 자신의 애완동물

이 자신에게 익숙해지도록 한 노력의 결과로 애완동물을 손으로 들 수 있게 되었다는 내용이므로 빈칸에는 Finally(마침내)가 알맞다.

2 '…할 수 있다'를 뜻하는 be able to는 조동사 can으로 바꿔 쓸 수 있다. be동사가 과거형이므로 could가 알맞다.

3

> 어느 인플루언서가 소셜 미디어에 멋진 야구모자 사진을 올린다. 그러면, 많은 폴로어들은 그것을 보고, 그 야구모자를 산다. 패션 인플루언서는 패션 동향을 만들어 낸다. 요즘에는, 세계 인구의 약 40퍼센트가 매일 소셜 미디어를 사용한다. 이들은 소셜 미디어에서 인플루언서들을 우러러보며 결정을 할 때 그들을 따른다. 유명인들, 블로거들, 유명한 작가들, 그리고 정치인들이 인플루언서가 될 수 있다. 그들은 우리를 이끌면서 동시에 잘못 이끌 수 있다. 그러므로 소셜 미디어 사용자들은 그들이 소셜 미디어에서 읽는 것에 대해 비판적인 사고를 가져야 한다.

주어진 문장은 소셜 미디어에서 읽는 것에 대해 비판적 사고를 가져야 한다는 문장 앞에 들어가는 것이 적절하다.

4

> 제주도의 전통적인 주택에는 특별한 대문인 정낭이 있었다. 그것은 집의 입구에 놓인 길고 두꺼운 통나무들로 만들어졌다. 정낭은 3개의 통나무로 이루어져 있다. 3개의 통나무가 모두 내려져 있으면 집주인은 집에 있다. 만약 3개의 통나무가 모두 제자리에 있다면, 집에는 아무도 없다. 통나무 2개가 제자리에 있는 것은 집주인이 오랫동안 돌아오지 않을 것임을 의미한다. 그러면 마을 주민들은 그 집에 들러서 거기 있는 소들과 돼지들을 돌보아 주곤 했다. 만약 통나무 1개만 제자리에 있다면, 그러면 그것은 주인이 곧 돌아올 것임을 의미한다.

④ 집주인이 오랫동안 집을 비우면, 마을 주민들이 들러서 가축들을 돌봐 주곤 했다고 언급되어 있다.

Expression Test

pp. 100~101

1 What is, like **2** ④ **3** ⑤ **4** ① **5** ② **6** (B) → (A) → (C)

1 인물의 특징을 묻는 표현은 What is ... like?이다.

2 외모를 묻는 질문으로 What do(es) ... look like? 또는 How do(es) ... look?을 쓸 수 있다.

3 밑줄 친 부분은 우울해 보이는 B에게 왜 그런지 묻는 표현이므로 ⑤ Why are you so disappointed?로 쓸 수 있다.

4 ① Bobby가 누군지 묻는 질문에 대해 그가 똑똑하다고 답하는 것은 어색하다.

5 ② 시험을 잘 못 본 사람에게 격려하는 표현이 들어가야 알맞다.

6 너는 형제자매가 몇 명 있니? – (B) 나는 두 명의 오빠와 한 명의 언니가 있어. – (A) 너의 언니는 어떻게 생겼니? – (C) 그녀는 굉장히 예뻐. 그녀는 단발머리야.

서술형 평가

p. 102

1 (1) What's the matter? (2) You'll do fine. **2** (1) must not eat or drink (2) must turn off your cell phone **3** (1) is able to (2) have to **4** (1) had better not eat (2) used to live with us **5** (1) used to (2) have to (3) may (4) should

1 (1) 기분이 안 좋아 보인다고 했으므로 무슨 일인지 상황을 묻는 표현 What's the matter?가 알맞다. (2) 걱정하지 말라는 말 다음에 격려하는 표현을 쓰는 것이 자연스럽다.

2 (1) 음식 섭취 금지 표시이므로 〈must not+동사원형〉을 써서 금지를 나타낸다. (2) 전화 통화 금지 표시이므로 〈must+동사원형〉을 써서 의무(전화를 꺼야 한다)를 나타낸다.

3 (1) can은 능력을 나타내는 조동사로 be able to와 같은 의미이다. (2) must는 '…해야 한다'라는 의무를 나타내는 조동사로 have to와 같은 의미이다.

4 (1) had better not+동사원형: …하지 않는 게 좋다 (2) used to+동사원형: …했었다, …하곤 했다

5 (1) used to+동사원형: (예전에) …했었다 (2) have to+동사원형: …해야 한다 (3) may not+동사원형: …이 아닐지도 모른다 (4) should+동사원형: …해야 한다

Final Test

pp. 103~107

01 ② **02** ② **03** ⑤ **04** ④ **05** ⑤ **06** is wearing **07** ③ **08** What does he look like? **09** ① **10** used to **11** ⑤ **12** ④ **13** (1) was able to (2) ought(has) to (3) should **14** (1) D (2) D (3) S **15** (1) getting → get (2) has to → must **16** ④ **17** ① **18** had better not **19** ⑤ **20** ⑤ **21** I couldn't **22** ⑤ **23** ① **24** (a) must be (b) may be **25** ① **26** ⑤ **27** ① **28** ② **29** ③ **30** ③

01 어떤 사람의 성격이나 생각에 대해 좋은 의견을 지니는 것은 '존경하다'는 뜻이다.

02 make a noise: 시끄럽게 하다 / make a mistake: 실수하다

03 ①, ②, ③, ④는 격려하는 표현이고, ⑤는 경고하는 표현이다.

04 인물의 특징을 묻는 표현이므로 How can you describe ...? 또는 What kind of person is ...?로 바꿔 쓸 수 있다.

05 ⑤ 'Oscar는 무엇을 찾고 있니?'라는 말에 '그는 선글라스와 모자를 쓰고 있어.'라고 대답하는 것은 어색하다.

06 A가 B에게 여동생의 외모에 대해 물었으므로 She is wearing ....을 써서 안경을 착용한 모습을 설명한다.

07 A의 질문에 대해 B가 Scott의 성격을 말하고 있으므로, 인물의 특징을 묻는 내용이 되도록 각각 What, like를 쓴다.

08 How does he look?은 외모를 묻는 표현이므로 What does he look like?로 바꿔 쓸 수 있다.

09 ① 불확실한 추측을 나타낼 때는 may 또는 might를 쓴다.

10 〈used to＋동사원형〉은 '(예전에) …했었다(지금은 아니다)'란 뜻으로, 과거 한때 지속된 상태를 나타낸다.

11 비행기가 이륙할 예정이어서 안전 벨트를 해야 하는 상황이므로 첫 번째 빈칸에는 의무를 나타내는 must가 알맞다. 두 번째 빈칸에는 '(예전에) …했었다'의 뜻으로 과거의 지속적인 상태나 사실을 나타내는 used to가 알맞다.

12 첫 번째 빈칸은 유리창이 더러워서 청소해야 하는 상황이다. 앞 문장이 과거시제이므로 had to가 알맞다. 두 번째 빈칸에는 a few years ago라는 과거 부사구가 있으므로 과거형 could가 알맞다.

13 (1) could는 was(were) able to로 바꿔 쓸 수 있다. (2) should는 ought to, 또는 have to로 바꿔 쓸 수 있다. (3) had better를 이용한 충고하는 말은 should를 써서 바꿔 쓸 수 있다.

14 (1) (a) 추측 (b) 허락 (2) (a) 능력 (b) 허락 (3) (a), (b) 의무

15 (1) used to 다음에는 동사원형을 쓴다. (2) must는 '…임에 틀림없다'의 뜻으로 강한 추측을 나타낸다. 이때는 〈have to＋동사원형〉과 바꿔 쓸 수 없다.

16 〈used to＋동사원형〉은 '(이전에) …했었다(지금은 아니다)'라는 뜻이므로 앞의 사실과 반대인 '극장이 없다'라는 내용이 와야 자연스럽다.

17 ① 〈had better＋동사원형〉의 부정은 〈had better＋not＋동사원형〉이다. (→ You'd better not go there.)

18 '…하지 않는 편이 좋겠다'는 〈had better not＋동사원형〉으로 나타낸다.

19 had better＋동사원형: …하는 편이 좋겠다

20 ⑤ had to의 부정은 didn't have to이다.

21 Could you ...?에 대한 부정의 응답은 No, I couldn't.이다.

22 과거의 습관을 나타내므로 used to가 알맞다.

23 첫 번째 빈칸은 지난주의 일이므로 had to가 알맞고, 두 번째 빈칸은 '…하는 편이 좋겠다'의 뜻으로 had better가 알맞다.

24 (a) 앞의 내용으로 볼 때 틀림없는 확신을 나타내는 말이 와야 한다. (b) 잘 모르는 상황이므로 불확실한 추측이 와야 한다.

25

> 우리는 선 자세에서 시작할 거예요. 첫째로, 여러분의 무게 중심을 오른발로 옮기세요. 왼쪽 무릎을 굽히고 왼발을 올리세요. 왼쪽 발목을 오른손으로 잡고 오른쪽 허벅다리 안쪽에 놓으세요. 이제 여러분은 오른발로만 서 있습니다. 균형을 조심히 유지하세요. 마지막으로 가슴 앞쪽에 기도하는 모양으로 두 손바닥을 맞대고 미세요. 이 자세의 이름을 추측할 수 있나요? 이것은 나무 자세입니다.

다리 자세를 완성한 후 두 손을 맞대고 밀어 기도하듯이 가슴 앞으로 손을 모으라고 했으므로 ①은 내용과 일치하지 않는다.

[26~27]

> 저는 예전에 머리가 길어서 아침에 시간을 아끼기 위해 이 헤어드라이어를 샀습니다. 그것은 강하고 제 머리카락을 5분 안에 빠르게 말립니다. 저는 그것을 2년 전에 구입했고 그것은 여전히 좋은 상태입니다. 저는 최근에 머리를 잘라서 예전만큼 자주 드라이어를 사용하지 않습니다. 저는 그것을 30달러에 팔기를 원합니다. 당신이 저의 집에 드라이어를 가지러 오거나 제가 배송 서비스로 그것을 보내줄 수 있습니다. 210-4567 번호로, Julie Benz에게 연락해 주세요.

26 ⑤ 구매자가 글쓴이의 집에 드라이어를 가지러 오거나 글쓴이가 배송 서비스로 보내줄 수 있다고 했다.

27 ⓐ 〈used to＋동사원형〉: …하곤 했다(지금은 아니다)

28

> **Tom** 스케이트 강습에 관한 정보를 알 수 있을까요?
> **점원** 그럼요. 초보이신가요?
> **Tom** 네, 그렇습니다.
> **점원** 좋습니다. 저희는 1일 기초 강습을 제공합니다. 강습 후에 바로 스케이트를 타실 수 있을 거예요.
> **Tom** 알겠습니다. 언제 시작하나요?
> **점원** 오늘 3시예요. 강습을 들으시려면 먼저 이 양식을 작성해 주세요. 한 가지 더요. 헬멧을 꼭 쓰셔야 해요.
> **Tom** 네. 제 헬멧을 가져왔습니다.
> **점원** 좋습니다. 양식을 다 작성하신 후에, 그것을 상자에 넣어 주세요.

마지막에 직원이 양식을 작성해서 상자에 넣으라고 했으므로, Tom은 양식을 작성할 것이다.

[29~30]

> 나는 오랫동안 도시와 도시를 돌아다녔다. 나는 여행하는 게 아니라 일하고 있다. 귀신의 집에 적합한 곳을 찾기 시작한 지 2주가 되었다. 여러분은 내가 어떤 종류의 직업을 가지고 있는지 추측할 수 있는가? 나는 야외 촬영 관리자이다. 나는 영화나 텔레비전 드라마를 위한 장소를 찾아다닌다. 야외 촬영 관리자가 되기 위해, 여러분은 여행을 많이 해야 하고 장소와 분위기를 보는 좋은 안목을 키워야 한다. 사진을 찍고 장소들에 관한 메모를 하는 것도 많은 도움이 될 것이다.

29 글쓴이는 야외 촬영 관리자로서 영화나 드라마의 촬영 장소를 알아보는 일을 한다고 했다.

30 '…해야 한다'의 의미인 have to는 must와 바꿔 쓸 수 있다.

듣기 실전 모의고사

01회 듣기 실전 모의고사

pp. 112~119

01 ① 02 ② 03 ④ 04 ⑤ 05 ② 06 ② 07 ⑤ 08 ⑤
09 ④ 10 ⑤ 11 ④ 12 ③ 13 ② 14 ③ 15 ⑤ 16 ④
17 ⑤ 18 ④ 19 ③ 20 ①

Dictation Test

01 weather forecast, outdoor, stop, shine **02** looking for, sells, pictures **03** wrong, worried, kidding, serious, Check **04** wearing, birthday present, special **05** runny nose, fever, get better **06** let, in, worried, holding, shoes **07** shopped, walked, baseball game **08** leaving, project, heavily, ride **09** never heard, successful, by herself **10** useful, belong to, transfer **11** first thing, worse, worse, plant **12** change, order, found, delivery **13** costs, discount, cash, credit card **14** driving at, speed limit, ticket **15** for help, solve, lifesaver **16** free, showing, look after **17** check out, fantasy, library **18** open, all kinds, parking lot **19** hiking, sunbathed, warmer, else **20** favorite, noisy, must, classical

01 ①

M Good morning. It's time for today's weather forecast. In Seoul, it will be sunny all day long, so you will be able to enjoy outdoor activities. In Daejeon, it will be cloudy and there will be showers in the afternoon. In Busan, it will rain in the morning, but the rain will stop and the sun will shine in the afternoon.

남 안녕하세요. 오늘의 일기 예보 시간입니다. 서울은 하루 종일 화창하겠으니 야외 활동을 즐기실 수 있겠습니다. 대전은 흐리고 오후에 소나기가 내리겠습니다. 부산은 오전에는 비가 오겠으나, 오후에는 비가 그치고 해가 비치겠습니다.

02 ②

M How may I help you?
W I'm looking for a white T-shirt.
M What about this one over here? It sells very well.
W Umm.... I don't like the square neck.
M Then how about this one? It has a round neck.
W I don't want any pictures on it. I need a simple one.
M Maybe this is the one you're looking for. Right?
W Perfect! I'll take it.

남 무엇을 도와드릴까요?
여 흰색 티셔츠를 찾고 있어요.
남 이쪽에 있는 이것은 어떠세요? 매우 잘 팔리거든요.
여 음…. 목이 네모 모양으로 파인 것은 좋아하지 않아요.
남 그러면 이건 어떠세요? 목이 둥글게 파인 것입니다.
여 아무 그림도 없으면 좋겠어요. 저는 단순한 걸 원하거든요.
남 아마도 이것이 찾고 계신 것 같네요. 그렇죠?
여 맞아요! 그걸로 할게요.

03 ④

W Dongmin, what's wrong? You look worried.
M I've been looking for my backpack, but I can't find it.
W Where did you put it?
M It was right here. But now it's gone.
W Really? Are you kidding me?
M Why? I'm very serious.
W Well. You're carrying it right now. Check your back.
M Oops! I didn't know that.

여 동민아, 무슨 일이야? 걱정스러워 보이는데.
남 내 배낭을 찾고 있는데, 찾을 수가 없어.
여 어디다 두었는데?
남 바로 여기에 있었어. 그런데 지금은 사라졌어.
여 정말? 농담하는 거지?
남 왜? 나는 정말 진지해.
여 음. 네가 지금 그것을 메고 있잖아. 네 등을 확인해봐.
남 이런! 몰랐어.

04 ⑤

M Sujin, you're wearing a nice muffler.
W Thanks.
M Where did you get it? Did you buy it at the mall?
W No, not really. I went to my grandmother's house yesterday, and she gave it to me as a birthday present.
M That's a really special present. Happy birthday, by the way.
W Thanks. Can you come to my birthday party

tomorrow?

M Of course I can.

남 수진아, 멋진 목도리를 하고 있구나.

여 고마워.

남 어디에서 났니? 쇼핑몰에서 샀니?

여 아니. 어제 할머니 댁에 갔었는데, 할머니께서 생일 선물로 그것을 나에게 주셨어.

남 정말 특별한 선물이다. 그건 그렇고, 생일 축하해.

여 고마워. 내일 내 생일 파티에 올 수 있니?

남 당연히 갈 수 있지.

05 ②

W What's the matter?

M I have a runny nose and I'm coughing a lot.

W Do you have a fever, too?

M No, I guess not.

W Then, take these pills three times a day. Be sure to take them after meals.

M I see.

W If you don't get better tomorrow, you should go see a doctor.

M Okay, I will.

여 어디가 아프신가요?

남 콧물이 나고, 기침을 많이 해요.

여 열도 있으신가요?

남 아뇨, 그렇지 않은 것 같아요.

여 그러면 이 알약을 하루에 세 번 복용하세요. 반드시 식사를 하신 후 복용하세요.

남 알겠습니다.

여 내일 좋아지지 않으시면, 병원에 가보셔야 합니다.

남 네, 그렇게 하겠습니다.

06 ②

W You look angry, Juho. What happened?

M I went to the supermarket with my pet dog, but they didn't let me in.

W Why? Because of your dog?

M Yes. They said that no animals were allowed inside the supermarket.

W Umm.... They might be worried about animals eating the food there.

M But I was holding my dog in my arms.

W Come on. Put yourself in their shoes, and you will understand.

여 너 화가 나 보인다, 주호야. 무슨 일 있어?

남 내 애완견과 슈퍼마켓에 갔는데, 그들이 나를 들여보내 주지 않았어.

여 왜? 네 애완견 때문에?

남 응. 그들은 어떠한 동물도 슈퍼마켓 안으로 들일 수 없다고 말했어.

여 음…. 아마도 그곳의 음식을 먹는 동물들에 관해 걱정하나 보네.

남 하지만 나는 내 애완견을 팔에 안고 있었는걸.

여 그러지 말고 그들의 입장에서 생각해봐. 그러면 이해가 될 거야.

07 ⑤

M Kate, are you having fun here in Korea?

W Yeah, I'm having a wonderful time here.

M You arrived two days ago. What did you do?

W Well. On the first day I shopped for clothes and then I went to an art gallery in Insadong.

M I see. What about yesterday?

W I first went to Gyeongbokgung in the morning and walked around Cheonggyecheon in the evening.

M Sounds fun. What's your plan for today?

W I'm going to watch a baseball game at the ballpark.

M I hope you will have a lot of fun there.

남 Kate, 여기 한국에서 즐거운 시간을 보내고 있니?

여 응, 나는 여기에서 멋진 시간을 보내고 있어.

남 너는 이틀 전에 도착했잖아. 무엇을 했니?

여 음. 첫째 날에는 옷을 사고 그 다음에 인사동에 있는 미술관에 갔어.

남 그렇구나. 어제는?

여 먼저 아침에는 경복궁에 가고 저녁에는 청계천 주변을 걸었어.

남 재미있었겠다. 오늘 계획은 뭐니?

여 야구장에서 야구 경기를 관람할 거야.

남 그곳에서 매우 재미있기를 바라.

08 ⑤

M Mom, I'm leaving.

W Where are you going?

M I'm going to meet my friends at the library. We have to finish the social studies project together.

W Are you going to ride your bike? It's raining heavily outside.

M Really? I didn't know that. Then I guess I'll take the bus.

W I'd better give you a ride. Wait just a few minutes.

M All right. Thanks, Mom.

남 엄마, 저 나가요.

여 어디에 가는 거니?

남 도서관에서 친구들을 만날 거예요. 함께 사회 프로젝트를 끝내야 하거든요.

여 자전거를 탈 거니? 밖에 비가 많이 오고 있단다.

남 정말요? 몰랐어요. 그러면 버스를 타야겠어요.

여 내가 너를 태워다 주는 게 좋겠다. 잠시만 기다리렴.

남 네. 감사해요, 엄마.

09 ④

W Did you read the article about Jina Lee?

M No, I've never heard about her. Who is she?

W She is a successful business person. She's only 30 years old, but she is already the CEO of a huge fashion company.

M That's amazing. I bet she majored in business administration.

W That's not true. She graduated from high school, and then she started a small business all by herself. Now she has more than 10,000 employees.

M Wow! I want to be a great CEO like her.

여 너 Jina Lee에 대한 기사를 읽었니?

남 아니, 나는 그녀에 대해 들어본 적이 없어. 그녀는 누구니?

여 그녀는 성공한 사업가야. 겨우 서른 살이지만, 이미 대형 패션 회사의 최고 경영자야.

남 놀랍다. 그녀는 분명 경영학을 전공했을 거야.

여 그렇지 않아. 그녀는 고등학교를 졸업하고 나서 혼자서 작은 사업을 시작했어. 지금은 만 명이 넘는 직원들을 두고 있어.

남 와! 나도 그녀처럼 멋진 최고 경영자가 되고 싶다.

10 ⑤

M This is useful when you can't visit a bank. You can take out money any time you want with a bank book or a bank card. It doesn't have to belong to your bank. You can also transfer the money in your account to another account using it. It is like a small bank that you can visit anytime, anywhere.

남 이것은 여러분이 은행에 방문할 수 없을 때 유용합니다. 여러분은 통장이나 은행 카드로 원하면 언제든지 돈을 인출할 수 있습니다. 그것은 여러분의 은행에 속해 있을 필요가 없습니다. 여러분은 또한 그것을 이용하여 여러분의 계좌에서 다른 계좌로 돈을 보낼 수도 있습니다. 그것은 마치 여러분이 언제 어디서든 방문할 수 있는 작은 은행과 같습니다.

11 ④

W What is the first thing you do in the morning? In my case, I check the weather forecast. To be more exact, I check the level of fine dust. Fine dust is getting worse and worse. To deal with this problem, everyone should work together. We can start by using public transportation instead of driving. We can also plant more trees. Let's not blame other countries but do something about it.

여 당신이 아침에 일어나서 가장 먼저 하는 일은 무엇인가요? 저의 경우에는 일기 예보를 확인합니다. 보다 정확하게는, 미세먼지의 정도를 확인합니다. 미세먼지가 점점 더 악화됩니다. 이 문제를 해결하려면, 모든 사람이 협력해야 합니다. 우리는 운전을 하는 대신에 대중교통을 이용함으로써 시작할 수 있습니다. 우리는 또한 더 많은 나무를 심을 수 있습니다. 다른 나라를 탓하기보다는 그 문제에 관해 뭔가를 합시다.

12 ③

W Hello. Find Wood Furniture. How may I help you?

M I'm calling to change my order.

W May I have your name, please?

M This is Mike Sullivan. I ordered a closet last Sunday.

W Yes, I found your order. What do you want to change?

M The delivery date. Can I get it this Wednesday instead of Saturday? I will be out of town during the weekend.

W No problem. We will deliver it to you on July 4th, Wednesday.

M Thank you very much.

여 여보세요. Find 원목 가구입니다. 무엇을 도와드릴까요?

남 주문을 변경하기 위해 전화를 했습니다.

여 성함을 알 수 있을까요?

남 Mike Sullivan입니다. 지난 일요일에 옷장을 주문했습니다.

여 네, 손님의 주문을 찾았습니다. 무엇을 변경하기 원하시나요?

남 배송 날짜요. 이번 주 토요일 대신에 수요일에 받을 수 있을까요? 주말 동안 도시를 떠나있을 거여서요.

여 문제없어요. 7월 4일 수요일에 배송해드리겠습니다.

남 대단히 감사합니다.

13 ②

W May I help you, sir?

M Yes. I would like to buy five tickets to the aquarium.

W The ticket costs 10,000 won per person. But we offer a ten percent discount to those who are over 65 or under seven years old.

M That's good. My mother is 67 and my youngest daughter is only six.

W Then you can get a discount for two people. Will you pay in cash or by credit card?

M By credit card.

W All right. Here are your tickets.

여 도와드릴까요, 선생님?

남 네. 수족관 입장권 5장을 구입하고 싶습니다.

여 입장권은 1인당 만원입니다. 하지만 65세 이상이나 7세 미만은 10퍼센트 할인을 해드립니다.

남 좋네요. 저희 어머니께서는 67세이시고 막내딸은 겨우 6세입니다.

여 그러면 두 사람에 대해 할인을 받으실 수 있어요. 현금으로 계산하시겠습니까, 아니면 신용카드로 하시겠습니까?

남 신용카드요.

여 알겠습니다. 여기 입장권을 드리겠습니다.

14 ③

M Excuse me, ma'am. You were speeding.

W Did I? I was driving at 40 kilometers per hour.

M You are in the school zone. The speed limit in this area is under 30 kilometers.

W Is that so? I didn't know that.

M May I see your driver's license?

W Here you are. Please let it go this once for me.

M Okay, but be careful when you drive. Next time you will get a ticket.

남 실례합니다, 부인. 과속하셨습니다.

여 제가요? 저는 시속 40킬로미터로 달리고 있었는데요.

남 당신은 어린이보호구역에 있습니다. 이 구역에서의 속도 제한은 30킬로미터 이하입니다.

여 그런가요? 몰랐어요.

남 운전면허증을 보여 주시겠습니까?

여 여기요. 제발 한 번만 봐주세요.

남 알겠습니다. 하지만 운전하실 때는 주의하세요. 다음번에는 교통 위반 딱지를 받으실 겁니다.

15 ⑤

[Telephone rings.]

M Hi, Jian. It's Yuchan.

W Hi. What's up?

M I called you to ask for help.

W What kind of help do you need?

M We have a math test tomorrow. But I can't solve any of the problems in the textbook. Please help me. I know you're good at math.

W Okay. I will come over to your house in half an hour.

M Thanks a lot. You're a lifesaver!

[전화 벨소리가 울린다.]

남 안녕, 지안아. 나 유찬이야.

여 안녕. 무슨 일이야?

남 도움을 요청하려고 전화했어.

여 어떤 도움이 필요하니?

남 내일 수학 시험이 있잖아. 그런데 교과서에 있는 어떤 문제도 풀 수가 없어. 나 좀 도와줘. 너는 수학을 잘하잖아.

여 그래. 30분 후에 너희 집으로 갈게.

남 너무 고마워. 너는 내 구세주야.

16 ④

M Are you free tonight? Let's go watch a movie. The new Spiderman movie is showing now.

W I really want to see it, but I can't go out tonight.

M Why is that?

W My little brother is sick. I have to look after him.

M What about your mom?

W She has to work late, so she asked me to take care of him.

M I see. We can watch the movie some other day.

남 오늘 밤에 한가하니? 영화 보러 가자. 새로운 스파이더맨 영화가 지금 상영 중이야.

여 정말 보고 싶은데, 오늘 밤에 외출할 수가 없어.

남 왜?

여 내 남동생이 아파. 내가 돌봐 줘야 해.

남 너희 어머니는?

여 엄마는 늦게 일하셔야 해서 나에게 동생을 돌봐 달라고 부탁하셨어.

남 그렇구나. 다른 날에 보러 가면 돼.

17 ⑤

① M How much do they cost all together?
W They're 20,000 won.
② M Are you going to check out now?
W Yes, here is my room key.
③ M How many books do you read a month?
W I usually read two to three books.
④ M What are you reading?
W I'm reading a fantasy novel.
⑤ M I want to check out this book.
W Okay. Please give me your library card.

① 남 다 합해서 얼마인가요?
여 20,000원입니다.
② 남 지금 체크아웃하시는 건가요?
여 네, 여기 제 방 열쇠요.
③ 남 너는 한 달에 몇 권의 책을 읽니?
여 나는 보통 두세 권 읽어.
④ 남 무엇을 읽고 있니?
여 공상 소설을 읽고 있어.
⑤ 남 이 책을 대출하고 싶습니다.
여 네. 도서관 회원증을 주세요.

18 ④

W Welcome to Green Supermarket. We're open from 9 a.m. to 10 p.m. every day. On the first floor, you can find all kinds of fresh and processed foods. On the second floor, there are stationery and home decoration items. We have a big parking lot on the basement floor. You can park your car there for two hours for free. Enjoy your shopping at Green Supermarket.

여 Green 슈퍼마켓에 오신 것을 환영합니다. 저희는 매일 오전 9시부터 오후 10시까지 영업을 합니다. 1층에서 여러분은 모든 종류의 신선 식품과 가공식품을 찾으실 수 있습니다. 2층에는 문구류와 실내 장식 상품들이 있습니다. 지하층에는 큰 주차장이 완비되어 있습니다. 2시간 동안 무료로 주차를 하실 수 있습니다. Green 슈퍼마켓에서 즐거운 쇼핑하세요.

19 ③

M How was your trip to Jeju Island?
W It was fantastic. The weather was great, and everyone in my family had a lot of fun.
M What did you do there?
W I went hiking to Hallasan and sunbathed on the beautiful beaches.
M Sounds great. Wasn't it cold?
W Not at all. It's much warmer there.
M What else did you do?

남 제주도 여행은 어땠니?
여 환상적이었어. 날씨가 좋았고, 가족 모두 너무 즐거워했어.
남 거기에서 무엇을 했니?
여 한라산으로 하이킹을 가고 아름다운 해변에서 일광욕을 했어.
남 좋았겠다. 춥지 않았니?
여 전혀. 그곳은 훨씬 더 따뜻해.
남 또 무엇을 했어?

20 ①

W What are you looking at, Minho?
M Look! My favorite hip hop group just released a new album.
W Do you like hip hop music? I didn't know that.
M Yeah. It's my favorite music genre. Don't you like it?
W Not really. I don't like noisy music.
M You must like classical music then.

여 무엇을 보고 있니, 민호야?
남 봐! 내가 가장 좋아하는 힙합 그룹이 방금 새 앨범을 출시했어.
여 너 힙합 음악을 좋아하니? 몰랐어.
남 응. 그것은 내가 가장 좋아하는 음악 장르야. 너는 힙합을 좋아하지 않니?
여 별로 안 좋아해. 나는 시끄러운 음악을 좋아하지 않거든.
남 그렇다면 클래식 음악을 좋아하겠구나.

>> 02회 듣기 실전 모의고사 pp. 120~127

01 ③ 02 ⑤ 03 ④ 04 ⑤ 05 ④ 06 ② 07 ② 08 ④
09 ③ 10 ① 11 ③ 12 ④ 13 ② 14 ① 15 ⑤ 16 ⑤
17 ① 18 ② 19 ④ 20 ⑤

Dictation Test

01 sunny, hard, until tomorrow **02** popular, recommend, prefer, expensive **03** no school, news, fair **04** sick, broke, leg, turns taking **05** package, express, regular mail, stamps **06** lunch, How, you, spicy **07** speech, improve, once, week, well **08** Help yourself, recipe, address **09** by subway, free, bring, uniform **10** indoors, put, into, dribbling **11** be held, amazing, miss **12** What brought, attend, thanks to **13** practice, cafeteria, begins, quarter **14** stomachache, skipped, bad, medicine, better **15** hungry, tired, want, better, wake **16** wrong, return, lost, my point **17** allowed, open, forward, seeing **18** flight time, arrive, temperature **19** mean, pay, right expression **20** playing against, sure, makes, think

01 ③

W Hello, everyone. Welcome to the World Weather Report. In New York, it's sunny and the temperature is around 18 degrees Celsius. A pleasant day is expected in London as well. In Tokyo, it's raining hard and the rain will continue until tomorrow. In Beijing, it will be cold and windy. Don't forget to wear a jacket when you go out.

여 안녕하세요, 여러분. 세계 일기예보에 오신 것을 환영합니다. 뉴욕은 화창하고 기온은 섭씨 18도 가량입니다. 런던에서도 쾌적한 날이 예상됩니다. 도쿄에서는 비가 많이 내리고 있고, 이 비는 내일까지 계속되겠습니다. 베이징은 춥고 바람이 불겠습니다. 외출하실 때 외투를 입는 것을 잊지 마세요.

02 ⑤

W What can I do for you, sir?
M I'm looking for a cake for my daughter.
W Okay. What about this one? It's popular among girls.
M She doesn't like chocolate. I need a whipped-cream cake.
W Then, I recommend this one with fruit toppings.
M Umm... I prefer that one with fruit toppings and flower decorations in the middle.
W It's a little expensive. Is it okay?
M No problem. I'll take it.

여 무엇을 도와드릴까요, 선생님?
남 딸에게 줄 케이크를 찾고 있어요.
여 네. 이것은 어떠세요? 여자아이들 사이에서 인기가 있어요.
남 제 딸은 초콜릿을 좋아하지 않아요. 저는 생크림 케이크가 필요해요.
여 그러면, 이 과일 토핑이 있는 것을 추천합니다.
남 음… 저는 과일 토핑과 가운데에 꽃 장식이 있는 저것이 더 좋아요.
여 그건 약간 비쌉니다. 괜찮으신가요?
남 문제없어요. 그것으로 할게요.

03 ④

M I have good news for you!
W What is it?
M We have no school tomorrow!
W Is that so? That's news to me. Why is that?
M Tomorrow is May 1st. Everyone has a day off that day.
W That's only for workers. We are students, not workers. So we have school that day. You didn't know that.
M What? That's not fair!

남 너에게 좋은 소식이 있어!
여 그게 뭐야?
남 내일 학교에 안 가도 돼!
여 그러니? 그거 몰랐는걸. 왜 그런 건데?
남 내일은 5월 1일이잖아. 모두가 그날은 쉬어.
여 그건 노동자들에게 해당되는 거야. 우리는 노동자가 아니라 학생이잖아. 그러니까 우리는 그날 수업이 있어. 너 그건 몰랐구나.
남 뭐라고? 그건 불공평해!

04 ⑤

M Jisu, I heard you were going camping with your family.
W Yeah, that was my plan. But I couldn't go.
M Why? Were you sick or something?
W Actually, my father was. He fell down the stairs and broke his leg.

M What a pity! Is he okay now?

W Yes, my mom and I took turns taking care of him at the hospital during the weekend. Now, he's at home.

M I hope he gets well soon.

W Thank you.

남 지수야, 너 가족들과 캠핑을 간다고 들었는데.

여 응, 그게 나의 계획이었지. 하지만 못 갔어.

남 왜? 아프거나 뭐 그랬니?

여 사실은, 아버지께서 편찮으셨어. 계단에서 넘어지셔서 다리가 부러지셨거든.

남 어떡해! 아버지께서는 지금은 괜찮으시니?

여 응, 엄마와 내가 주말 동안 번갈아가며 병원에서 아버지를 돌봐 드렸어. 지금은 집에 계셔.

남 곧 쾌차하시길 바라.

여 고마워.

05 ④

W How may I help you?

M I need to mail this package to Mokpo, please.

W Okay, let's see how much it weighs.... It's about 2 kilograms. You can send it by express mail or regular mail.

M Regular mail, please. How much will that be?

W Five thousand won. Do you need anything else?

M Oh, yeah! I almost forgot. I need a book of stamps, too.

W Okay, your total comes to 8,000 won.

여 무엇을 도와드릴까요?

남 이 소포를 목포로 보내고 싶어요.

여 네, 무게가 얼마나 나가는지 보도록 하죠?. 약 2킬로그램이네요. 속달 우편이나 일반 우편으로 보내실 수 있습니다.

남 일반 우편으로 보내겠습니다. 얼마일까요?

여 5,000원입니다. 더 필요하신 게 있으신가요?

남 오, 네! 거의 잊을 뻔 했네요. 우표책 한 권도 필요해요.

여 네, 다 합쳐서 8,000원입니다.

06 ②

M Oh, it's noon already. Let's have lunch.

W Okay. What do you want to eat?

M I'd like to have Chinese food today.

W Let's go to the new restaurant down the street. I ate there with my family last weekend.

M Really? How did you like it?

W The *jjajangmyeon* was very delicious, but the *jjamppong* was a little bit spicy.

M Umm.... Then, we'd better not go there.

남 오, 벌써 정오다. 점심 먹자.

여 그래. 뭐 먹고 싶니?

남 오늘은 중국 음식을 먹고 싶어.

여 길 아래에 있는 새로운 식당에 가자. 지난 주말에 거기에서 가족들과 식사를 했거든.

남 정말? 어땠어?

여 짜장면은 정말 맛있었는데, 짬뽕은 약간 매웠어.

남 음…. 그러면, 그곳에 가지 않는 게 좋겠다.

07 ②

M Yuna, that was an amazing speech. I didn't know that you were such a good English speaker.

W Thanks. I'm still trying to improve my English speaking.

M How do you practice?

W Well, I read a lot of English books, and I listen to an English radio program every morning.

M Wow. That's a lot of effort.

W I also joined an English debate club. We have a regular meeting once a week. I try to think in English as well.

M I don't think I could do all that.

남 유나야, 정말 멋진 연설이었어. 네가 그렇게 영어를 잘하는지 몰랐어.

여 고마워. 나는 영어 말하기 실력을 향상시키기 위해서 지금도 노력하고 있어.

남 어떻게 연습하니?

여 음, 나는 영어 책을 많이 읽고, 매일 아침 영어 라디오 방송을 들어.

남 와, 정말 많은 노력을 하고 있구나.

여 나는 영어 토론 동아리에도 가입했어. 우리는 일주일에 한 번 정기적으로 만나. 또한 나는 영어로 생각하려고 노력해.

남 내가 그걸 다 할 수는 없을 것 같다.

08 ④

M Thanks for inviting me to the party.

W I'm glad you could come. Help yourself to pizza.

M Umm.... This is so delicious. Did you make it yourself?

W Yeah. This is the first time I made pizza.

M Really? How did you make it?

W I just followed the recipe on the blog. There's a useful cooking blog I visit very often.

M Tell me the address. I'll visit there right now.

W Okay. Check this out.

남 파티에 초대해줘서 고마워.

여 네가 와줘서 기뻐. 피자 많이 먹어.

남 음…. 이거 너무 맛있다. 네가 직접 만들었니?

여 응. 내가 피자를 만든 건 이번이 처음이야.

남 정말? 어떻게 만들었니?

여 그냥 블로그의 요리법을 따라했어. 내가 자주 방문하는 유용한 요리 블로그가 있거든.

남 주소 좀 알려 줘. 지금 당장 거기에 방문해 봐야겠다.

여 그래. 여기 봐봐.

09 ③

W Hello, this is your homeroom teacher. Tomorrow, we're going to visit the National Museum. We will go there by subway, so please come to the subway station by 8 o'clock in the morning. You can enter the museum for free, but you must bring your transportation fee and lunch with you. Everyone should wear the school uniform.

여 안녕하세요, 담임 교사입니다. 내일, 우리는 국립 박물관을 방문할 예정입니다. 지하철을 타고 갈 것이니, 오전 8시까지 지하철역으로 오세요. 박물관은 무료로 입장할 수 있지만, 교통비와 점심 식사는 가져와야 합니다. 모두가 교복을 입어야 합니다.

10 ①

M This is a sport that can be played indoors or outdoors. Each team has five players. They have to put the ball into the other team's basket to score points. The team with the most points wins. A player with the ball can't take more than 3 steps without dribbling it.

남 이것은 실내에서 혹은 실외에서 하는 운동입니다. 각 팀에는 5명의 선수가 있습니다. 그들은 점수를 얻기 위해 공을 상대 팀의 바스켓에 넣어야 합니다. 점수가 가장 많은 팀이 이기게 됩니다. 공을 들고 있는 선수는 드리블을 하지 않으면 세 걸음 이상 걸을 수 없습니다.

11 ③

W Hello, everyone. I'm the school president, Kim Suyeon. I'm happy to make this announcement. The annual school festival is going to be held next week. It will begin at 4 p.m. on July 20th. Please come to our auditorium by 3:50. There will be amazing performances by the school band and the dance group. Also, there will be free snacks and beverages. Don't miss this exciting event!

여 안녕하세요, 여러분. 저는 학생회장인 김수연입니다. 이것을 알리게 되어 기쁩니다. 연례 학교 축제가 다음 주에 열릴 예정입니다. 축제는 7월 20일 오후 4시에 시작될 것입니다. 강당으로 3시 50분까지 와 주세요. 학교 밴드와 댄스 그룹의 멋진 공연이 있을 것입니다. 또한, 무료 간식과 음료도 있을 것입니다. 이 신나는 행사를 놓치지 마세요!

12 ④

W Hi, Mark. It's good to see you here in Korea.

M Hi, Mira. I'm glad to see you again, too.

W What brought you here? Are you going to take the Korean language classes like last year?

M Not really. My uncle is going to get married this weekend. I'm here to attend his wedding.

W Wow, that's good news.

M Yeah. By the way, my Korean improved a lot thanks to the Korean language classes I took last year.

W Really? Why don't you say something in Korean?

M All right. Give me a topic, then I'll talk about it.

여 안녕, Mark. 한국에서 너를 봐서 좋다.

남 안녕, 미라야. 나도 너를 다시 봐서 기뻐.

여 무슨 일로 온 거야? 작년처럼 한국어 수업을 들을 예정이니?

남 아니. 삼촌이 이번 주말에 결혼을 하실 거야. 삼촌의 결혼식에 참석하려고 왔어.

여 와, 그거 좋은 소식이다.

남 응. 그건 그렇고, 작년에 들은 한국어 수업 덕분에 내 한국어 실력이 많이 늘었어.

여 정말? 한국어로 뭔가 말해보는 게 어때?

남 좋아. 주제를 줘 봐, 그러면 그것에 대해 말해 볼게.

13 ②

[Cell phone rings.]

W Hi, Tony. This is Jenny.

M Hi, Jenny.

W You know we have to practice the role play for the English class tomorrow.

M I know, but I have no time at all today. Why don't we practice before class tomorrow?
W That's a good idea. What time shall we meet?
M Let's meet at the school cafeteria at 8 o'clock.
W But tomorrow is Monday. The first class begins at 8:30. I'm afraid we would be late for class.
M Then, how about a quarter to eight?
W That would be nice. See you tomorrow.

[휴대전화 벨소리가 울린다.]
여 안녕, Tony. 나 Jenny야.
남 안녕, Jenny.
여 우리 내일 영어 수업의 역할극을 연습해야 하는 거 알지?
남 알고 있지만, 난 오늘은 시간이 전혀 없어. 내일 수업 전에 연습하는 게 어때?
여 그거 좋은 생각이다. 몇 시에 만날까?
남 학교 식당에서 8시에 만나자.
여 근데 내일은 월요일이잖아. 1교시가 8시 30분에 시작해. 수업에 지각할까봐 걱정이 돼.
남 그러면, 8시 15분 전은 어때?
여 그거 좋겠다. 내일 봐.

14 ①

W What's wrong with you, Minsu?
M I have a stomachache and I feel dizzy.
W What did you eat for breakfast?
M I skipped breakfast. I guess the milk I drank last night was bad.
W Oh, my! Did you visit the school nurse?
M Yes, I took the medicine she gave to me already, but I don't feel better.
W Okay, I think you should go home now. Let me call your mom.

여 어디가 아프니, 민수야?
남 배가 아프고 어지러워요.
여 아침 식사로 뭘 먹었니?
남 아침은 걸렀어요. 어젯밤에 마신 우유가 상했던 것 같아요.
여 오, 이런! 보건 선생님께 가 봤니?
남 네, 보건 선생님께서 주신 약을 이미 먹었는데, 나아지지 않아요.
여 그래, 내 생각에는 네가 지금 집에 가야 할 것 같구나. 어머님께 전화를 드릴게.

15 ⑤

M Mom, I'm home.
W How was school, Jinsu?
M I had a long day. I'm so hungry and tired.
W Do you want me to make you a sandwich or something?
M Thanks, Mom. But I think I'd better get some sleep first. I can't move at all.
W Okay. Then go get some sleep.
M Can you wake me up in an hour?
W Of course I can. I will get your sandwich ready by then.

남 엄마, 저 집에 왔어요.
여 오늘 학교는 어땠니, 진수야?
남 하루가 너무 길었어요. 너무 배고프고 피곤해요.
여 샌드위치나 뭐 다른 거 만들어 줄까?
남 감사해요, 엄마. 하지만 먼저 잠을 좀 자야겠어요. 전혀 움직일 수가 없어요.
여 그래. 그러면 가서 좀 자거라.
남 한 시간 뒤에 깨워 주실 수 있으세요?
여 물론이지. 그때까지 샌드위치를 만들어 놓을게.

16 ⑤

M Sora, you look upset. What's wrong?
W One of my friends borrowed my English textbook last week, but he didn't give it back to me until now.
M We have an English test next week. You should ask him to return it.
W I already did. But he told me that he had lost it.
M Oh, no. You need the book for the test!
W That's my point. I'm so mad.
M Come on, let's see what we can do.

남 소라야, 너 화가 나 보인다. 무슨 일이야?
여 내 친구 중 한 명이 지난주에 내 영어 교과서를 빌려 갔는데, 지금까지 나에게 돌려주지 않았어.
남 우리는 다음 주에 영어 시험이 있잖아. 그에게 그것을 돌려 달라고 얘기해야지.
여 벌써 했지. 그런데 그 아이가 그것을 잃어버렸다고 했어.
남 오, 이런, 시험을 위해서 그 책이 필요한데!
여 내 말이 그 말이야. 나 너무 화가 나.
남 진정해, 우리가 뭘 할 수 있는지 생각해 보자.

17 ①

① W I'm sorry. No food or drink is allowed here.
M Oh, I didn't know that.

② W When is the museum closed?
M The museum is open all year round.
③ W How may I help you?
M I'd like to buy tickets to the special exhibition.
④ W Welcome to the National Art Museum.
M Thank you. I'm looking forward to seeing the artworks here.
⑤ W What are you drinking?
M I'm drinking soda.

---

① 여 죄송합니다. 이곳에는 음식이나 음료를 반입하실 수 없습니다.
남 오, 몰랐어요.
② 여 박물관은 언제 휴관합니까?
남 박물관은 연중 내내 문을 엽니다.
③ 여 무엇을 도와드릴까요?
남 특별 전시회의 표를 사고 싶습니다.
④ 여 국립 미술관에 오신 것을 환영합니다.
남 감사합니다. 이곳의 예술품들을 보는 것이 기대됩니다.
⑤ 여 무엇을 마시고 있니?
남 탄산음료를 마시고 있어.

18 ②

M Ladies and gentlemen, good afternoon. Welcome aboard Peace Airlines. This is your captain speaking. Our flight time today will be three and a half hours and we will arrive in Bangkok at 4 p.m. The weather is good. The temperature in Bangkok is now 28 degrees Celsius. We wish you a pleasant flight. Thank you.

남 신사 숙녀 여러분, 안녕하세요. Peace 항공사의 비행기에 탑승하신 것을 환영합니다. 저는 기장입니다. 오늘 저희는 세 시간 반을 비행하여 오후 네 시에 방콕에 도착할 것입니다. 날씨는 좋습니다. 현재 방콕의 기온은 섭씨 28도입니다. 즐거운 비행이 되시기를 바랍니다. 감사합니다.

19 ④

W Are you finished? I'm done.
M Me, too. The food here is really great.
W I agree. By the way, let's Dutch pay today.
M Dutch pay? What do you mean?
W I mean let's pay individually.
M Ah ha. Dutch pay is not the right expression.
W Then, how should I say it?

여 다 먹었니? 나는 다 먹었어.
남 나도. 여기 음식 정말 훌륭하다.
여 동의해. 그건 그렇고, 오늘은 더치페이하자.
남 더치페이? 그게 무슨 뜻이야?
여 내 말은 각자 계산하자고.
남 아하. 더치페이는 옳은 표현이 아니야.
여 그러면, 어떻게 말해야 해?

20 ⑤

W What are you thinking about so hard?
M Oh, I'm thinking about the soccer match tomorrow.
W The Korean national soccer team is playing against Germany, right?
M Yeah, I made a bet on the match with my father.
W Who do you think will win?
M I'm sure the Korean team will win the match.
W Really? But the German team is one of the top-ranked teams. What makes you think our team will win?

여 무엇에 대해 그렇게 골똘히 생각하고 있어?
남 오, 내일 있을 축구 경기에 대해 생각하고 있어.
여 한국 국가대표 축구팀이 독일이랑 경기하지, 그렇지?
남 응, 아버지와 그 경기에 대해 내기를 했어.
여 누가 이길 거라고 생각해?
남 나는 한국 팀이 경기에 이길 거라고 확신해.
여 정말? 하지만 독일 팀은 최상위권 팀들 중 하나잖아. 어째서 우리 팀이 이길 거라고 생각해?

>> 03회 듣기 실전 모의고사 pp. 128~135

01 ③ 02 ④ 03 ① 04 ⑤ 05 ② 06 ① 07 ③ 08 ①
09 ② 10 ④ 11 ⑤ 12 ③ 13 ③ 14 ⑤ 15 ⑤ 16 ③
17 ③ 18 ④ 19 ⑤ 20 ④

Dictation Test

01 chance, clear skies, rain **02** subway, shoulder, laptop, hanging **03** good at, missed, proud, son **04** came up, hurt, serious **05** ticket, passport, or, seat number, begin **06** painting, homework, after, own **07** sports, both, same, soccer, settled 08 took, month, How, student discount, get **09** flea, Anyone, playground, buyer **10** trash problem, solve, waste, difference **11** how long, climbs up, strong, feed **12** ordered, change, instead of, pick, up **13** popular, expensive, off, recommend 14 dirty, replace, with, piece, wait **15** finish, cleaned, laundry, forget **16** enough sleep, study, rest **17** park, car coming, heavy **18** turn off, a noise, mark **19** farm work, potatoes, wish, had 20 forgot, throw, party, need

01 ③

M Good morning, everyone. It's Monday morning and here's the weather report for this week. Now, it's very sunny and cool. In the afternoon, there is a chance of some rain. Tomorrow, we will see clear skies again and the pleasant weather will continue until Friday. The rain will start again on Saturday morning.

남 안녕하세요, 여러분. 월요일 아침에 이번 주의 일기 예보를 말씀드리겠습니다. 지금은 화창하고 시원합니다. 오후에는 비가 좀 내릴 가능성이 있습니다. 내일은 다시 맑은 하늘을 보겠고 화창한 날씨는 금요일까지 계속되겠습니다. 토요일 아침에 비가 다시 시작되겠습니다.

02 ④

W Seoul Station's Lost and Found. May I help you?
M I left my bag on the subway and I'm looking for it.
W What kind of bag is it?
M It's a yellow shoulder bag. It is as big as a laptop.
W I see. Is there anything else you want to tell us about it?
M Well. It's all yellow and has no patterns on it. But there is a puppy key chain hanging on it.
W Okay. If we find the bag, we will contact you.

여 서울역 분실물 취급소입니다. 무엇을 도와드릴까요?
남 지하철에 가방을 놓고 내려서 찾고 있어요.
여 어떤 종류의 가방인가요?
남 노란색 숄더백이에요. 노트북 컴퓨터만큼 커요.
여 그렇군요. 가방에 대해서 더 말씀해주시고 싶으신 게 있나요?
남 음. 그것은 전체가 노란색이고 무늬가 없어요. 하지만 강아지 열쇠고리가 달려있어요.
여 네. 가방을 찾으면, 연락드리겠습니다.

03 ①

W Wow! Look at that boy! He's really good at soccer. No wonder his nickname is Messi!
M Is that so? I didn't know that.
W The first half didn't end yet, but he has scored three goals until now.
M That's a lot. I just arrived, so I missed all of them.
W His parents must be very proud of him.
M Actually, I am his father.
W Really? You have such a great son.
M Yes, I think so too.

여 와! 저 소년 좀 보세요! 정말 축구를 잘하네요. 별명이 왜 Messi인줄 알겠어요!
남 그런가요? 몰랐어요.
여 아직 전반전이 끝나지도 않았는데, 지금까지 세 골을 넣었어요.
남 그거 많네요. 저는 이제 막 도착해서, 그것을 다 놓쳤어요.
여 저 소년의 부모님은 참 자랑스러우시겠어요.
남 사실은, 제가 그의 아버지입니다.
여 정말요? 정말 훌륭한 아드님을 두셨어요.
남 네, 저도 그런 것 같아요.

04 ⑤

M Did you have a good time at Janet's party yesterday?
W Yes, we had fun. How come you didn't come to the party?
M I was going to go, but something just came up.
W Was it something bad?
M Yeah. My father hurt his leg while cutting a tree.
W Oh, no! Is he all right?
M Yes. Fortunately, it was not that serious. I took

him to the hospital right away, and he's getting better now.

남 어제 Janet의 파티에서 좋은 시간 보냈니?
여 응, 재미있었어. 넌 왜 파티에 안 온 거야?
남 가려고 했는데, 일이 생겼어.
여 안 좋은 일이었니?
남 그래. 아버지께서 나무를 자르시다가 다리를 다치셨어.
여 오, 이런! 아버지께서는 괜찮으시니?
남 응. 다행히도, 그렇게 심각하지 않았어. 난 아버지를 즉시 병원에 모셔다드렸고, 지금은 회복 중이셔.

05 ②

W Can I see your ticket and passport?
M Sure. Here they are.
W Okay. How many suitcases will you be checking in?
M Just one suitcase.
W Would you like a window or aisle seat?
M A window seat, please.
W This is your seat number and the departure gate.
M What time will we be boarding?
W We will begin boarding at six. Enjoy your flight.

여 표와 여권 좀 보여 주시겠어요?
남 그럼요. 여기 있습니다.
여 네. 여행 가방은 몇 개나 부치실 건가요?
남 한 개입니다.
여 창가 쪽 좌석이 좋으신가요, 복도 쪽 좌석이 좋으신가요?
남 창가 쪽으로 주세요.
여 여기 좌석 번호와 출발 탑승구를 확인하세요.
남 몇 시에 탑승하나요?
여 여섯 시에 탑승을 시작합니다. 즐겁게 여행하세요.

06 ①

M Can you do me a favor?
W What is it?
M I have to finish painting this picture today. Can you do it for me?
W It's your art homework. Why are you asking me to do it?
M I have to go out in 30 minutes. I'm going to play soccer with my friends.
W Then you can do it after you play soccer.
M But you're my sister. Please do it for me just this once.
W Kevin, I'm your big sister, and I love you. Still, you should do your own work.

남 부탁 좀 들어줄 수 있어?
여 뭔데?
남 이 그림 그리는 것을 오늘 끝내야 해. 해 줄 수 있어?
여 그건 네 미술 숙제잖아. 왜 나한테 해 달라고 부탁하는 거니?
남 난 30분 안에 나가야 해. 친구들이랑 축구하기로 했어.
여 그러면 축구하고 나서 하면 되잖아.
남 하지만 누나는 내 누나잖아. 이번 한 번만 나를 위해 해 줘.
여 Kevin, 나는 네 큰 누나고 너를 사랑해. 그래도 네 일은 네가 해야 해.

07 ③

M Look here! The timetable for the after-school classes just came out. I'd like to take one, but I can't decide what to take.
W What are you interested in?
M I'm interested in sports, but I think I should take the science class, too.
W Then you can take both of them.
M But most sports classes are on Monday which is the same day as the science class.
W Look! There is a soccer class on Friday. So, you can take it with the science class.
M You're right. Now, it's settled.

남 여기 봐! 방과 후 수업 시간표가 방금 나왔어. 하나 듣고 싶은데, 무엇을 들을지 결정할 수가 없네.
여 너는 무엇에 관심이 있니?
남 나는 운동에 관심이 있어. 하지만 과학 수업도 들어야 할 것 같아.
여 그러면 둘 다 들으면 되잖아.
남 하지만 대부분의 운동 수업이 월요일에 있는데, 과학 수업과 같은 날이야.
여 봐! 금요일에 축구 수업이 있어. 그럼 그것을 과학 수업과 들으면 되겠다.
남 네 말이 맞아. 이제 정해졌네.

08 ①

W Minsu, where are you going?
M I'm going to the community center. I'm thinking about taking a yoga class.
W Oh, I took the class last month.
M How did you like it?
W It was great. By the way, you know we can get a

student discount, don't you?

M No, I didn't know that. How can I get the discount?

W You only have to show your student ID.

M Oh, I think I have to go back home to get it.

여 민수야, 어디에 가고 있니?

남 문화 센터에 가고 있어. 요가 수업을 들을까 생각 중이야.

여 오, 나 지난달에 그 수업을 들었어.

남 어땠어?

여 좋았어. 그건 그렇고, 우리가 학생 할인을 받을 수 있는 거 알고 있지?

남 아니, 몰랐어. 어떻게 할인을 받을 수 있어?

여 학생증을 보여 주기만 하면 돼.

남 오, 집에 돌아가서 가져와야겠다.

09 ②

W Adam, did you hear about the school flea market?

M No, I didn't. Can you tell me about it?

W The school is holding a flea market for students.

M Sounds interesting. Can I join it?

W Sure. Anyone can join. If you want to sell something, just apply for it on the school website.

M When and where will it be held?

W It's going to be held at the playground at 2 p.m. on May 2nd.

M It's this Saturday. I think I should join it as a buyer.

여 Adam, 학교 벼룩시장에 대해서 들었니?

남 아니, 못 들었어. 그것에 대해 나에게 말해줄 수 있어?

여 학교에서 학생들을 위해 벼룩시장을 개최한대.

남 재미있게 들린다. 내가 참여할 수 있어?

여 물론이지. 누구나 참여할 수 있어. 뭔가를 팔고 싶으면, 학교 홈페이지에서 신청하면 돼.

남 언제 어디에서 열릴 예정이니?

여 5월 2일 오후 두 시에 운동장에서 열릴 거야.

남 이번 주 토요일이네. 구매자로서 참여해야겠다.

10 ④

W Yesterday, I saw a documentary about the trash problem in our country. They say we don't have enough space to bury the trash now. What can we do to solve the problem? The most important thing is not to make waste. We have to recycle and reuse things. We should also try not to waste food too. The little things we do can make a big difference.

여 어제, 저는 우리나라의 쓰레기 문제에 관한 다큐멘터리를 봤습니다. 우리는 이제 쓰레기를 묻을 충분한 공간이 없다고 합니다. 이 문제를 해결하기 위해 우리는 무엇을 할 수 있을까요? 가장 중요한 것은 쓰레기를 만들지 않는 것입니다. 우리는 물건을 재활용하고 재사용해야 합니다. 우리는 또한 음식을 버리지 않도록 노력해야 합니다. 우리가 하는 작은 일들이 큰 차이를 만들 수 있습니다.

11 ⑤

W Everyone knows baby koalas live in their mothers' pouches. But do you know how long they stay there? When a koala is born, it climbs up to its mother's pouch and grows there for about six months. When it grows strong enough, the baby moves to its mother's back and stays there another six months. They still use their mothers' pouches to feed.

여 아기 코알라가 어미의 주머니 속에서 산다는 것은 누구나 알고 계실 것입니다. 하지만 얼마나 오랫동안 그곳에 머무는지 아시나요? 코알라가 태어나면, 그것은 어미의 주머니로 올라가 그곳에서 약 6개월 동안 자랍니다. 충분히 튼튼해지면, 아기 코알라는 어미의 등으로 옮겨가 그곳에서 6개월을 더 지냅니다. 그들은 여전히 어미의 주머니를 먹이를 먹기 위해 이용합니다.

12 ③

[Telephone rings.]

W Hello. This is Charlie's Bookstore.

M Hello. My name is Daniel Thomson. I ordered three books at your store yesterday.

W Yes. Is there anything I can help you with?

M Actually, I want to change something in my order.

W What would you like to change?

M I want to order *Holes* by Louis Sachar instead of *Matilda* by Roald Dahl.

W That's possible. But *Holes* is not in stock now. It will arrive in three days. Is it okay for you?

M No problem. I'll pick them up this weekend.

[전화 벨소리가 울린다.]

여 여보세요. Charlie 서점입니다.

남 안녕하세요. 제 이름은 Daniel Thomson입니다. 어제 그

서점에서 세 권의 책을 주문했습니다.

여 네. 도와드릴 일이 있는지요?

남 사실은, 제 주문에서 뭔가를 변경하고 싶습니다.

여 무엇을 변경하고 싶으신가요?

남 Roald Dahl의 'Matilda' 대신에 Louis Sachar의 'Holes'를 주문하고 싶습니다.

여 가능합니다. 하지만 'Holes'는 현재 재고가 없습니다. 3일 후에 도착할 것입니다. 괜찮으신가요?

남 문제없습니다. 이번 주말에 찾으러 가겠습니다.

13 ③

M Do you need help?

W Yes, I'm looking for a shirt for my dad.

M What about this one? It's very popular.

W I like it. But it looks expensive.

M Don't worry. It's on sale now. Its regular price is 40,000 won, but it's 50 percent off now.

W Really? That's great! Then can you recommend a necktie, too? I think I can buy a shirt and a tie.

M Sure. What about this one? It's only 10,000 won now.

W Perfect. I will take them.

남 도움이 필요하신가요?

여 네, 아버지께 드릴 셔츠를 찾고 있어요.

남 이것은 어떠세요? 매우 인기가 있습니다.

여 마음에 드네요. 하지만 비싸 보여요.

남 걱정 마세요. 지금 할인 중이에요. 그것의 정가는 4만원인데, 지금은 50퍼센트를 할인해 드립니다.

여 정말요? 좋네요! 그러면 넥타이도 하나 추천해 주실래요? 셔츠와 넥타이를 살 수 있을 것 같아요.

남 물론이죠. 이거 어떠세요? 지금 겨우 만원이에요.

여 완벽해요. 그것들로 할게요.

14 ⑤

M What is the matter?

W Look. The printout has spots and is dirty.

M Umm... I think it's because of the toner. Let me replace it with a new one.

W Okay.

M Let's print out a piece of paper for a test. Look. Now it's clean.

W That's right.

M Is there any other problem?

W Oh, one more thing. The paper gets jammed sometimes.

M Let me check the printer. Please wait.

남 무엇이 문제인가요?

여 보세요. 인쇄물에 얼룩이 있고 더러워요.

남 음… 제 생각에는 토너 때문인 것 같습니다. 새것으로 갈아드릴게요.

여 네.

남 시험 삼아 종이 한 장을 출력해 보죠. 보세요. 이제 깨끗하네요.

여 맞네요.

남 또 다른 문제가 있나요?

여 오, 한 가지 더요. 가끔씩 종이가 걸려요.

남 프린터를 점검해 보겠습니다. 기다려 주세요.

15 ⑤

W Are you going out, Minho?

M Yes, I am. I'm going to hang out with my friends.

W Did you finish your homework?

M Yes, Mom. I cleaned my room, too.

W Good job. By the way, can you do me a favor?

M Of course I can. What is it?

W On your way home, stop by the cleaner's and pick up the laundry, will you?

M Sure. I won't forget.

여 밖에 나가는 거니, 민호야?

남 네. 친구들과 놀기로 했어요.

여 숙제는 끝냈니?

남 네, 엄마. 제 방도 청소했어요.

여 잘했구나. 그건 그렇고, 부탁 하나 해도 될까?

남 물론이죠. 뭔데요?

여 집에 오는 길에, 세탁소에 들러서 세탁물 좀 찾아오겠니?

남 물론이죠. 잊지 않을게요.

16 ③

M Juha, you look tired. Didn't you get enough sleep last night?

W Yeah. I stayed up all night yesterday.

M Why did you do that? Did you study for the test?

W Not really.

M Then why did you stay awake?

W I just couldn't go to sleep. I usually drink just one cup of coffee, but I drank two cups yesterday.

M That's it. You couldn't sleep because of the caffeine. Why don't you get some rest?

W I think I should.

남 주하야, 피곤해 보인다. 어젯밤에 잠을 충분히 못 잤니?
여 그래. 어제 밤을 샜어.
남 왜 그랬어? 시험에 대비해 공부했니?
여 그런 건 아니야.
남 그러면 왜 깨어 있었어?
여 그냥 잠을 이룰 수가 없었어. 보통 때는 커피를 한 잔 마시는데, 어제는 두 잔을 마셨거든.
남 그거네. 넌 카페인 때문에 잠을 잘 수 없었던 거야. 좀 쉬는 게 어때?
여 그래야 할 것 같아.

17 ③

① W I'm sorry. You can't park here.
M Sorry. I didn't see the sign.
② W Where is the nearest post office?
M Cross the road here. Then you will see it on your right.
③ W Watch out! There's a car coming.
M Oops! I didn't see it. Thanks.
④ W What are you doing?
M I'm just waiting for my friends.
⑤ W The traffic is too heavy today.
M You're right. We're going to be late.

---

① 여 죄송합니다. 여기에 주차하시면 안 됩니다.
남 죄송해요. 표지판을 못 봤어요.
② 여 가장 가까운 우체국이 어디에 있나요?
남 여기에서 길을 건너세요. 그러면 오른편에 보일 겁니다.
③ 여 조심해요! 차가 오고 있어요.
남 이런! 못 봤어요. 감사합니다.
④ 여 뭐 하고 있어요?
남 그냥 친구들을 기다리고 있어요.
⑤ 여 오늘 차가 많이 막힌다.
남 맞아. 우리 늦겠다.

18 ④

M Before we start the English listening test, I will give you some instructions. First, make sure to turn off your cell phones before the test. Second, try to read the questions before you listen to the conversations. Next, don't make a noise during the test. Finally, don't forget to mark your answers with a pencil. Good luck to you.

남 영어 듣기 평가를 시작하기에 앞서, 몇 가지 유의 사항을 말씀드리겠습니다. 첫째, 시험 전에 휴대전화를 반드시 꺼 주세요. 둘째, 대화를 듣기 전에 질문을 읽도록 노력하세요. 다음으로, 시험 중에는 소음을 내지 마세요. 마지막으로, 답을 연필로 표시하는 것을 잊지 마세요. 행운을 빕니다.

19 ⑤

M What did you do last weekend?
W I went to my grandmother's farm and helped her with farm work.
M What kind of work did you do?
W Well, I dug out potatoes and picked up peppers. I sweated a lot, but it was fun.
M My grandmother lives in a city. I wish I had a farm to visit.
W You can come with me if you want.

남 지난 주말에 무엇을 했니?
여 난 할머니의 농장에 가서 농장 일을 도와 드렸어.
남 어떤 종류의 일을 했는데?
여 음, 감자를 캐고 고추를 땄어. 땀은 많이 났지만, 재미있었어.
남 우리 할머니는 도시에 사시는데. 나도 방문할 농장이 있으면 좋겠다.
여 원하면 나랑 같이 가도 돼.

20 ④

M Tomorrow is Mother's Day.
W Oh, I almost forgot. What should we do?
M Why don't we throw a party for mom?
W That's a great idea. Do you have any plans for it?
M I think we need a cake and a card. I can bake a cake.
W Okay. What do you want me to do?

남 내일은 어머니의 날이야.
여 오, 거의 잊을 뻔했네. 무엇을 해야 하지?
남 엄마를 위해 파티를 열어드리는 게 어때?
여 좋은 생각이다. 그것에 대한 계획이 있니?
남 내 생각에는 케이크와 카드가 필요한 것 같아. 내가 케이크를 구울 수 있어.
여 좋아. 나는 무엇을 하면 좋을까?

04회 듣기 실전 모의고사 pp. 136~143

01 ③ 02 ② 03 ① 04 ⑤ 05 ② 06 ④ 07 ④ 08 ⑤
09 ⑤ 10 ③ 11 ④ 12 ④ 13 ④ 14 ④ 15 ③ 16 ⑤
17 ① 18 ① 19 ② 20 ②

Dictation Test

01 bright, fine dust, clear **02** placed, square, under, meaningful **03** second, win, honest, regrets **04** walk, amusement, have, exam **05** choose, died, water, often, show **06** major, changed, scolds, practice, real **07** allowance, expect, rest, snacking, wisely **08** dye, worrying, search, instead **09** hospital, prepare, introducing, scissors **10** legs, avoid, straight, patterns, concerned **11** plastic, regular, polluted, sort, out **12** secret, asleep, off, dark **13** ballet, loves, lecture, hurt, starts **14** volunteer, taking, need to, special **15** bought, leftovers, options, delicious, fridge **16** bunch, closely, up, dipped **17** gave birth, have, corner, center **18** thinner, alike, voices, confused **19** artwork, seems, twinkling, unlighted **20** recently, huge, always, tea

01 ③

W Good morning. Here's today's weather forecast. It's a bright sunny Saturday and I think many people plan to hang out outside. However, the air is not so clear with high levels of fine dust. Fortunately, it is expected to rain tomorrow and it will clear up the air by Monday.

여 안녕하세요. 오늘의 일기 예보입니다. 밝고 맑은 토요일이기에 많은 분들이 밖에서 시간을 보낼 계획이실 것 같습니다. 하지만 대기는 높은 미세먼지 수치로 인해 그다지 깨끗하지 않습니다. 다행히도, 내일은 비가 올 것으로 예상되며 월요일 경에는 공기가 깨끗해질 것입니다.

02 ②

M Hi, Cindy.
W Hey, Mark. I like your bag.
M This is the eco bag that I designed myself.
W Really? I like the way you placed the white fish in the middle of the black square.
M Thanks. What do you think about the logo under the square?
W Wow, it says, "Love Your Life."
M Right. I hope people start thinking about a meaningful life.
W You are amazing.

남 안녕, Cindy.
여 안녕, Mark. 네 가방 마음에 든다.
남 이건 내가 직접 디자인한 에코백이야.
여 정말? 검정 정사각형 가운데에 흰 물고기를 배치한 방식이 마음에 들어.
남 고마워. 정사각형 아래에 있는 로고는 어떻게 생각하니?
여 와, '당신의 인생을 사랑하라.'라고 쓰여 있네.
남 맞아. 난 사람들이 의미 있는 삶에 대해 생각하기 시작하면 좋겠어.
여 너 정말 대단하다.

03 ①

M Sarah, did you do well on the contest yesterday?
W I got second place.
M What? I was sure you would win first place.
W Well, thanks for comforting me.
M No, I'm not just saying it. I'm honest.
W I was also disappointed but now I feel so refreshed.
M How so?
W I did my best, and there are no regrets.
M Good for you.

남 Sarah, 어제 대회에서 잘했니?
여 난 2등을 했어.
남 뭐라고? 네가 1등을 할 거라고 확신했는데.
여 음, 위로해줘서 고마워.
남 아냐, 그냥 하는 말이 아니야. 진심이라고.
여 나도 실망했었는데, 이제는 너무 후련해.
남 어째서?
여 난 최선을 다했고, 그래서 후회가 안 남거든.
남 잘됐네.

04 ⑤

M Sarah, how about a badminton game after school?
W Sorry, I can't. I can't even walk well.
M What's wrong? Did you work out hard during the weekend?
W No, I went to the amusement park yesterday and I walked around for almost 12 hours.
M You must have had fun, though.

W I rode a roller coaster and a few others. They're fun.
M Let's go there together after the exam.
W Alright.

남 Sarah, 방과 후에 배드민턴 한 게임 어때?
여 미안하지만, 난 못해. 나 잘 걸을 수도 없어.
남 무슨 일이야? 주말에 운동을 열심히 했니?
여 아니, 어제 놀이공원에 가서 거의 열두 시간을 걸어 다녔어.
남 그래도 재미있었겠다.
여 롤러코스터와 몇 가지 다른 것들을 탔어. 재미있더라.
남 시험 끝나고 함께 거기에 가자.
여 좋아.

05 ②

W Good afternoon. How can I help you?
M I need some flower seeds.
W You can choose from this shelf.
M Thanks. By the way, the rubber tree I bought here last month almost died.
W Hmm... how often did you water it?
M Every day.
W Maybe that's why. You watered it too often.
M Alright. Do you have small pots? I want to plant the seeds.
W Follow me. I'll show you where they are.

여 안녕하세요. 무엇을 도와드릴까요?
남 꽃씨가 좀 필요해요.
여 이 선반에서 고르시면 됩니다.
남 감사합니다. 그나저나 지난달에 여기서 산 고무나무가 거의 죽었어요.
여 흠… 얼마나 자주 물을 주셨나요?
남 매일요.
여 그래서 그런 것 같아요. 너무 자주 물을 주셨어요.
남 알겠습니다. 작은 화분들 있으세요? 씨앗을 심고 싶어서요.
여 따라오세요. 어디 있는지 알려드릴게요.

06 ④

W Dad, I want to quit piano lessons.
M Are you serious? You've always said you wanted to major in piano in college.
W Yes, but I changed my mind.
M Can you tell me what happened?
W My piano teacher scolds me whenever I don't practice enough.
M Do you want to have a different teacher? Or you don't want to practice?
W Well, I don't know.
M Try to think about the real reason. Then we will talk about it again.

여 아빠, 피아노 레슨을 그만두고 싶어요.
남 진심이니? 넌 대학교에서 피아노를 전공하고 싶다고 늘 말해 왔잖니.
여 네, 하지만 마음이 바뀌었어요.
남 무슨 일이 있었는지 말해줄래?
여 제가 연습을 충분히 안 할 때마다 피아노 선생님이 혼내세요.
남 다른 선생님께 배우고 싶은 거니, 연습을 하기가 싫은 거니?
여 음, 모르겠어요.
남 진짜 이유를 생각해보려무나. 그런 후에 이것에 대해 다시 이야기하자.

07 ④

M Mom, can I get some money? I need to buy a T-shirt.
W I gave you the allowance last week, remember?
M I used it up in buying some books.
W You don't expect me to believe that, do you?
M I really bought a couple of books and magazines.
W And where's the rest of the money?
M I bought a birthday present for Mina and spent some money on snacking and playing Internet games.
W I think you need to learn to spend money wisely.

남 엄마, 돈 좀 주실래요? 티셔츠를 사야 해요.
여 지난주에 용돈 줬잖니, 기억하지?
남 책 사는 데 다 썼어요.
여 그걸 믿을 거라고 생각하진 않겠지?
남 정말로 책이랑 잡지를 두어 권 샀어요.
여 그러면 나머지 돈은 어디에 있니?
남 미나의 생일 선물을 사고, 간식 사 먹고 인터넷 게임 하는 데 돈을 썼어요.
여 돈을 현명하게 쓰는 법을 배워야겠구나.

08 ⑤

W Brian, have you bought the presents for Parents' Day yet?
M I'm still thinking what to buy. Have you?
W I haven't yet, either. But I've been thinking of buying a bottle of hair dye.

M Are you planning to help your parents get their hair dyed?
W Yeah. I heard my Mom worrying about her grey hair.
M That's sad. I think you're a good daughter.
W Thanks. Can I use your cell phone? I want to search for a good hair dye.
M It's out of battery now. You can use my laptop instead.
W Thanks so much.

여 Brian, 어버이날 선물은 샀니?
남 뭘 사야 할지 아직 생각 중이야. 넌 샀어?
여 나도 아직 안 샀어. 하지만 염색약을 한 통 살까 생각 중이야.
남 부모님 머리 염색하는 것을 도와 드릴 계획이니?
여 응. 엄마가 흰머리에 대해 걱정하시는 걸 들었거든.
남 슬프다. 넌 좋은 딸인 것 같아.
여 고마워. 네 휴대전화 좀 써도 될까? 좋은 염색약을 검색하고 싶어서.
남 지금 배터리가 다 떨어졌어. 대신 내 노트북 컴퓨터를 써도 좋아.
여 정말 고마워.

09 ⑤

W Luke, how's your leg? Are you still in the hospital?
M I am. But I'll be able to go to school by next Tuesday.
W I'm so glad to hear that.
M Is there anything I need to prepare for school?
W Yeah. We are taking the art performance test on Tuesday.
M Oh, is it about the collage work introducing one's hero?
W Exactly. So you need to bring a picture of your hero and some newspaper.
M Anything else?
W You need scissors and a glue stick, too.
M Thanks.

여 Luke, 다리는 좀 어떠니? 아직도 병원이야?
남 응. 하지만 다음 주 화요일쯤에는 학교에 갈 수 있을 거야.
여 정말 다행이다.
남 학교 갈 때 준비해야 할 게 있을까?
여 응. 우린 화요일에 미술 수행평가를 봐.
남 아, 그게 자신의 영웅을 소개하는 콜라주 작품에 대한 거니?
여 맞아. 그래서 너의 영웅의 사진과 신문지를 좀 가져가야 해.
남 다른 거는?
여 가위랑 풀도 가져가야 하고.
남 고마워.

10 ③

M Let me tell you some tips to resolve your concerns. First, choose pants with narrow legs. Wider pants make you look shorter. Second, wear slimmer shoes and avoid bulky ones. The point is to make a long straight line from your waist to your toes. Third, stay away from shirts with large patterns. Keep these in mind if you are concerned about your height.

남 여러분의 걱정을 해결할 수 있는 몇 가지 조언을 해 드리겠습니다. 첫째, 폭이 좁은 바지를 고르세요. 폭이 넓은 바지는 여러분을 작아 보이게 만듭니다. 둘째, 볼이 좁은 신발을 신고 부피가 큰 신발은 피하세요. 요점은 허리부터 발가락까지 길고 곧은 선을 만드는 것이랍니다. 셋째, 커다란 무늬가 있는 셔츠는 멀리하세요. 키 때문에 걱정이시라면 이 점들을 유의하세요.

11 ④

W Let me tell you about recycling. Recycling companies come and take usable garbage on Mondays. They do not take plastic bags. So please put plastic bags in regular garbage bags. Also, the companies do not take polluted styrofoam or plastic bottles. So if they got dirty, please clean them before you sort them out.

여 재활용에 대해 말씀드리겠습니다. 재활용 업체는 월요일마다 와서 사용 가능한 쓰레기를 수거합니다. 그들은 비닐봉지는 수거하지 않습니다. 그러니 비닐봉지는 일반 쓰레기봉투에 담아주세요. 또한 재활용 업체는 오염된 스티로폼이나 플라스틱 병은 수거하지 않습니다. 그러므로 더러워졌다면 분리 배출하기 전에 그것들을 씻어주세요.

12 ④

M Your babies grew taller recently. What's the secret?
W I make them go to bed early.
M When do you get them to sleep?
W My kids go to bed at eight thirty in the evening and fall asleep by nine.

M That early? How is it possible?

W I make them ready for bed and turn off all the lights at eight o'clock.

M What good is it to turn off the lights?

W They get the feeling that it's dark outside and that it's time to go to bed.

남 당신의 아기들이 최근에 더 자랐네요. 비결이 뭔가요?

여 저는 아이들을 일찍 재워요.

남 몇 시에 재우시는데요?

여 제 아이들은 저녁 여덟 시 반에 자러 가서 아홉 시쯤 잠들어요.

남 그렇게 일찍요? 그게 어떻게 가능한가요?

여 전 아이들이 잠잘 준비를 하도록 하고 여덟 시에 모든 불을 꺼요.

남 불을 끄는 게 어떤 도움이 되는 거죠?

여 아이들은 바깥이 어두워졌고, 잘 시간임을 느끼게 되죠.

13 ④

W Jeffrey, why don't you join the ballet lesson?

M Are you kidding?

W No, I'm serious. There is a boy in my class and he loves it too.

M I am not of the kind.

W Come on. Try out the free lecture next Wednesday.

M I feel silly but trying wouldn't hurt. You mean on June 6th?

W No, on the 13th. It is the 8th today.

M Oh, you're right. What time is it?

W It starts at 6:30 p.m.

여 Jeffrey, 발레 수업에 들어오는 게 어때?

남 농담하니?

여 아니, 진심이야. 우리 반에 남자아이가 한 명 있는데 그 아이도 발레를 좋아해.

남 난 그런 사람이 아니야.

여 자, 다음 주 수요일에 하는 무료 강좌에 참여해 봐.

남 바보가 된 기분이지만 시도해서 나쁠 건 없지. 6월 6일 말하는 거니?

여 아니, 13일. 오늘은 8일이야.

남 아, 맞네. 몇 시에 하는데?

여 오후 6시 30분에 시작해.

14 ④

[Telephone rings.]

W Hello. How can I help you?

M Hi. I am a teacher at Daehan Middle School. Can I take my students to the welfare center to do some volunteer work?

W Sure. When do you plan to visit?

M Is April 20th okay with you?

W I guess. How many students are you taking?

M We have 15 students in our school volunteer club.

W Okay.

M Is there anything we need to prepare?

W Nothing special.

[전화 벨소리가 울린다.]

여 안녕하세요. 무엇을 도와드릴까요?

남 안녕하세요. 저는 대한 중학교 교사입니다. 복지관에 학생들을 데리고 가서 봉사 활동을 할 수 있을까요?

여 물론입니다. 언제 방문하실 계획이세요?

남 4월 20일 괜찮으신가요?

여 그럴 것 같습니다. 학생들을 몇 명이나 데리고 오시나요?

남 학교 자원봉사 동아리에 15명의 학생들이 있습니다.

여 알겠습니다.

남 준비해야 할 것이 있을까요?

여 특별히 없습니다.

15 ③

M Becky, why don't you eat some more?

W I'm so full. We should have bought less *samgyeopsal*.

M That's true. Let's just throw away the leftovers.

W No way.

M Do you have any other options?

W You can make delicious *kimchi-jjigae* with the meat.

M Really?

W Yeah. Let's keep it in the fridge. Could you get me a zipper bag?

M Alright.

남 Becky, 좀 더 먹지 그러니?

여 나 너무 배불러. 삼겹살을 좀 덜 샀어야 했는데.

남 맞아. 남은 음식은 그냥 버리자.

여 절대 안 돼.

남 다른 방안이 있니?

여 그 고기로 맛있는 김치찌개를 만들 수 있다고.

남 정말?

여 응. 그것을 냉장고에 넣어 두자. 지퍼백 하나 가져다줄래?

남 좋아.

16 ⑤

M Ruth, look at the bunch of flowers in the vase.
W They are so fresh and beautiful.
M Yeah, but look at it more closely.
W Oh, one of the flowers has dried up.
M You're right.
W What happened to that flower?
M Only that flower hasn't been dipped into the water.
W I can see that.

남 Ruth, 꽃병에 있는 꽃다발 좀 봐.
여 너무 신선하고 아름답다.
남 응, 하지만 좀 더 자세히 봐봐.
여 어머, 꽃들 중 한 송이가 말라버렸네.
남 맞아.
여 그 꽃은 어떻게 된 거니?
남 그 꽃만 물에 담가져 있지 않았거든.
여 그렇구나.

17 ①

① W Look! The mommy fish finally gave birth to a school of baby fish.
M It's amazing.
② W Happy birthday, Brian. Here's your birthday present.
M Thanks. I've always wanted to have this toy.
③ W Have you fed the fish yet? They must be hungry.
M I totally forgot.
④ W Where did you buy this toy fish?
M I bought it at the store around the corner.
⑤ W Which T-shirt looks better on me?
M The one with the big fish in the center looks better.

---

① 여 봐! 엄마 물고기가 마침내 아기 물고기 떼를 낳았어.
남 놀랍다.
② 여 생일 축하해, Brian. 여기 네 생일 선물이 있어.
남 고마워. 늘 이 장난감을 가지고 싶었어.
③ 여 물고기 밥 줬니? 배고프겠다.
남 깜빡했네.
④ 여 이 장난감 물고기를 어디서 샀니?
남 모퉁이에 있는 상점에서 샀어.
⑤ 여 어떤 티셔츠가 나한테 더 잘 어울리니?
남 가운데에 커다란 물고기가 있는 게 더 잘 어울려.

18 ①

M This is a picture of my dad 30 years ago. As you see, I resemble him a lot. He was not as tall as I am and he was much thinner but people say we look so alike. My eyes, nose, and even ears are from him. Besides our voices are similar. Sometimes my uncles get confused when I get phone calls for my father.

남 이것은 30년 전 우리 아버지의 사진입니다. 보시다시피, 저는 아버지를 많이 닮았어요. 아버지는 저처럼 크지도 않으셨고 훨씬 마르셨지만 사람들은 우리가 많이 닮았다고 합니다. 제 눈, 코, 그리고 심지어 귀마저도 아버지께 물려받았지요. 게다가 우리는 목소리도 비슷해요. 때때로 제가 아버지 대신 전화를 받으면 저희 삼촌들도 헷갈리세요.

19 ②

W Look at this picture.
M It's *The Starry Night* by Van Gogh.
W Right. It's my favorite artwork.
M It seems that the tree is alive and the stars are actually twinkling.
W Yeah. Doesn't the unlighted church look so lonely?
M Is there a church in the picture?

여 이 그림 좀 봐.
남 반 고흐의 '별이 빛나는 밤'이구나.
여 맞아. 내가 가장 좋아하는 미술 작품이야.
남 나무는 살아있고 별들은 실제로 반짝이는 듯해.
여 응. 불 꺼진 교회는 너무 외로워 보이지 않니?
남 그림 속에 교회가 있니?

20 ②

M What's in the box?
W It is the tent I bought recently.
M The box is too small for a tent.
W Yeah, but there is a huge tent folded up inside.
M It's amazing. By the way, why did you buy it?
W I've always wanted to go camping with my family.
M Really? Well.... Camping is not my cup of tea.

남 박스에 뭐가 들어 있니?
여 내가 최근에 산 텐트야.
남 텐트가 들어가기에는 박스가 너무 작은데.

여 응, 하지만 안에 커다란 텐트가 접혀 있어.
남 놀랍다. 그나저나, 그걸 왜 산 거니?
여 난 늘 가족과 캠핑을 가고 싶었거든.
남 정말? 음…. 내 경우에는 캠핑을 좋아하지 않아.

>> 05회 듣기 실전 모의고사 pp. 144~151

01 ② 02 ④ 03 ② 04 ③ 05 ③ 06 ⑤ 07 ④ 08 ①
09 ④ 10 ④ 11 ④ 12 ④ 13 ③ 14 ① 15 ④ 16 ④
17 ⑤ 18 ② 19 ② 20 ⑤

Dictation Test

01 through, short shower, rainy **02** tomato plant, prefer, grow, bigger **03** apartment building, hurt, extinguished **04** background photo, celebrating, wearing, ordered **05** pool, baseball cap, next to **06** stepped on, throw away, donate **07** bazaar, sold out, I bought **08** violin lesson, battery, give, ride **09** check, shut off, cancel, plug **10** poster, theme, designs, participate in **11** costume, laundry basket, possible **12** clean, allowance, laugh **13** sunburn, two, one for each **14** purchased, my toes, widen, less than **15** write a letter, translator, correct, read through **16** donate, passed, wait for **17** enough, order, plastic bag, cash **18** title, topic, support, synonyms **19** grill, boiled, water **20** turned on, upstairs, sneezing, move to

01 ②

W Here's the weather forecast for this week. The rain will stop by Monday morning and we'll have clear skies through the week. However, a short shower is expected on Thursday and you'll have another set of cold rainy days from Friday. So enjoy the nice weather for a couple of days.

여 이번 주 일기 예보입니다. 월요일 아침까지는 비가 그치고 주중에는 맑은 하늘이 이어지겠습니다. 하지만, 목요일에는 잠깐 소나기가 올 것으로 예상되고 금요일부터 춥고 비 오는 날들이 다시 시작되겠습니다. 그러므로 이삼 일간 좋은 날씨를 즐기시기 바랍니다.

02 ④

M Can I help you?
W I want to buy a flower pot to plant a tomato plant.
M How about this square-shaped pot?
W I prefer bright colors. This white round-shaped pot looks cute.
M Tomato plants grow really tall. So you'd better buy a bigger one.
W Then would this white tall rectangular one be okay?
M That'll do.
W Great. I'll take it.

남 도와드릴까요?
여 토마토를 심을 화분을 하나 사고 싶어요.
남 이 정사각형 모양의 화분은 어떠세요?
여 저는 밝은 색깔을 선호해요. 이 동그란 모양의 흰색 화분이 귀엽네요.
남 토마토는 키가 정말 높이 자라요. 그래서 더 큰 것을 사는 게 좋을 거예요.
여 그러면 이 흰색 긴 직사각형 화분은 괜찮을까요?
남 그거면 될 거예요.
여 좋아요. 그걸로 할게요.

03 ②

M Good morning, Mia.
W Hi. Did you see the fire engines in front of our apartment building last night?
M No, I didn't. What happened?
W There was a fire on the 10th floor.
M Oh, my. Did anybody get hurt?
W No, I heard that it was a small fire and it was extinguished soon.
M Oh, thank God.

남 안녕,Mia.
여 안녕. 너 어젯밤에 우리 아파트 앞에 있는 소방차들 봤니?
남 아니, 못 봤어. 무슨 일이 있었니?
여 10층에서 불이 났었어.
남 세상에. 다친 사람이 있니?
여 아니, 작은 불이어서 금방 진화됐대.
남 정말 다행이다.

04 ③

M Phoebe, did you change the background photo of your smartphone?
W Yeah, it's the picture of my family.
M When did you take it?
W We took it last week, celebrating my parents'

anniversary.

M I like the T-shirt all your family members are wearing.

W Thanks. I ordered them a month ago.

M Cool. You all look so happy.

남 Phoebe, 너 스마트폰 배경 사진 바꿨니?

여 응, 우리 가족사진이야.

남 언제 찍은 거니?

여 우리 부모님의 결혼기념일을 축하하는 의미에서 지난주에 찍었어.

남 너희 가족 모두가 입고 있는 티셔츠가 마음에 든다.

여 고마워. 한 달 전에 주문한 거야.

남 멋지다. 모두 행복해 보여.

05 ③

W Excuse me, sir.

M Yes?

W You cannot enter the pool without a swimming cap.

M I am wearing a baseball cap instead.

W I'm sorry but we don't allow baseball caps.

M I see. Where can I borrow one?

W You can borrow one next to the front desk.

M Thanks.

여 실례합니다.

남 네?

여 수영 모자 없이는 수영장에 들어가실 수 없어요.

남 대신 야구 모자를 썼는데요.

여 죄송하지만 야구 모자는 허용되지 않습니다.

남 알겠습니다. 어디에서 수영 모자를 빌릴 수 있죠?

여 안내 데스크 옆에서 대여하실 수 있습니다.

남 감사합니다.

06 ⑤

W Ouch!

M Are you alright, Mom?

W I stepped on your toy cars again, Philip.

M Oh, I'm sorry. I was just about to clear them up.

W You said the same thing last time. Do you remember what I said?

M That you were going to throw away mine?

W Not quite. I said I was going to donate them to children in need.

M You can do so next time, really.

여 아야!

남 괜찮으세요, 엄마?

여 내가 네 장난감 자동차들을 또 밟았구나, Philip.

남 아, 죄송해요. 막 치우려던 참이었어요.

여 너 지난번에도 같은 말 했잖니. 내가 뭐라고 했는지 기억나니?

남 제 걸 버리신다고요?

여 아니. 도움이 필요한 아이들에게 그것을 기부할 거라고 했어.

남 다음번에는 정말로 그렇게 하셔도 돼요.

07 ④

M How did the bazaar go, Linda?

W I had so much fun. My hairpins were sold out, you know.

M I'm happy for you. Did you buy some stuff too?

W Yeah. These party balloons, magnets, books and the teaspoon set are what I bought today.

M You did buy a lot of stuff.

W You know what? I bought all of them with just 3,000 won.

M I can't believe it.

남 바자회는 어땠니, Linda?

여 너무 재미있었어. 내 머리핀은 다 팔린 거 있지.

남 나도 기쁘다. 물건도 좀 샀니?

여 응. 이 파티용 풍선, 자석, 책, 그리고 티스푼 세트가 내가 오늘 산 것들이야.

남 정말 많이 샀구나.

여 그거 아니? 나 이 모든 것들을 겨우 삼천 원에 샀어.

남 믿을 수가 없다.

08 ①

W David, why are you still home? Isn't it time for you to take the violin lesson?

M I still have 30 minutes to go. It's 4 o'clock now.

W No, it's 5 o'clock.

M What?

W The clock must be out of battery.

M Oh, no. I must not be late today.

W Hurry up, David.

M Grandma, could you give me a ride?

W Alright.

여 David, 너 왜 아직도 집에 있니? 바이올린 레슨 받는 시간 아니니?

남 가려면 아직 30분 남았어요. 지금 4시잖아요.

여 아냐, 지금 5시야.

남 뭐라고요?
여 시계 배터리가 다 됐나보다.
남 안 돼. 오늘 절대로 늦으면 안 되는데.
여 서두르렴, David.
남 할머니, 저 차로 태워다 주시겠어요?
여 알겠다.

09 ④

W Are we all ready to go? We don't want to miss the plane.
M Wait. We have to check some things before we depart.
W Like what?
M We should put all the food into the fridge, shut off the gas valves, and so forth.
W You're right. Let me cancel the newspaper subscription for the week.
M Thanks. Are there some other things we need to do?
W Maybe we can pull out the plug for all of the electronics.
M Great. I guess we are now ready for a trip.

여 우리 갈 준비 다 됐나? 비행기 놓치면 안 돼.
남 잠깐만. 출발하기 전에 몇 가지를 확인해야 해.
여 어떤 거야?
남 모든 음식을 냉장고에 넣어야 하고, 가스 밸브를 잠가야 하고, 기타 등등을 해야지.
여 맞네. 일주일간 신문 구독을 취소할게.
남 고마워. 해야 할 다른 일이 또 있을까?
여 모든 가전제품의 플러그를 뽑을 수 있을 것 같아.
남 좋아. 이제 여행할 준비가 된 것 같다.

10 ④

W Here is an announcement regarding the poster design contest for the school festival. The theme of our school festival this year is Disney World. Keep that in mind and try to come up with creative poster designs. If you want to participate in the contest, please visit the teacher's office on the first floor.

여 학교 축제 포스터 디자인 대회 관련 안내입니다. 올해 우리 학교 축제의 주제는 디즈니 월드입니다. 그것을 염두에 두고 창의적인 포스터 디자인을 생각해 보세요. 대회에 참여하기를 원하면, 1층 교무실에 방문해 주세요.

11 ④

M Have you seen my black T-shirt, Mom?
W Which one?
M The one I bought for my Halloween costume last year.
W I don't quite remember. Can you describe it?
M It is the one with jack-o'-lantern at the back.
W Oh, that one. I don't know where it is. Maybe it's in the laundry basket.
M That's not possible. I haven't worn it recently.

남 엄마, 제 검정 티셔츠 보셨어요?
여 어떤 것 말이니?
남 작년 핼러윈 의상으로 샀던 거요.
여 기억이 잘 안 나네. 설명해 볼래?
남 등에 호박등이 그려져 있는 거요.
여 아, 그거. 어디에 있는지 모르겠네. 세탁물 바구니에 있을지도 모르겠다.
남 그건 불가능해요. 최근에 입은 적이 없거든요.

12 ④

M Mia, look what I did.
W Wow, did you finally clean your room?
M Not only that. I also cleaned up the bathroom.
W Were you planning to ask for a raise in your allowance?
M No, I wanted to make Dad happy.
W That's enough to make a cat laugh.
M I'm serious. It's Parents' Day soon.

남 Mia 누나, 내가 한 일 좀 봐.
여 와, 드디어 방을 치웠니?
남 그뿐만이 아니야. 화장실도 청소했어.
여 용돈을 더 올려 달라고 할 계획이었니?
남 아니, 아빠를 기쁘게 해드리고 싶었어.
여 지나가던 개가 웃겠다.
남 진짜야. 곧 어버이날이잖아.

13 ③

M It's so hot. You'll get a sunburn if you stay out there just for five minutes.
W You can say that again. Would you care for some ice cream?
M Why not? Let me go get some ice cream.
W Thanks. Please buy two ice cream cones for me.
M That'll make three including mine.

W Oh, Jenny and Jack will be arriving soon. Would you get one for each of them?
M Sure.

남 정말 덥다. 5분만 밖에 있어도 햇볕에 심하게 탈 거야.
여 같은 생각이야. 아이스크림 좀 먹을래?
남 좋지. 가서 아이스크림 좀 사 올게.
여 고마워. 나는 아이스크림콘 두 개 사다 줘.
남 내 것까지 합하면 세 개가 되겠네.
여 아, Jenny와 Jack이 곧 도착할 거야. 걔들 것도 하나씩 사다 줄래?
남 물론이지.

14 ①

M How can I help you?
W I've purchased these high heels here a week ago and they are very uncomfortable.
M How are they uncomfortable?
W The room for my toes is too tight and my toes hurt.
M In that case, I can widen the part with a special tool.
W That'll be nice. Do I have to come and grab them later?
M No, you can just wait here. It takes less than ten minutes.
W Awesome.

남 무엇을 도와드릴까요?
여 일주일 전에 이곳에서 이 하이힐을 구매했는데요, 너무 불편해요.
남 어떻게 불편하세요?
여 발가락 부분의 공간이 너무 좁아서 발가락이 아파요.
남 그렇다면 특별한 도구로 그 부분을 넓힐 수 있어요.
여 그러면 좋겠네요. 다음에 와서 찾아가야 하나요?
남 아뇨, 여기서 기다리시면 됩니다. 10분도 안 걸려요.
여 좋네요.

15 ④

M Are you still learning Chinese, Ellen?
W I am. It's so interesting.
M Can you help me write a letter to my Taiwanese friend?
W Why don't you use a translator program on the Internet?
M Actually, I did use it and I'm not sure if the translated version is correct.
W So you want me to read through the translation, right?
M That's right.

남 여전히 중국어 배우고 있니, Ellen?
여 응. 정말 재미있어.
남 내 대만 친구에게 편지 쓰는 걸 좀 도와줄래?
여 인터넷 번역기 프로그램을 사용하지 그러니?
남 사실, 그것을 사용했는데 번역본이 맞는지 확실히 모르겠어.
여 그래서 번역본을 읽어봐 달라는 거지?
남 맞아.

16 ④

M Amy, do you have plans for the weekend?
W I'm planning to donate my blood. Do you want to join?
M I'd like to, but I can't.
W Aren't you 17 years old yet? I thought your birthday was in February.
M Yeah, my 16th birthday already passed. It's just that I already made a blood donation last month.
W Oh, you need to wait for another month to be able to donate blood.
M That's right.

남 Amy, 주말에 계획 있니?
여 헌혈할 생각이야. 같이 갈래?
남 가고 싶은데, 안 돼.
여 너 아직 열일곱 살 안 됐니? 네 생일이 2월인 줄 알았는데.
남 그래, 내 열여섯 번째 생일은 이미 지났어. 지난달에 이미 헌혈을 해서 그런 거야.
여 아, 헌혈을 할 수 있으려면 한 달은 더 기다려야겠구나.
남 맞아.

17 ⑤

① W How much is it total?
M Let me pay this time.
② W Would you like to have some more chicken?
M No, thanks. I've already had enough.
③ W I'd like to order two boxes of fried chicken.
M Okay. Tell me your address, ma'am.
④ W Where can I throw away the bones?
M Let's put them in this plastic bag.
⑤ W Oops, I don't have any cash. Can I pay by credit card?

M Of course you can.

① 여 모두 다 해서 얼마죠?
남 이번에는 제가 낼게요.
② 여 치킨 좀 더 드실래요?
남 아뇨. 이미 많이 먹었어요.
③ 여 프라이드치킨 두 상자 주문할게요.
남 네. 주소를 알려 주세요.
④ 여 뼈는 어디에 버리면 될까요?
남 이 비닐봉지에 넣기로 하죠.
⑤ 여 어머, 현금이 없네요. 신용카드로 계산해도 될까요?
남 물론 가능합니다.

18 ②

M Let me give you some tips for writing. First, you need to give it an interesting title that attracts the readers' attention. Next, you should start with a good topic sentence. Then, write the sentences that support the topic sentence. Lastly, use synonyms to avoid repeating certain words.

남 글쓰기를 위한 팁을 좀 알려드릴게요. 먼저, 독자의 관심을 끌 수 있는 흥미로운 제목을 붙이셔야 합니다. 다음으로, 좋은 주제문으로 시작하셔야 해요. 그런 다음에는 주제문을 뒷받침하는 문장들을 쓰세요. 마지막으로, 특정 단어를 반복하는 것을 피하기 위해 유의어를 사용하세요.

19 ②

W Brandon, come and have some corn.
M They are so delicious. Did you grill them with butter?
W No, I boiled them in water.
M It didn't taste the same when I boiled them last time.
W You shouldn't put too much water when boiling.
M I didn't. How are they so tasty?

여 Brandon, 와서 옥수수 좀 먹어.
남 정말 맛있다. 버터를 발라 구웠니?
여 아니, 물에 삶았어.
남 지난번에 내가 삶았을 때는 같은 맛이 아니었는데.
여 삶을 때 물을 너무 많이 넣으면 안 돼.
남 그러지 않았어. 이건 어떻게 이렇게 맛있는 거지?

20 ⑤

M Where is this noise from?
W I've turned on the air conditioner.
M It's not the air conditioner. Is your phone vibrating?
W Hmm, no. I guess it's from upstairs.
M You mean you even can hear your neighbor's phone vibrating?
W I can sometimes hear them sneezing, you know.
M Maybe you should move to another apartment.

남 이 소리가 어디서 나는 거지?
여 내가 에어컨을 켜 놨어.
남 에어컨 소리가 아닌데. 네 전화기의 진동이 울리고 있니?
여 흠, 아니. 위층에서 나는 것 같아.
남 너 이웃의 전화기 진동 소리마저 들을 수 있단 말이니?
여 때때로 그들이 재채기하는 소리도 들을 수 있어.
남 너 다른 아파트로 이사 가야겠다.

All that 올댓·중학·영어 중학영어의 모든 것이 들어 있는 올댓으로 학교 시험 완벽 대비!

대표전화 1544-0554
주소 서울특별시 구로구 디지털로33길 48 대륭포스트타워 7차 20층